New York Guitar Method
Primer
Book One

By
Bruce Arnold

Muse Eek Publishing Company
New York, New York

ISBN 1594899126

Printed in the United States

This publication can be purchased from your local bookstore or by contacting:
Muse Eek Publishing Company
New York, NY, USA
Fax: 212-473-4601
http://www.muse-eek.com
sales@muse-eek.com

Table Of Contents

Acknowledgments

The author would like to thank Gabriel Cummins for his many hours of help in writing and editing this latest series of books.   I would also like to thank Michal Shapiro for proof reading and helpful suggestions and finally Ronald Andryshak for his administrative assistance.

About the Author

Born in Sioux Falls South Dakota, Bruce Arnold began his music training at the University of South Dakota. After three years of study he transferred to the Berklee College of Music where he received a Bachelor of Music degree in Composition. While doing undergraduate work at Berklee College of Music Bruce received the Harris Stanton award for outstanding guitarist of the year. He continued with further study in improvisational and compositional methods with Charlie Banacos and Jerry Bergonzi. Bruce received the outstanding teacher of the year award at Berklee in 1984 and went on to teach at the New England Conservatory of Music, and Dartmouth College.

Upon moving to New York City, Bruce found himself preoccupied with the possibilities of applying the twelve tone theoretical constructs of Schoenberg and Berg to American improvised music. His first CD, "Blue Eleven" contained the seeds of those ideas he was to develop further in his following critically acclaimed works: "A Few Dozen" and "Give 'Em Some." In this vein, his music is remarkably tonal, and the results give proof that inventive improvisation is possible within this format.

Bruce currently plays with his own band, "The Bruce Arnold Trio" and with "Spooky Actions" a jazz quartet that performs his transcriptions of Webern and other classical masters. In addition, Bruce has performed with such diverse musicians as Gary Burton, Joe Pass, Joe Lovano, Randy Brecker, Peter Erskine, Stuart Hamm, Boston Symphony Orchestra, and The Absolute Ensemble under the baton of Kristjan Järvi.

Bruce currently teaches at Princeton University, New York University and the New School. Upon his arrival at NYU he set about to improve the music education program, and instituted NYU's first sight-reading program for jazz guitarists. He started writing music education books to fill a need he perceived in formal jazz education.

As an author, Bruce has written 50 books on music education. These books cover many of the important aspects of mastering high performance skills for both the advanced music student with professional goals, and the dedicated beginner. To view the complete catalogue, please log on to his publisher's website at: http://www.muse-eek.com.

Foreword

The New York Guitar Method series is structured to enable a total beginner to learn the tools necessary to become a master musician from the ground up. This Primer Book One should be used as a first step toward New York Guitar Method Primer Book Two and Primer Ensemble Book Two. All three books are prerequisites for students entering NYU as a jazz guitar major and for students wishing to go to the New York Guitar Summer Program at NYU.

Because some readers may be skipping back and forth between chapters, I have provided a great deal of repetition in this book to make sure no information is overlooked. For some this repetition may feel annoying but for others it can be a learning tool.

There is a developing online resource including midifiles and FAQs that can be found on the title page of the muse-eek.com website. You will also find additional help files in the member's area. The member's area is a part of the muse-eek website that offers free access for book owners. You will find audio and video files which supplement the information presented in this book. To register for a username and password please go to:

http://www.muse-eek.com/books/members/members1.html

You will be sent a username and password via email

If you have any problems with gaining access please send the following information to muse-eek via email to info@muse-eek.com

full name
address
city
state
country
email address

Bruce Arnold

A Word to the Wise

I'd like to say a few words about how I believe a student should approach being a musician, a guitarist and an artist.

The first thing that comes to mind is the old joke:
Q: How many guitarists does it take to change a light bulb?
A: Two, one to change it and one to say they could have done it better.

Competitiveness in music is destructive to the accused, to the accuser and to the musical community. Each person projects their own voice through their instrument. Granted this voice can be anywhere from weak and ineffective to revolutionary and technically astounding. The important thing to realize is that all great musicians were once weak and ineffective. It is dedication, knowing the right thing to practice and artistic vision that eventually makes a musician great. Another counter production is the notion that this guitarist is better than that guitarist. This is such an absurd line of thought. Who is better; Django Reinheirt or Charlie Christian? —Pat Metheny or John Scofield? Obviously they all have brought their own unique language of music and one is not "greater" than the other. Therefore, look for the uniqueness in a guitarist and remember their voice may be only just beginning to emerge. And of course, all musical taste is subjective. Keep in mind that you might not like a certain style of music which is absolutely fine. Conversely, you may like music that other people don't like or simply cannot relate to. Remember that an opinion is not a fact.

Secondly, I'd like to make some comments about being a student. While respect for your teacher is a given, the best and most effective student is one who thinks on their own and questions both their preconceptions and the information their teachers give them. The worst thing you can do is just figure "my teacher plays better than me, therefore I should do everything he or she says without questioning its validity." This doesn't mean you have to enter into a contentious relationship with your teacher, it means you need to think logically about what they are asking you to do and ask honest questions if you are uncertain that their advice is the best. Another common mistake I see among students is thinking that studying with the most famous person will net them the best information and therefore they will achieve their goals more quickly. Someone's ability on their instrument and certainly their popularity doesn't make them a good teacher. A good teacher is above all someone who cares whether you improve and then has the insights to convey assignments tailored to your needs along with a deep understanding of all aspects of working towards mastering an instrument. This is usually a rare commodity and isn't something that is automatically inherent in a musician that is famous.

Thirdly, be a buddy. Jon Damien, a great teacher at Berklee College of Music, had a buddy system he promoted there. It's such a simple concept, but it can lay the foundations for the right attitude towards practice and interaction with the other members of your musical community. And that's as crucial as any other part of your development. Here's the concept: seek out other guitarists to play and practice with. This will help you develop and let you see other musical possibilities through your buddy's eyes and ears. It will also help you build a community of people that may even eventually support you in your career. This very closely relates back to the first point I made. It's important to keep yourself open and nonjudgemental. Remember you don't want to play only with someone you feel is more developed than you. Someone not quite as developed as you in the ways you currently feel are important may have other aspects of their playing that could influence you positively. Look for the strong points in your fellow musicians and learn from them.

Fourth, and unfortunately too common with guitarists, is the notion that fast equals good. Anyone can tell if someone is playing fast—that's not even something you need to be a musician to do. Someone who bases their analysis of a musician on their technique is someone who doesn't understand first, what art is, and secondly, what good music is. Your evaluation of a musician should be based on whether this person has an affinity with your artistic vision and says something through their instrument that touches you in a deeper way. In conjunction with this remember your artistic vision is always a work in progress so your analysis has to be always tempered by the fact that someone's playing may not mean something to you at your current state of development, but may speak to you later on.

Lastly a few tidbits of advice:

Try not to tell another musician that their music or playing sounds like "X" person. A true artist is trying as hard as they can to find their own personal sound, so this kind of statement is not what they really want to hear. You will most likely get an unenthusiastic "thank you" and a glazed look. Keep in mind that your current state of development might be telling you that they sound like someone else but later on you may find that they have something unique to offer.

It's good to have heroes, and to emulate the way that they play, but you are who you are, and you should not start out trying to sound like anyone else. Each day try to find something in your practicing that can define your voice. This can start with the smallest thing but can grow into a singular vision.

What works for one person may not work for another. If you have a good teacher, your assignments will be tailor made for you, and would not necessarily be relevant for another student. The converse is true—what another person is working on may not have any value for you.

Just because someone famous has a lack of knowledge of music theory and sight reading doesn't mean that you should follow in their footsteps. The requirements of a musician's success change over time along with the era in which they may have gotten their greatest career boost. Things are a lot more demanding these days, and you would be best served to have all the "tools of the trade" at your command when you assail the walls of professional music.

Important Background Information

Care of Your Guitar

Guitar Technique

Tuning the Guitar

Notes Found on the Guitar

Quick Start

There are many ways to approach this book. The important thing is that sooner or later you should read and understand everything presented. Each individual works differently and is at a different level, so here are some possible ways of approaching this book.

TOTAL BEGINNER: I have no previous experience playing the guitar or with music in general.

1. Read pages 1-4 while referring to the pictures on pages 51-2 and video files on muse.eek.com
2. Tune your guitar using method on pages 5-6 or use internet guitar tuning files on muse-eek.com
3. Read pages 18-19 and start learning the chords on pages 19-26.
4. When you take a break start reading the music theory section on page 9-17 and the understanding rhythm on pages 32-5
5. As you feel more comfortable with the chords and understand rhythm start learning the chord progressions on pages 37-48.

INTERMEDIATE BEGINNER: I have played a while but know very little.

1. Read pages 1-4 while referring to the pictures on pages 51-2 understand that one the of reasons you
   might have had problems in the past playing the guitar is because your technique is flawed. Look for your problems by comparing notes with the book and looking in a mirror to see how you are playing. Also check video files on muse.eek.com
2. Check page 18 for explanation of chord diagrams and then proceed to explanation of chord progression on page 36.
3. Begin working on chord progression on pages 37-48 refer to pages 32-35 if you have rhythm problems.

ADVANCED BEGINNER: I know most "open" position chords but can't play songs yet.

1. Read pages 1-4 while referring to the pictures on pages 51-2 and video files on muse.eek.com and start to correct any discrepancies you find in your technique.
2. Read page 36 and start learning the chord progressions.
3. When you take a break start reading the music theory section on page 9-17 and the Understanding Rhythm on pages 32-5.
4. Read pages 27-28 and learn all barre chords on pages 29-31 using the cycle 5 progression.
5. Start with the 3 notes per string scales found on page 176.

Master These Things Over Time

1. Read and reread the music theory section on pages 9-17 until in makes sense to you.
2. Learn all "open" chords and use the cycle 5 progression on 28 to memorize all "barre" chords
3. Read and reread the Understand Rhythm section of page 32-5 until you can play the examples.
4. Keep rereading pages 1-4 and check your technique in a mirror or with a video camera.
5. Start to memorize the notes of the guitar fretboard on page 8.

Hint: When I was first trying to memorize the notes on the guitar fretboard, I photocopied a page like page 8 and carried it around with me. I would quiz myself while walking, or sitting on a train. For example: What note is on the 6th fret of the D string? I would then check my answers with the diagram of the fretboard to make sure I was correct.

Important Background Information

If you have just purchased a guitar or received one as a present it is important to first understand some basic general information that will help you get off on the right foot. The concepts presented here are really the most important thing you will ever learn on the guitar. It is sad but true that with most of the new students I receive, I usually spend the first year correcting problems. Nine out of ten times these problems were caused by not knowing the proper technique to use on the guitar or not understanding the right way to process music both intellectually and aurally. This book will help you get started in the right way so you can develop to your full potential, and bypass the problems.

A picture is worth a thousand words, so for many of the concepts presented here you will find pictures on pages 174-175 and short videos on the muse-eek.com website found under the book's title listing. Some exercises can also be found as midifiles or mp3 files so you can hear what the exercise should sound like and see the techniques discussed with your own eyes. I urge you to download these pictures and videos to your computer so you can examine them closely and refer back to each file for further refinement of each technique presented. As previously stated. as an owner of this book you have free access to the "Member's Section." Take advantage of this, because you will find other information and educational files to help you develop as a musician.

The first step in playing the guitar is to learn such basic information as how to tune a guitar, hold your pick properly and position your hands and body in relationship to the guitar to help you play correctly and avoid any repetitive stress injuries. We will also discuss some of the basic concepts of strumming the guitar and where notes are located on the guitar neck. A music theory section is also included to get you started thinking about music in a structured way. This theory section will be quite challenging for the beginning student. Don't feel like you have to master the music theory before moving on to the chords and chord progressions. If you have problems with the music theory, just relax and keep rereading it until it makes sense to you. The important thing to remember is that you have all the information to get you started in the right direction in this book.

This book can't cover every subject at the depth you will need. Along the way I will recommend other books for study which will help you correct problems or enrich your understanding. Don't automatically figure you are untalented if you run into a road block. If you have a particular problem try using some of the books or e-books I recommend for further study. You could also check the FAQ section for this book and see if others have had similar problems, or contact me and I will make suggestions to help you get on the right track again.

Care of your Guitar

Let's discuss the care of your guitar. It's your "baby" so take care of it.

Store your guitar in the case. If you leave it sitting out anywhere, you are inviting problems, from having some bozo grabbing your guitar and messing it up, to things getting dropped on it, to falling over it and breaking it. Why take the chance?

In the winter time don't store your guitar near an active heater. Dry air will crack the wood of your instrument. Try to keep you house or apartment between 30 and 40 percent humidity. If this is impossible, buy a humidifier for your guitar. You can find these in any music store. They are very cheap but they do the trick.

If you lean your guitar against a wall (which I don't recommend) put the string side facing the wall, not the back. This usually gives the guitar more stability and makes it less likely to fall over.

Try to avoid extreme changes in temperature when transporting your guitar. If you take your guitar to a friend's house in the winter time, let the guitar warm up for 15 to 20 minutes before taking it out of the case.

All these tips will go a long way towards keeping your guitar safe and in one piece for many years.

Holding the Guitar

There are two methods of holding the guitar. Your basic position will either be sitting or standing. If you are sitting you want to place the guitar across your lap and rest the inward curving section of the guitar on your right or left leg. (See picture 7 or video clip 3 for different views of this position) The "classical" technique for holding the guitar is to place it on the left leg, spreading your legs and allowing the rest of the body of the guitar to fall between your two legs. I recommend using this technique if you are sitting down. This will help you maintain the proper position for both your right and left hands. You should also raise up your left leg about 3 to 5 inches. This can be done by placing your foot on the guitar case. The height of this foot rest will vary from person to person. As a basic guideline you don't want to put the foot rest so high that you are forced to raise your left shoulder to reach up to the neck. Anything that will support your leg is fine. There are adjustable guitar footrests that you can purchase in any music store which are obviously the best to have, because you can get the exact height that is comfortable for you. If you put a strap on later and stand up, your guitar should be in the same position on your body as it was when your were sitting.

Practice the way you will perform. I get many guitarists who can't figure out why they play so much better when they are sitting at home in a chair, than they do when performing or rehearsing standing up. It's because they are holding their guitar in one position when they are practicing, and a different position when performing. It's just common sense to practice the way you will perform but you'd be amazed how many people don't realize this. If you are playing an electric guitar you can use the same technique but quite honestly, you would be much better off standing and using a strap. It's very seldom that an electric guitarist performs sitting down, so don't practice while sitting down. You should adjust your strap so that the middle of the back of the guitar falls around your belly button. Each person is built differently so exact placement will have to be found but a good indicator is actually what your left hand position ends up being on the guitar. (See photo 10)

The Left Hand/Arm Position

Your left hand should come around the neck from below it. Your shoulder should be relaxed. (See photo 1,5,7 and 10 or video clip 3) It is very common for students to raise, clench or hold their shoulder up. If your strap is too high you will find you are raising your shoulder. You will also find your shoulder is to high if you are sitting and you have your left foot raised too high. Your fingers should be relaxed. I often tell students to first put your hand down by your side and let it relax. Then bring the hand up to the guitar neck. Your hand should remain in the same relaxed position. Fingers should be relaxed, and the wrist should be straight. (See photo 1 -6 and video clip 3) If you find that your wrist is getting bent at more than a 10 to 20 degree angle when you are playing notes on the guitar, you need to raise the height of the guitar up so your wrist will not be forced into that angle. People who play over long periods of time with their wrist bent at too much of an angle will find that they develop pain, and sooner or later a repetitive stress injury. (See photos 1-4, 5, 6 and video clip 3 for proper wrist angle)

A common mistake students make is to stretch their fingers out so that one finger is covering each fret. Don't do this. I give students this example when considering how to place your left hand on the guitar: Hold your left hand out in front of you and stretch your fingers apart. Now try and move your fingers and feel how flexible they are. Next, relax your hand by the side of your body and then bring it out in front of your body. Now try moving your fingers. You will find that a relaxed hand allows your fingers to move more quickly and with less tension. This is how your hand should be when you are playing the guitar. Relaxed, with fingers relatively close to each other. (See video clip 7)

There are of course examples of particular melodies and chords that will require you to stretch your fingers out. (I sometimes get students who bring me a particular musical example where they don't understand how it could be played without stretching the fingers out.) But your basic position should always be one of relaxed fingers fairly close together. I have never seen a great guitarist who played with a tense hand. One last point to keep in mind is that each person is different. If you have very short fingers a stretch for you might not be a stretch for someone with very long fingers.

The next common question is: How do I move from one note to another if I don't stretch my hand out? This is accomplished by a combination of elbow and shoulder action that moves your hand up and down the neck to reach each fret. This technique will take some time to develop but it keeps your fingers in the same relationship to the neck as you play each note. At this point it can't be over emphasized how important it is to keep your hand and fingers in a consistent relationship to the guitar fretboard. Many students play the guitar differently depending where they are on the guitar neck. This makes playing the guitar a lot harder. By maintaining the same position you are homing in on one technique, and by maintaining a consistent, relaxed technique you will develop speed and precision on the guitar. (See video clip 2-7)

The Left Hand Finger Position

You will be playing using the tips of your fingers and your fingers should be slightly arched. (See photos 1-2,12 and video clip 2-7) This is the usual position of your hand when it is relaxed by the side of your body. When you press down on a note you want to press between the frets to make a note sound. You only want to press hard enough to make the note sound. Most students press too hard with their left hand when playing notes. Spend some time analyzing the way your hand is working and make sure you are not pressing too hard. The harder you press, the slower you will play, and the sooner your hand will tire.

The Right Hand/Arm Position

Your right hand should come over the body of the guitar. (See photos 7 and 10.) Keep your shoulders relaxed and guard against the tendency to raise them up. Your arm from the elbow to the tips of your fingers should be straight using your elbow to raise or lower your arm to play each string. (See photos 7 and 10 and video clip 2.) The forearm (the area between the wrist and elbow) should be used to pick each string. This forearm movement is the same movement used to drink a glass of water, turn a screw driver or open a door. Another way to experience this movement is to lay your arm flat on a table and lift your thumb up using your forearm. Don't use the muscle in your thumb but allow your forearm to pick your thumb up off the table. This technique will seem a little awkward to begin with but by using the big muscle group in your forearm you will have the power and endurance to play for long periods of time without injury. (See video clip 8)

It should be mentioned that many students use their wrists to pick each note. I have found that though this technique will work, you do run the risk of injury. The wrist contains very small muscles and they are easily damaged. Also a tendency to hold your arm stationary and just move your wrist up and down to play each string is inviting disaster. This is the same motion that creates Carpal Tunnel Syndrome when using a mouse on a computer.

Many guitarists try to rest one or more of their fingers against the body of the guitar to help them get a "feel" for where the strings are. I have seen nothing but problems develop later on using this technique. I strongly recommend that you not rely on your hand touching the guitar. Keep your fingers relaxed. Your arm from the upper forearm to the elbow should be the only place where your arm touches the guitar. This will allow your lower forearm, wrist and hand to move freely. (See photo 7)

Using a Guitar Pick

The type of pick you use is a personal preference. Go to a local music store and buy one light , one medium and one heavy gauge pick. They are very cheap, so by a bunch if you're up for it. Try each pick for a week or two and see which one feels the best and which one sounds the best. I use an extra heavy pick because I like the resistance, sound and feel. But that is just me. You are the final judge as to what feels and sounds best for you; There is no right or wrong pick weight.

You should hold the pick either between your thumb and first finger, or the thumb and your first and second finger together. (See photos 8-9) Students commonly press their fingers together too tightly while gripping the pick. This can cause tension in the forearm. Keep the rest of your fingers relaxed. If you start to feel pain or stress in your fingers or forearm you are probably holding the pick too tightly.

When you pick the string you do not want to dig your pick too far into the strings, because this will slow you down. Compare photos 15 and 16. In photo 16 the pick is picking too far into the string. Photo 15 is the correct method.

To recap: your right arm/elbow combination will be doing the work of strumming. Strumming refers to the technique you use to play all the notes in chords. You usually start from the lower in pitch strings and move the pick across the strings in a downward motion. You can also strum with an upward motion. You will need both as you start to play the chords to different songs. You can initiate the strum from your elbow or your forearm. I use mostly my forearm and a little movement of the elbow. When picking individual strings you will use your forearm and then your elbow to move up or down to the next string. (See video clip 1, 2 and 8.)

Applying Right and Left Hand Techniques

For a technical application of right and left hand technique I would recommend the following: First, overall try to apply your new technique to everything you have learned so far on the guitar. For some this is a daunting task especially if you have been playing for a while. But you will find that whether you are a beginner or a seasoned pro after a while this technique will feel natural and music that you already know will quickly fall into place. More specifically for both left and right hand technique I recommend downloading the major scales, arpeggios and sweeps from the "Music Workshop" at www.arnoldjazz.com, following the directions on each page. Also for right hand technique I have written a book called "Right Hand Technique for Guitar Volume One" ISBN 096486326X. This book will give you hundreds of right hand exercises.

Pictures and Videos

Along with the pictures found on pages 174-75 you will find video clips under this book's title on the muse-eek.com website. Take full advantage of these visual aids as they will help you understand the proper technique on the guitar. An extra few weeks spent refining your basic interface with the guitar will help you to progress more productively. You will also find that any music you play sounds better when your muscles are relaxed and being used in the right way. You will also avoid the injuries that can arise from incorrect technique.

Other Guitar Information

Change your guitar strings at least once every six months. New strings bring life back into an instrument. There are many different gauges and types of strings. The lighter the strings the easier they are to play but you sacrifice tone and volume as you use lighter and lighter strings. Bring your guitar with you when you buy your first set and have the clerk help you with string selection. Guitar strings come in pre gauged sets. These sets of 6 strings are listed as different gauges. In general I would recommend medium to light string sets for both an acoustic and electric guitar.

Keep in mind that an acoustic guitar is traditionally harder to play than an electric guitar because of the higher string tension used. Therefore, if you are working through this book with an acoustic guitar give yourself some extra time for your hand to get used to the extra pressure needed to push down the strings.

Tuning the Guitar

First, let's look at the basic mechanics of the guitar before starting to tune. There are tuning pegs at the far end of the guitar neck. Turning these pegs will raise or lower the pitch of the string. Play each string with your right hand and locate the peg that changes the pitch of that corresponding string. Over time you will know which peg changes which string but it isn't unusual to be confused about these pegs when you are first starting out.

If you take your right hand and play each string without using your left hand, you are playing on what is referred to as the "open" strings. To play other notes you need to press your left hand down on a string. When you do this you need to place one of your fingers between one of the frets and play that corresponding string with your right hand. When you play a note in this manner you are said to be "fretting" a note. In order to tune the guitar you are going to use a combination of playing an open string and comparing it to a "fretted" pitch on a neighboring string. Figure 1 shows you a guitar neck with some of the basic information you will need to know to get started.

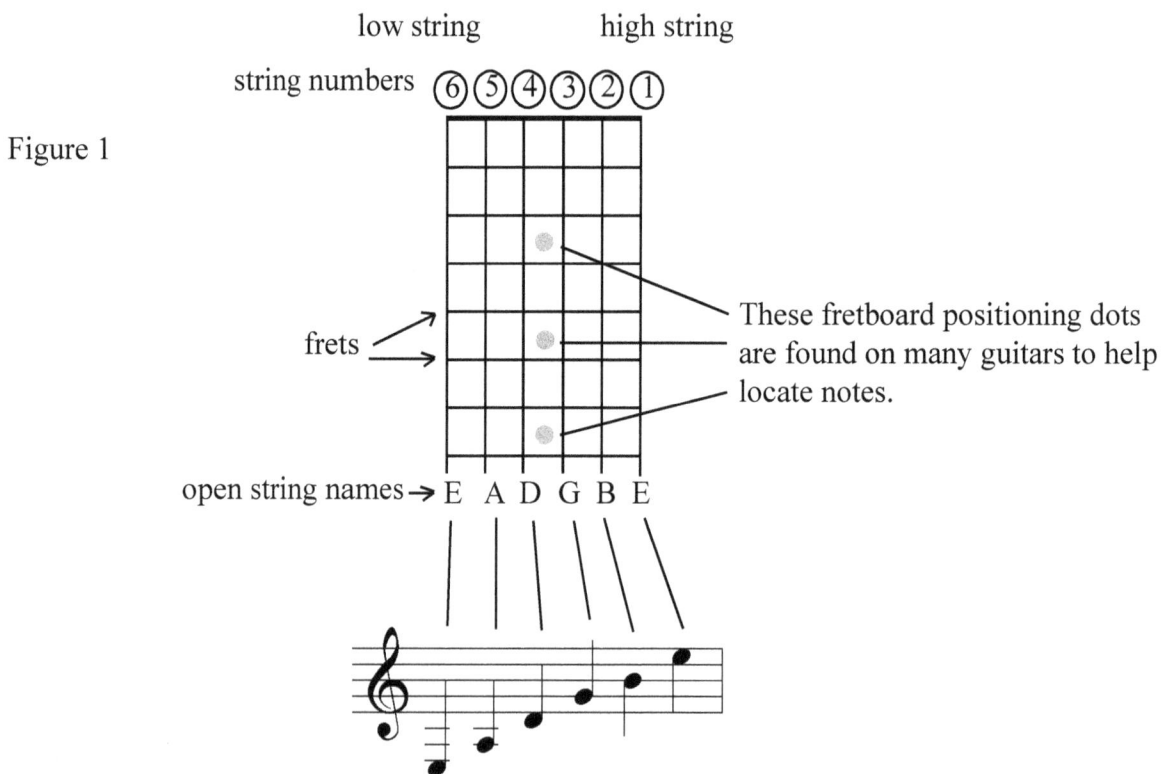

Figure 1

Notice that each string has a corresponding name and number. I've also included where you would find these open string pitches on a musical staff. We will discuss the music staff later.

There are many ways to tune a guitar. You can use an electronic guitar tuning device, or a pitch pipe, either of which can be purchased at a music store. Although I use an electronic guitar tuner when I perform I recommend you start to develop the ability to tune your guitar by hearing the sounds. For a beginner this can be a frustrating procedure. It takes time to develop your ear to recognize whether or not your guitar is in tune. The basic concept of tuning a stringed instrument is to make two pitches sound the same. In the case of the guitar we fret one string and play another to try to make the two notes, i.e. strings, sound the same. As you work on this you will find your ability to hear whether two notes sound exactly the same will improve. Don't worry if at first you feel like you are a lost cause. Many beginning students have problems discerning whether two pitches are the same and also have problems with the basic mechanics of the tuning process.

As a first step you will need to tune one of your strings to the correct pitch (often referred to as a "concert pitch." Do this by either using another instrument like a piano, tuning fork or guitar tuner. If none of these are immediately available you can tune your guitar anyway (as long as it is close to concert pitch) and it just won't be in the correct "concert pitch." This means that if you try to play with another guitarist you won't be tuned the same, and it will not sound good. If you are playing by yourself you may not notice any problem at all. **There is, however, a tuning pitch for each open string on the muse-eek.com website that you can play with the free downloadable midifile player. Most browsers like Netscape and Explorer will also play midifiles. In addition there are mp3 files of a guitar playing each open string to help you get your guitar in tune. You will find these files under the book's title listing.**

Using one of the previously mentioned methods, tune your 6th or low E string. As I mentioned you are going to play one "open" string and compare that pitch's sound to a fretted note on an adjacent string. To tune the A (5th string) you are going to play an A note on the low E string (6th string) by placing your index finger on the 5th fret of the low E string and then playing the open A string (5th string). (See Diagram 1). Play both strings. See if the A string sounds lower or higher in pitch. If the A string sounds lower in pitch raise the string up using the tuning peg for the A string until both strings sound the same. Conversely if the A string's pitch sounds too high in pitch, lower it using the tuning peg until both strings sound the same.

Diagram 1

Play this string "open"

string numbers ⑥⑤④③②①

fret this note with index finger ⟶ Ⓐ

string names E A D G B E

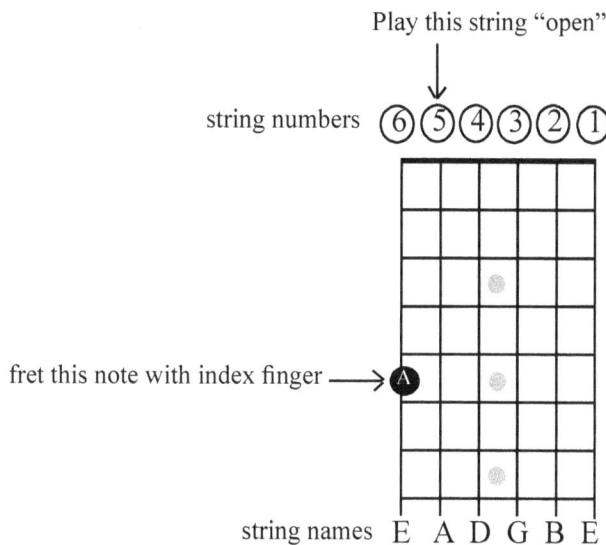

Continue this process for each string, always comparing the fretted string to the next higher "open" string. Notice that when you tune the G string to the B string you press on the 4th fret, **not** the 5th. (See Diagram 4 on the next page.)

Diagram 2

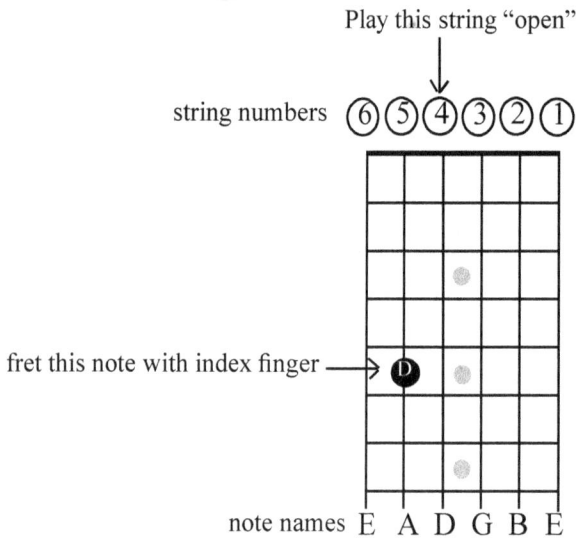

Diagram 3

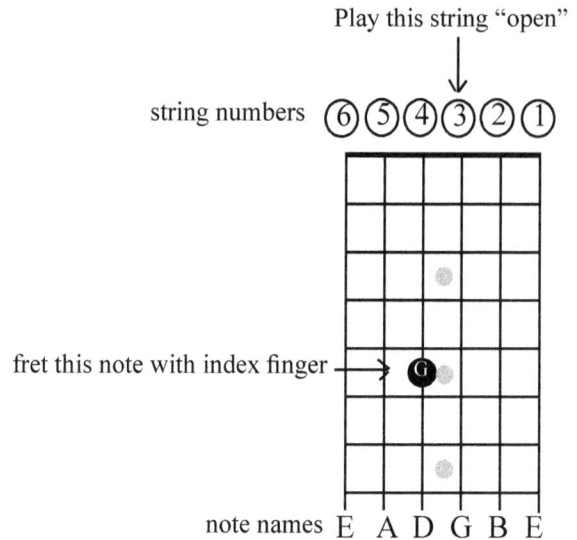

Diagram 4

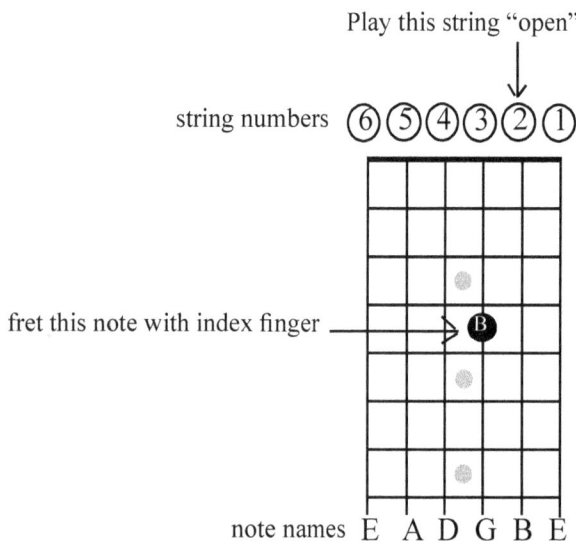

Diagram 5

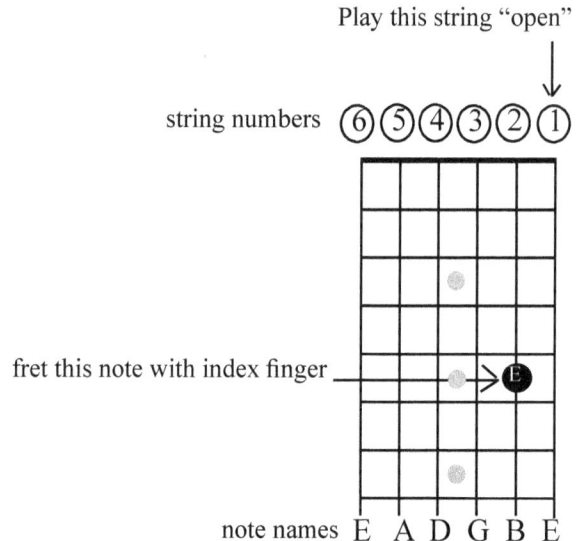

Tips:

You should always try to tune each string by raising the string's pitch up to the correct note rather than lowering the pitch down into the correct note. It's not the end of the world if you don't do this but it usually helps to keep the guitar in tune. Also if you have just put new strings on your guitar you will need to "stretch the string out" so it stays more consistently in tune. This is done by first tuning your guitar so that all your strings are to their correct pitches and then gently pulling on each string to stretch it. This is done by pulling each string up and away from the guitar. After each "pulling" you will find that the string has gone flat. Tune the string back up to the correct pitch and continue this until you can pull gently on each string and that string stays in tune. Do this to all 6 strings. This is a technique which is used by professionals to work around the problem that comes with changing strings. If you don't use this process you will find yourself constantly retuning your guitar for the first couple of days after replacing the strings. If you use this method you will find that your guitar stays in tune more consistently.

Notes Found on the Guitar

Below is a diagram showing you all the notes found on the guitar up to the 12th fret of each string. Some notes have two possible names. This is called its enharmonic spelling and is explained in the theory section found on the next few pages.

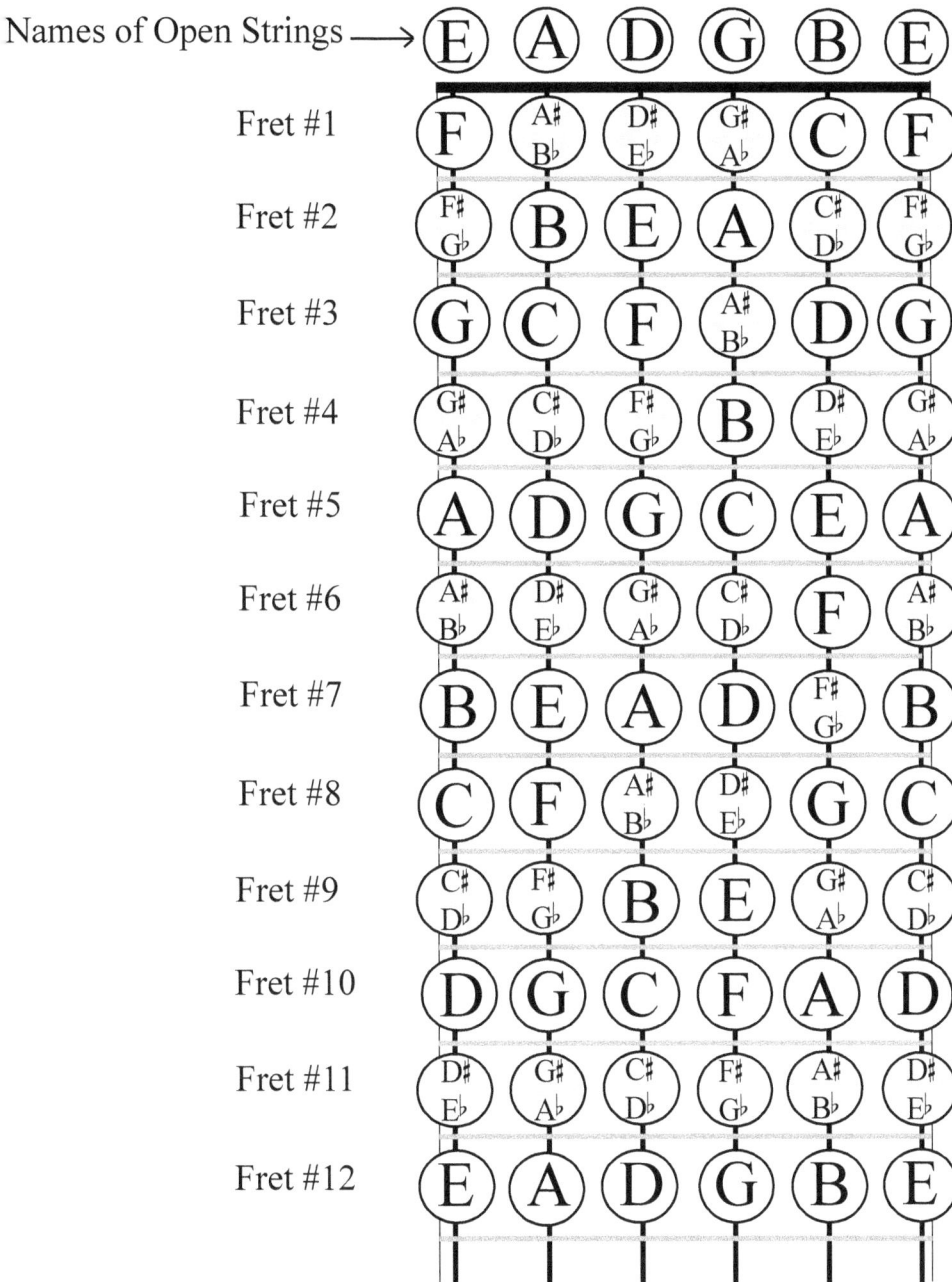

Names of Open Strings →

	E	A	D	G	B	E
Fret #1	F	A♯/B♭	D♯/E♭	G♯/A♭	C	F
Fret #2	F♯/G♭	B	E	A	C♯/D♭	F♯/G♭
Fret #3	G	C	F	A♯/B♭	D	G
Fret #4	G♯/A♭	C♯/D♭	F♯/G♭	B	D♯/E♭	G♯/A♭
Fret #5	A	D	G	C	E	A
Fret #6	A♯/B♭	D♯/E♭	G♯/A♭	C♯/D♭	F	A♯/B♭
Fret #7	B	E	A	D	F♯/G♭	B
Fret #8	C	F	A♯/B♭	D♯/E♭	G	C
Fret #9	C♯/D♭	F♯/G♭	B	E	G♯/A♭	C♯/D♭
Fret #10	D	G	C	F	A	D
Fret #11	D♯/E♭	G♯/A♭	C♯/D♭	F♯/G♭	A♯/B♭	D♯/E♭
Fret #12	E	A	D	G	B	E

It is important that you learn all these notes over time, but also remember it is important to understand the basics of music theory so you understand why these notes exist and how they relate to one another. The next section of this book will introduce you to basic music theory concepts. It is highly recommended that you read and reread these pages until this information is understood. You don't have to master <u>all</u> the music theory information before starting to learn the chords and chord progressions. Work back and forth until you can play the chords and chord progressions and reread the music theory section until its different components make sense to you.

Chapter One

Music Theory Introduction

The C Major Scale

The C Major Chord

Overall Purpose of This Method

Each chapter of this book will contain sections covering the important information you need to know to develop as a musician. The New York Guitar Method's main goal is to develop your skills to the level of a professional musician. Even though some of the material presented may not seem relevant to what you want to know right now, this material is what I have found professional musicians need to know to be successful.

Contents of Each Chapter

There are three major sections for each chapter in this book. These chapters are divided up into music theory, chords, and scales. The music theory section will give you background knowledge on a particular topic and then an exercise section which will help you apply this material directly to the guitar. The chord voicing and progression section will help you learn all the important chords on the guitar. This section contains tips on how to practice the chords along with chord progressions to apply your newly learned chords. A scale section will teach you all the important scales and how they relate to the chords you are learning. Fingerings will be supplied, along with further information on how to apply the scale.

How to Proceed

I think it makes logical sense to proceed through the chapters as written. However, you may want to learn the scale or chord for each chapter on the guitar first, so you can be practicing it as you learn the theory that applies to it. The theory will explain the construction of the scales and chords you are playing. It is also important to get both a physical, and emotional connection to the sounds of the chords and scales. If you feel this way of learning is better for you then I suggest you turn to pages 24-28 and look at the C major chord and the C major scale. You could then look back later at the theory section to help you understand the nuts and bolts of music. You should continue with whatever process helps you get the most out of this book.

How Much Music is Enough Music Theory

In the music theory sections of this book I have tried to be as thorough as possible because I am assuming you want to develop to a professional level with music. In many cases I have presented you with more information than you need to complete the theory exercises starting in Chapter Two. Along with reading each section I suggest you look at the music theory videos on-line to get a better idea of what is important to know now, and what can be learned over time. Keep in mind that if things stop making sense to you, it is most likely because you are skipping sections of this book in order to satisfy yourself. Some discipline when studying music is always a good rule of thumb in order to avoid confusion.

Remember There is Music Outside of This Book

The most successful students realize that they should be investigating music outside of this book. It is important to listen to music. You should experiment with the ideas presented here and come up with musical ideas of your own. Music is a creative art. Any creativity that you can bring to the table will only make you a better musician.

Music Theory

This section will start you with the building blocks for understanding music theory. Although not all of the information presented on the next couple of pages is crucial for successfully completing the exercises, it is important that you learn what the names of the notes are on the music staff. You should also understand that there are different octaves in music. Learn how a chromatic scale is built and how a major scale can be derived from using certain notes. You will find this information much easier to remember once you begin to apply it to the theory exercises starting in Chapter Two. With this in mind let's get started.

Learning the Notes of a Music Staff

The music staff is a series of lines and spaces employed to create a visual representation of sound. Each line and space corresponds to a pitch. Each pitch is given a name A, B, C, D, E, F, or G. A clef sign is also used to designate what names each line and space will receive. There are many types of clefs but we will only be using the treble in this book. The treble clef places the note in sequence in the order listed below. This complete system of lines and spaces with a clef sign is called a staff.

treble clef sign ——→

staff

The Use of Ledger Lines in Music

As can be seen in example 1, each line and space corresponds to a different tone. If you want to have pitches higher or lower than the 5 lines and four spaces you can extend the staff by using ledger lines. Ledger lines give you the ability to represent higher and lower pitches by extending the staff. These extended pitches are called ledger line notes. (See example below.)

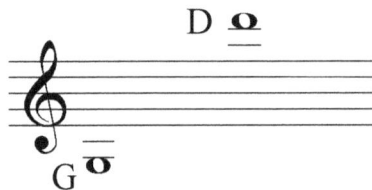

Learning the Concept of an Octave

If we look at our treble clef again we notice that there is an "e" on the first line and an "e" on the 4th space. Our ear recognizes these pitches as being the same pitch but the "e" on the 4th space sounds like a higher version of the low "e". In musical terminology the higher "e" is said to sound an octave higher than the lower "e". If we play these two "e's" on the guitar it would be the 2nd fret on the D string and fifth fret on the B string.

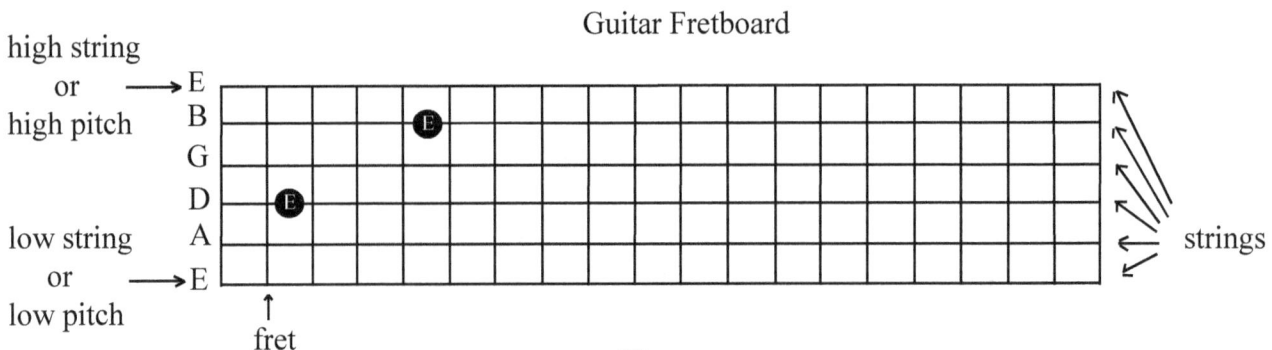

Guitar Fretboard

high string
or ——→ E
high pitch B
G
D
low string A
or ——→ E
low pitch

fret

strings

22

Summarizing What We Have Learned So Far

To summarize what we have learned so far:

1. There are 7 pitches which are represented on a staff with the letter names A,B,C,D,E,F,G.
2. These 7 pitches keep repeating themselves in different octaves.
3. To represent these notes in other octaves we need to use ledger lines or other clefs.

Learning All the Available Notes in Western Music

There are a total of 12 pitches used in western music which of course as we have learned can be found in many different octaves. To show all 12 notes in the system, "sharp" (♯) and "flat" (♭) symbols are used to represent the tones that occur between the letter names of the notes. For example between the note C and D there exists a pitch which can be called either C sharp or D flat. These notes are represented as follows C♯ or D♭. The (♯) and (♭) symbols work in the following way: a flat (♭) lowers the pitch and a sharp (♯) raises the pitch. If a note is sharped it is said to have been raised a half step, if it is flatted it is said to have been lowered a half step. **A half step is the smallest distance possible in western music.**

The Chromatic Scale

If we take all of the 12 available notes used in the western system of music and combine them on the staff within one octave we get what is called the chromatic scale. Two things to notice are: there is no sharp or flat between E and F, and B and C, and there are two ways to write out a chromatic scale. One way to write the chromatic scale uses sharps. The other way uses flats. You will also notice that the D in the chromatic scale with flats has a symbol in front of it. This symbol is called a natural sign. It is used to cancel the flat that appears before the previous D. **In written music, measures are used to delineate time, and sharps and flats carry through the whole measure until a new measure starts, unless a natural symbol is used to cancel it.**

Two Ways to Write a Chromatic Scale on a Staff

The 12 note chromatic scale can be represented in either of the two examples listed below. Remember a C♯ is the same note as a D♭ on the guitar. If you play on only one string of the guitar and move consecutively up each fret you will be playing a chromatic scale. If you were to play the above two examples of a chromatic scale you would start on the A string 3rd fret, and move up each fret until you reached the 15th fret to complete the chromatic scale.

Chromatic Scale

Seeing the Chromatic Scale on the Guitar

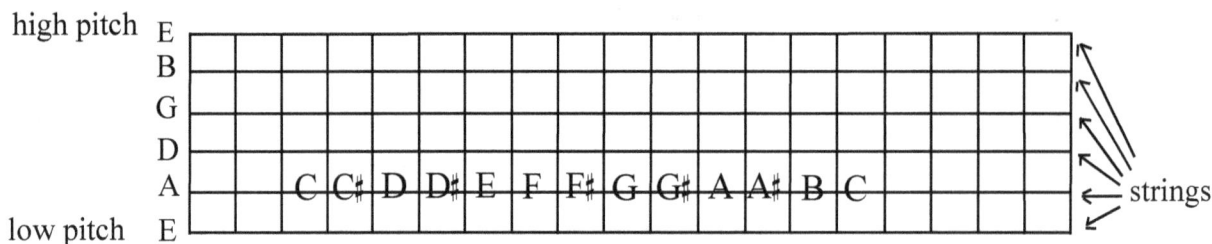

high pitch E

B

G

D

A   C C# D D# E F F# G G# A A# B C

low pitch E ← strings

Though the chromatic scale represents all 12 notes, much of western music of the last few centuries has been based around only 7 tones. If we extract these 7 notes as shown below we end up with a major scale.

Major Scale Derived from a Chromatic Scale

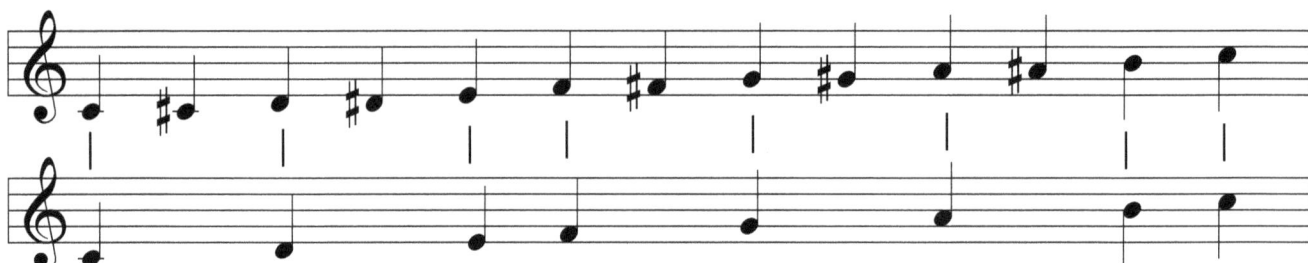

Chromatic Scale

Major Scale

Interval Relationships Found in a Major Scale

If we look at the distance in half steps between the notes of a major scale we see a pattern; whole, whole, half, whole, whole, whole, half. **All major scales are based on these intervals.**

C Major Scale

whole step   whole step   half step   whole step   whole step   whole step   half step

Seeing the C Major Scale on the Guitar

When we apply this to the guitar fretboard the information works out accordingly: start on any note on the guitar and move up on one string starting with a whole step (2 frets), whole step, half step (1 fret), whole step, whole step, whole step, half step. This is one way to play a major scale on the guitar.

Guitar Fretboard

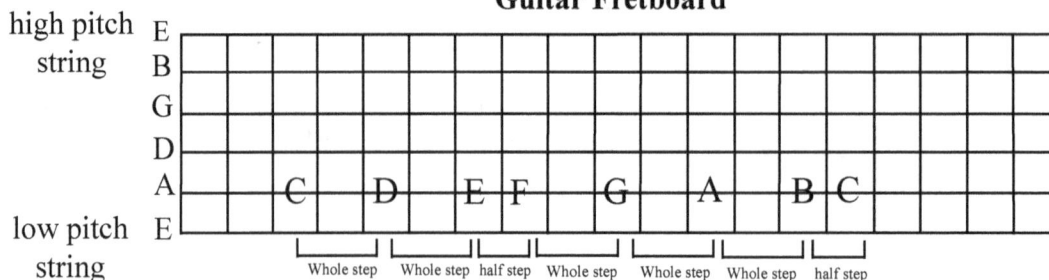

high pitch E
string
B

G

D

A   C   D   E F   G   A   B C

low pitch E
string
Whole step Whole step half step Whole step   Whole step Whole step half step

24

Practical Way to Play a C Major Scale on the Guitar

While it is easy to see how the major scale is built in the previous example, it is more common for a guitarist to employ multiple strings in order to play a scale. Keep in mind that there are numerous ways to play any scale on the guitar and the example below is just one. The C major scale below uses "open" strings on the D, G, and B strings. Therefore, when you come to the notes D, G and B you need to play an "open" string in order to hear the correct note. Learn the scale below slowly so you can play up and down the scale without hesitation. Be conscious of using proper technique. Please refer back to the technique section found on pages 13-15 if you are unsure. Play the scale slowly and try to make each note sound good and ring out as much as possible. Try to make each note *legato*. This means that you want the least amount of silence between each note. It should sound like one flows directly into the other.

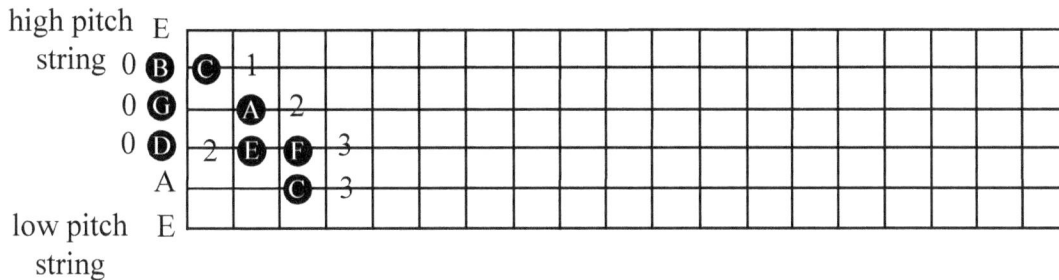

This knowledge of the chromatic scale, major scale and the construction of intervals is a valuable tool for understanding the internal structure of chords. Usually it takes a student around a year of study to remember all this information. If you do the exercises presented in this book and subsequent books in this series you will find that all this information becomes second nature.

Building Chords

So far we have discussed the chromatic and major scales and where to play one of these scales on the guitar fretboard. The C scale presented above is used when you play a C chord. So first we need to learn how to build and play a C chord so we can in turn use the C scale for improvisation.

In general a chord can be a combination of any 3 or more notes played at the same time. One of the most common ways to build chords is to stack up every other note of a scale. For example, if we took the C scale and used every other note we would extract C, E and G.

C Major Triad

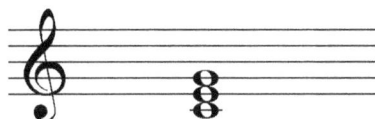

Building a C Major Chord

The structure below, C, E, and G, form what is called a major chord. If we measure the distance or interval between each note using our chromatic scale we can find the formula for building major chords. Between C and E there are 4 half steps. This is called a major third. Between E and G there are 3 half steps. This is called a minor third. Therefore, to create a major chord we need to combine a major third on the bottom and a minor third on the top.

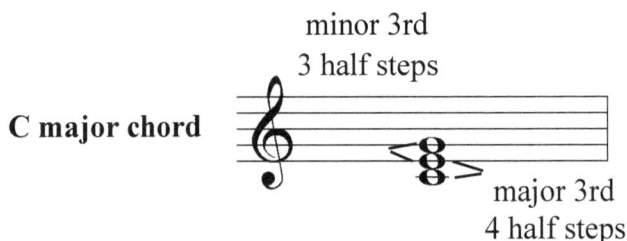

minor 3rd
3 half steps

C major chord

major 3rd
4 half steps

Playing a C Major Chord on the Guitar

The diagram below shows you how you would play this on the guitar. The tablature below shows fret location with the circled number, the fingering with the number next to the dots, and an X placed above to indicate which string is not played. Sometimes open circles will indicate that open strings are to be played (see example below). Index finger is 1, middle finger is 2, ring finger 3, little finger is 4.

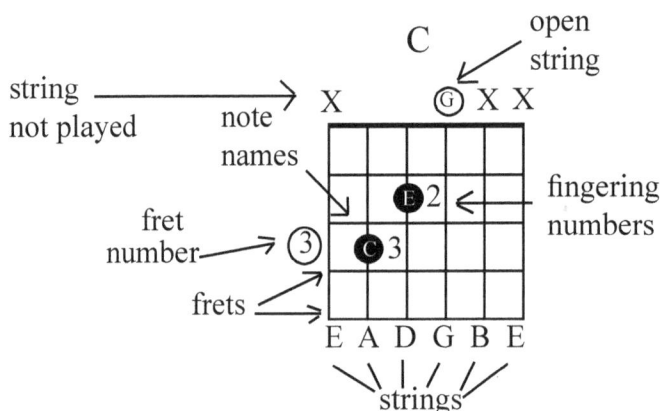

C

open
string

string
not played

note
names

X   Ⓖ X X

Ⓔ2 ←

fingering
numbers

fret
number

③   Ⓒ3

frets

E A D G B E

strings

Understanding a Chord Voicing

Although the chord above will work fine for a C major chord, guitarists oftendouble a few notes from the triad in order to make the chord sound more full. they are combined into a chord on the guitar which is both playable, and has a good sound.   So there are many ways to play any given chord depending on how many notes of the chord you use, and how many notes are doubled. **Each of these different combinations of notes is called a chord voicing.**

**Common chord voicing
for a C major.**

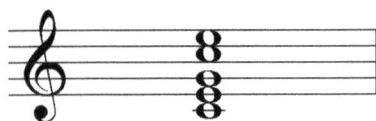

**This is how you would play
these notes on the guitar.**

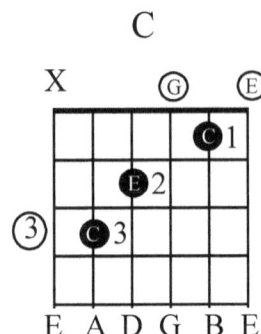

C

X   Ⓖ   Ⓔ

Ⓒ1

Ⓔ2

③   Ⓒ3

E A D G B E

Now it is Time to Play a Chord on the Guitar

On the next page you will find the fingering for a C major chord. With the theory information you have learned on the previous pages you should have a good idea on how this chord is constructed.

How to Practice the Strumming Exercises

With each new chord you will be given a short chord progression to play. This will help you develop your skills with playing the chord and strumming at the same time. I suggest you use the following tips to help you learn these strumming patterns in combination with the chord. You should realize that playing a chord is usually much easier than playing the chord and strumming a rhythm at the same time. Therefore, be patient with yourself, this is not easy to start with, but once you gain a little coordination you should find strumming chords becomes easy and fun.

1. Play each example slowly, using a metronome or a help file, or count the correct number of beats for each.
2. Follow the picking directions. (see below the exercise for explanation of picking symbols)
3. Speed up the example over a week of practice then proceed to the next level.

Reading Rhythms

Refer to pages 153-57 for an explanation on how to read rhythms.

If You Have Problems There is More Help Online at muse-eek.com

There are two different types of files available to you to help you master each strumming exercise. The midifiles (played by downloading a midifile player from the muse-eek.com website) will play each example at whatever tempo you select.

Using audio and midifiles can really speed up your progress on the guitar. Take the time to set up your computer so you can take advantage of these help files. You will also notice that the midifile player allows you to speed up and slow down the audio so you can gradually play the chords faster and faster.

Root Position Major Chords

Possible chord tones for major
1,3,5

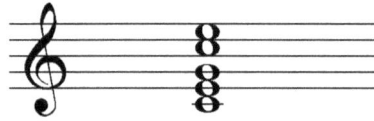

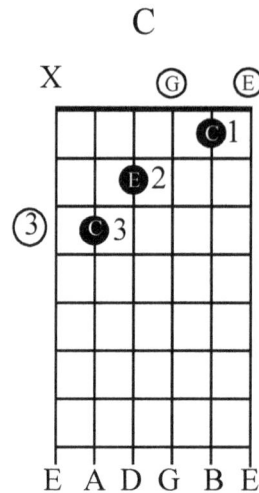

C

The C chord is usually one of the easier chords to play. It is common for a beginning student to have a problem keeping the 2nd finger curved enough to allow the "open" G string to sound. It is also common to have the same problem with the "open" high E string. Make sure to look at the video chord files found in the member's area of the muse-eek.com website for tips on how to play a C chord more proficiently and the common mistakes students make when learning the chord.

Applying the C Chord to a Strumming Pattern

Below you will find a strumming pattern which includes the rhythm. The rhythm is written with rhythmic notation. This is commonly used in professional situations to show a performer the rhythm of a chord progression with no regard to a specific pitch on the clef. Therefore, you will notice that diamonds and slashes are used only to designate the amount of time each chord is played and held. If you are confused by this type of notation I suggest you check out the rhythmic notation file found in the member's area, along with the audio files, so you can hear exactly what this should sound like.

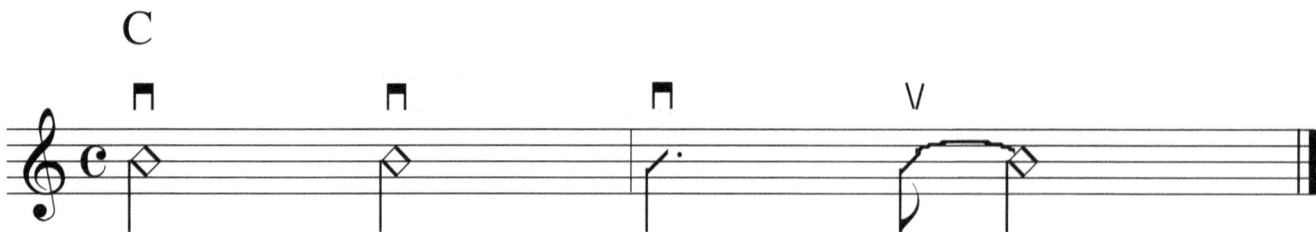

Explanation of Strumming Symbols

The following symbols are used to indicate an up or down stroke.

⊓ = Strum with a downward motion
V = Strum with an upward motion

Sight Reading

Each chapter in this book will include a sight reading example like the one on the following page. Sight reading is very important because it can open so many musical doors for you. For example, learning to sight read gives you access to literally millions of music books that include notation of music from every style all over the world. Also, if you want to play in bands, especially those that include original music, you will likely run into charts you will have to read. Conversely, if you wish to compose your own music to be played with others, learning to sight read will give you the potential to write for any instrument you wish. Simply stated, you will be afforded many more musical opportunities if you learn to sight read. That said, let us now talk about how to understand the sight reading examples in this book.

Understanding the Symbols in the Sight Reading Example

String Numbers

A number with a circle around it, located above the staff, indicates which string you will use to play a note. A series of notes will frequently be played one after another on the same string. In these cases the circled number will only appear above the first note. You should continue playing the subsequent notes on that same string until another circled number appears telling you to move to another string.

Fret Numbers

The number located directly below the staff indicates the fret location of the note.

Fingering Numbers

The bottom number of the two located below staff indicates which left hand finger you will use to play the note.

Examples

The examples below show you the string, fret and fingering location of the first two notes (E and G) played on beats one and two in the first measure of the sight reading example on the following page.

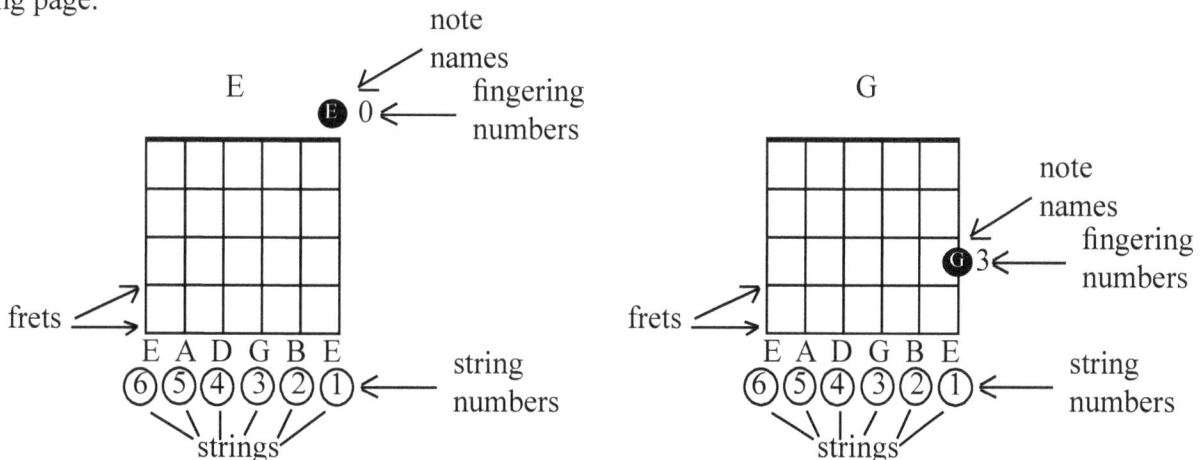

Chords

Many of the sight reading examples include chords you may not already know. They are included so you can come back when your chord knowledge improves and play the exercises as a duet with another guitarist. If you are studying with a teacher, he/she should play the chords while you play the melody. If you are studying on your own, there are help files online at www.muse-eek.com that will play the chords for you while you play the melody.

Understanding the Guitar as a Transposing Instrument

It must be mentioned that the guitar is a transposing instrument sounding an octave (12 half steps) lower than written. Therefore, middle C on a piano appears as the C one ledger line below the staff (Example 1) while the actual sound of middle C on the guitar is on the 1st fret on the B string (See Example 2). So if you see a middle C written for guitar (See Example 3) you will play it on the 3rd fret of the A string (See Example 4). **All staff notation in this book is already transposed.**

Example 1

Middle C

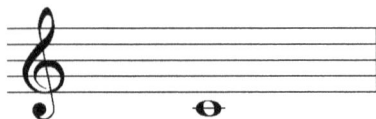

Example 3

Middle C in guitar notation

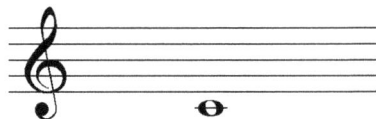

Example 2

Middle C

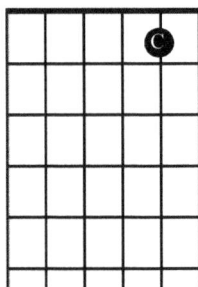

E   A   D   G   B   E

Example 4

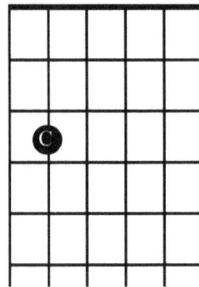

When you see middle C on the staff you play this note on the guitar.

E   A   D   G   B   E

The example below shows how the open strings on the guitar would be written.

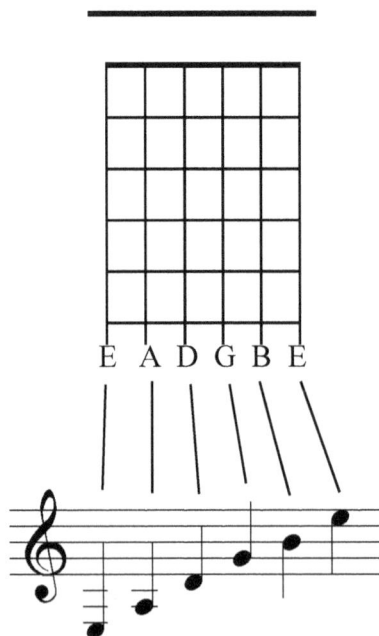

E   A   D   G   B   E

Sight Reading Exercise 1

See page 29 for an explanation on understanding the sight reading example.

Chapter Two

Music Theory Basic Intervals

The G Major Scale

The G Major Chord

More Theory Knowledge and How to Organize It

The next couple of pages address the various keys found in music. You will also learn about intervals. This is more information than you could learn in a week so it's important to realize what you need to learn, and what you can learn over time.

The important thing to get from the next page is how a major scale is built and how it is a modular system, so you can for instance, play a D major scale by sliding up a couple a frets on the guitar and playing the same interval patterns. It is not important that you memorize all the key signatures present on the next page right away. However, you will find that you can use key center knowledge to help you quickly figure out the notes in chords or scales. You can find further information on this in the Alternate Music Theory file found in the member's area.

Learning Your Intervals

In the next few pages you will begin to learn all your basic intervals. By learning this information you will begin to understand how chords are built. Since it's best to learn by applying information directly each chapter will provide you with a page of exercises to apply one specific aspect of music theory. In this case, it will be exercises to help you learn intervals and where these intervals are on the guitar fretboard.

The Best Way to Learn Music Theory

With each chapter you will be given music exercises to help you learn and memorize the material presented. I suggest that you do a few of the music theory exercises each day so that you are steadily reintroducing this information. By doing only two or three exercises each day it will help your mind to remember the information and in turn will help you memorize the theoretical concepts presented. It is also recommended that you play these examples on the guitar so you hear what they sound like, and begin to associate their shape with the various interval types.

What's Important to Learn First

You will find a lot of information presented on the next few pages. The important thing to learn is the half steps contained in each interval. The key signatures will be useful in the future but are only presented here for two reasons; so you understand there is more than one key, and that all major keys have the same interval content but start on different notes. Over time you can learn all the key signatures. This will happen naturally you we begin playing all the scales in every key. With all theoretical information it is best to learn it as you apply it. Therefore, I suggest you not worry about learning the intervals before you do the "basic interval" exercises, but learn the intervals as you do the "basic interval" exercise.

Playing Scales in All Keys and Key Signatures

The example below shows you once again, a major scale being played up and down the A string.

Guitar Fretboard

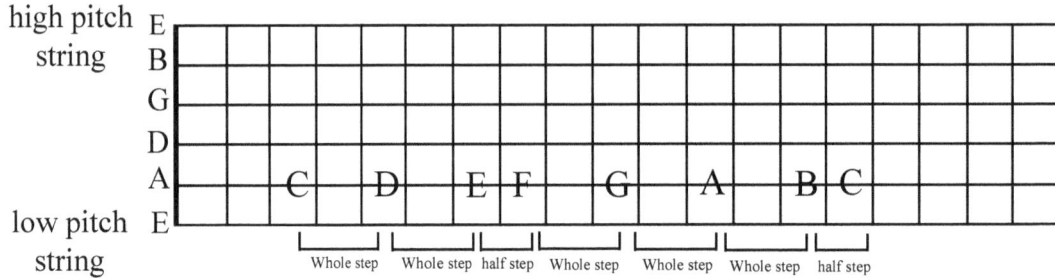

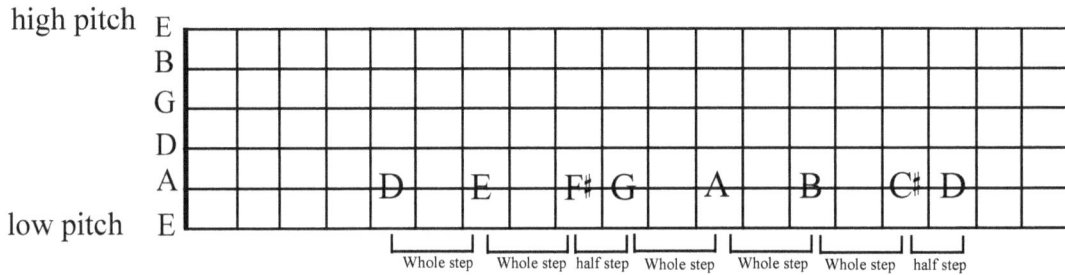

If we move up two frets, start on a D, and use the pattern of whole step, whole step, half step, whole step, whole step, whole step, half step this will form a D major scale.

Guitar Fretboard

The notes of a C major scale C, D, E, F, G, A, B are commonly referred to as the diatonic notes of the key of C major. If we take the key of D major, the diatonic notes would be D, E, F#, G, A, B, C#.

If we use the major scale formula (1,1,1/2,1,1,1,1/2) we can figure out every major scale. We will find that each key has a different number of sharps or flats. If a piece of music uses a particular key, it's key signature is placed at the beginning of the piece of music. The example below shows a list of all the sharps and flats found in various keys. These are commonly referred to as the key signatures. They occur after the clef sign and at the beginning of each line of music.

The Basic Intervals in Music

Whole steps and half steps are the basic building blocks for the major scale. The whole step equals two half steps. The distance between two notes is called an interval. For example the distance between C and D is a whole step. This is also called a major second interval. It is important to know intervals because chords are frequently named for the intervals in their internal structure. All two note interval combinations from the root of the major scale are listed below.

Major 2nd
2 half steps

Major 3rd
4 half steps

Perfect 4th
5 half steps

Perfect 5th
7 half steps

Major 6th
9 half steps

Major 7th
11 half steps

Octave
12 half steps

If we sharp any of these intervals we create an augmented interval. If we flat a major second, third, sixth, or seventh, we create a minor interval. If we flat a perfect fourth, a fifth, or an octave, we get a diminished interval, and *if we double flat the major 7th we have a diminished 7th.* * Below are some of the more common augmented, minor and diminished intervals.

augmented unison
1 half step

minor 2nd
1 half step

augmented 2nd
3 half steps

minor 3rd
3 half steps

augmented 4th
or tritone: 6 half steps

diminished 5th
or flat 5th: 6 half steps

augmented 5th
8 half steps

minor 6th
8 half steps

diminished 7th *
9 half steps

augmented 6th
10 half steps

minor 7th
10 half steps

Directions for Theory Exercises on Next Page

1. Find the specific interval above each note and write this on both the music staff and the guitar fretboard diagram.
2. Look at how many half steps are involved to make the interval by counting up half steps. Use the chromatic scale found on page 23.
3. If you are unsure of how many half steps are contained in the interval refer to the top of this page.
4. Remember that there is more than one correct answer for each exercise. This is because there are many repeated notes on the guitar. I have provided you with all the possible correct answers in the Alternate Music Theory Answers file found in the member's area of the www.muse-eek.com website.

* A double flat (♭♭) lowers a note two half steps. A double sharp (x) raises a pitch two half steps.

Basic Interval Exercises

Example

perfect 5   major 7   perfect 4   major 3

major 2   augmented unison   minor 2   augmented 2

minor 3   tritone   augmented 4   flat 5

diminished 5   augmented 5   minor 6   diminished 7

augmented 6   minor 7   perfect 5   major 7

major 6   perfect 4   major 3   major 2

augmented unison   minor 2   augmented 2   minor 3

tritone   augmented   flat 5   diminished 5

How to Proceed

On the next page you will see the music theory involved to make a G major scale. G major contains one sharp. That sharp is F Sharp. Once again jump to pages 39-41 if you want to first learn the scale and/or the G chord. Probably the single most important thing to do as you learn each chord is to develop the ability to switch between each chord fluently. This is by far the hardest hurdle a new student of guitar will face. Therefore, make sure to practice the chord progressions on pages 160-71.

Additional Techniques

Improvising with Each New Scale You Learn

As you learn each new scale I highly recommend that you improvise with this scale over the chord it is related to. This may feel very awkward when you start but over time you will find you will feel more and more comfortable with creating melodic ideas on the spot. In order to improvise you of course will need something to improvise over. If you go to the Member's Area you will find links to MP3's that you can use to apply these scales.

Adding Notes to Chords

Along with strumming patterns to help you learn new chords. I will also present ways to alter chords, or add notes between chords, to create more interest. On each new chord we will explore a different way to add scale notes to chords. These additional techniques, although physically difficult for some students, can help to create a much more satisfying musical experience. Because of the depth and beauty these notes can add to even the most common chords and progressions I urge you to explore these suggestions. If you are having problems simply playing the chord, you should wait until you have better technique before trying these ideas. Remember, each student is different. What is easy for you may not be for someone else, and visa versa.

G Major Scale Theory

Chromatic Scale Starting on G on the Guitar Fretboard

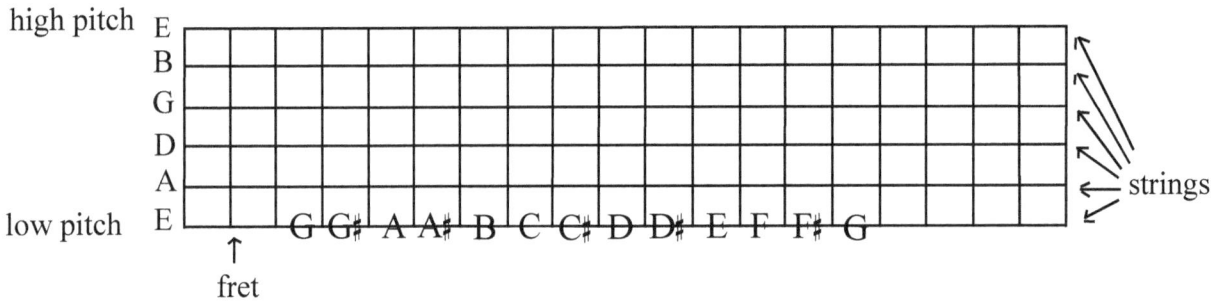

Extracting a G Major Scale from a Chromatic Scale

Just like the C major scale, the G major scale can be extracted from the chromatic scale. Below you can see how the notes of G major can be found.

Major Scale Derived from Chromatic Scale

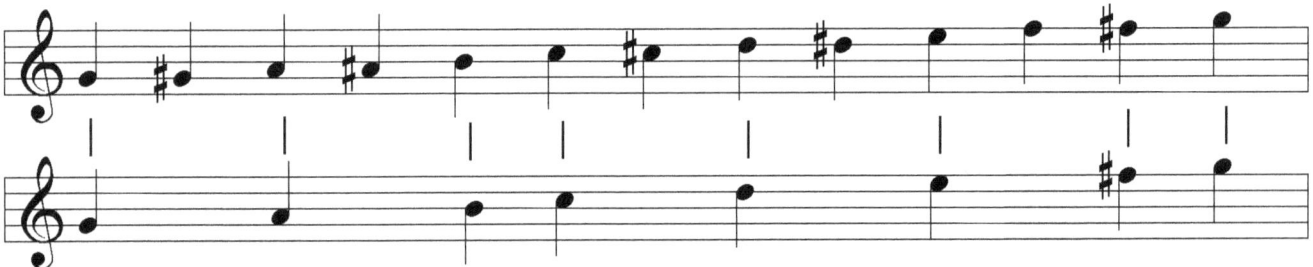

Interval Relationships Found in a Major Scale

If we look at the distance in half steps between the notes of a G major scale we see a pattern; whole, whole, half, whole, whole, whole, half. **All major scales are based on these intervals.**

G Major Scale

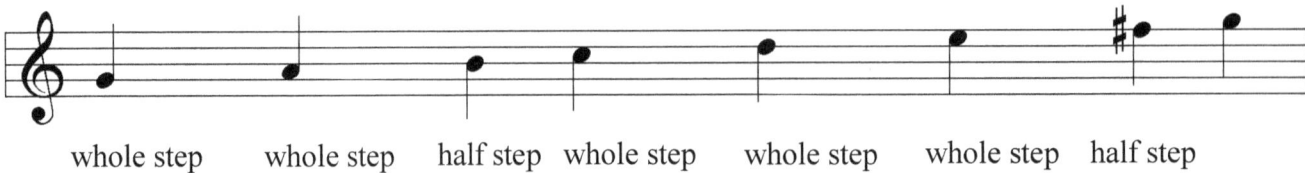

Seeing the G Major Scale on the Guitar

As we have seen in the previous chapter, if we apply this to the guitar fretboard the information works out accordingly: start on any note on the guitar and move up on one string starting with a whole step (2 frets), whole step, half step (1 fret), whole step, whole step, whole step, half step. This is one way to play a major scale on the guitar.

Guitar Fretboard

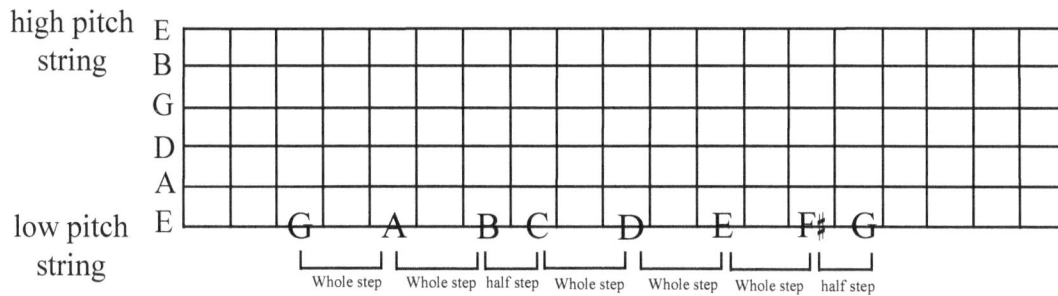

Another way to play this G Major scale on the guitar is to play it in "open" position by using the open strings, and in this case, the first four frets of the guitar as shown below.

Practical Way to Play a G Major Scale on the Guitar

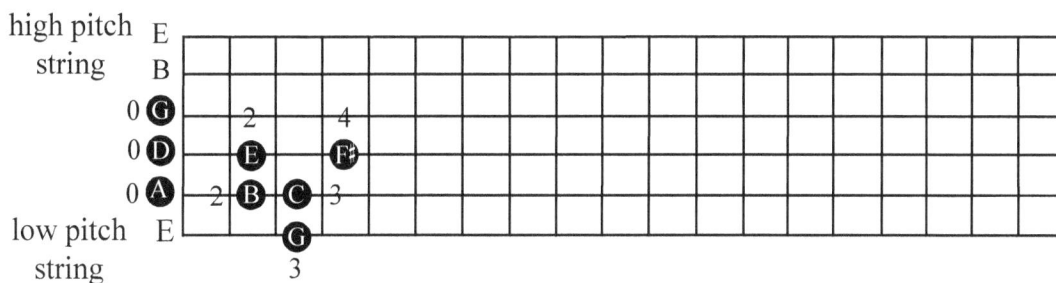

Building Chords

To review what you have learned so far, chords can be a combination of any 3 or more notes played at the same time. Western music builds chords using a wide variety of intervals. One of the most common ways to build chords is to stack up diatonic 3rd intervals. For example, if we took G in the key of G and stacked up 3rds we would get G, B, and D because all of those notes are in the key of G, and are a 3rd apart. **These structures built in thirds are commonly referred to as triads, and the G note is said to be the root of the chord**.

G Major Triad

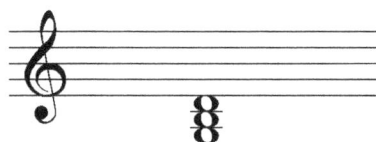

Building a G Major Chord

The structure below, G, B, and D, form what is called a major chord. If we measure the distance or interval between each note using our chromatic scale we can find the formula for building major chords. Between G and B is 4 half steps or a major third. Between B and D is 3 half steps or a minor third. Therefore, to create a major chord we need to combine a major third on the bottom, and a minor third on the top.

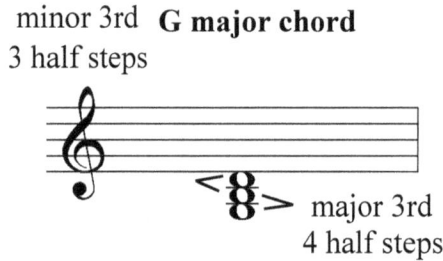

minor 3rd **G major chord**
3 half steps

major 3rd
4 half steps

Playing a G Major Chord on the Guitar

The diagram below shows you how you would play this on the guitar. The tablature below shows fret location with the circled number, the fingering with the number next to the dots, and an X placed above to indicate which string is not played. Sometimes open circles will indicate that open strings are to be played (see example below). Index finger is 1, middle finger is 2, ring finger 3, little finger is 4.

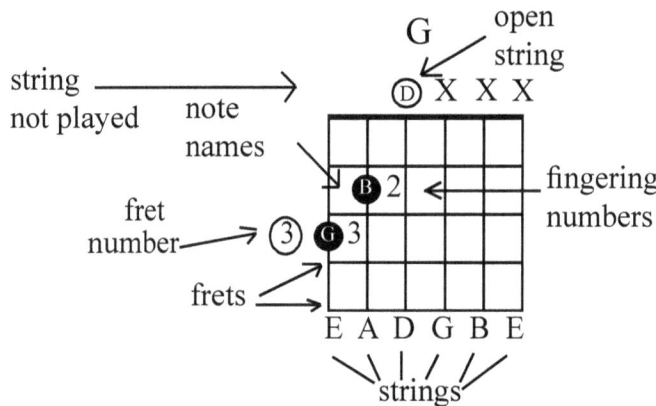

string
not played

note
names

G   open
string

Ⓓ X X X

B 2   fingering
numbers

fret
number   ③ Ⓖ 3

frets

E A D G B E
strings

Understanding a Chord Voicing

As shown in the previous chapter, although the chord above will work fine for a G major chord it is common for a guitarist to double a few notes from the triad in order to make the chord sound fuller. It is combined into a chord on the guitar which is both playable and has a good sound. So there are many ways to play any given chord depending on how many notes of the chord you use and how many notes are doubled. **Each of these different combinations of notes is called a chord voicing.**

Common chord voicing for a G major.

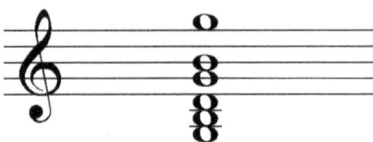

This is how you would play these notes on the guitar.

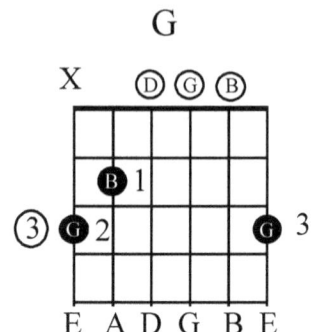

G

X   Ⓓ Ⓖ Ⓑ

B 1

③ Ⓖ 2   Ⓖ 3

E A D G B E

Root Position Major Chords

Possible chord tones for major
1,3,5

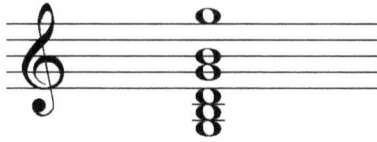

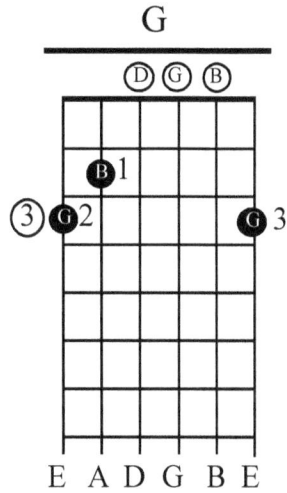

The G chord is usually one of the easier chords for a beginner but it is sometimes hard to change to it quickly in a chord progression. Make sure your "open" D, G and B strings ring out clearly. Make sure to look at the video chord files found in the member's area of the muse-eek.com website for tips on how to play a G chord more proficiently and the common mistakes students make when learning the chord.

Applying the G Chord to a Strumming Pattern

Below you will find a strumming pattern which includes the rhythm. If the rhythm is hard for you, start by using the rhythm we used for the C major chord. Then, practice the G rhythm when you are ready.

Once again the rhythm is written with rhythmic notation. See page 157 for more information on rhythmic notation.

Now let's try using both chords you have learned

Explanation of Strumming Symbols

The following symbols are used to indicate an up or down stroke.

⊓ = Strum with a downward motion

V = Strum with an upward motion

Additional Techniques

First, I must again stress if you are having problems just playing the chord, and the chord progressions on the previous page, you should wait until you have better technique before trying the ideas presented below. Remember, each student is different and what is easy for you may not be for someone else and visa versa.

3 Ways to Apply Scales to Chords

The most common ways a musician adds in these notes is by the 3 methods below:

1. Adding notes to chords as permanent additions
2. Adding notes to chords that create melodic movement while the chord is being played
3. Playing notes between chords

Depending on the chord you play and how you finger it, different methods work better for different chords. Theoretically, all methods work on every chord but may be physically hard to play. There are two types of notes you will add to chords. These notes are either called tensions* or avoid notes*. It's not that important that you totally understand these two types of notes theoretically right now.

For major chords the common tensions added are the 2nd and the 6th. It should be noted that the ♯4 is also an available tension and will be discussed in later volumes of this series.

Example of Applying Scales to Chords

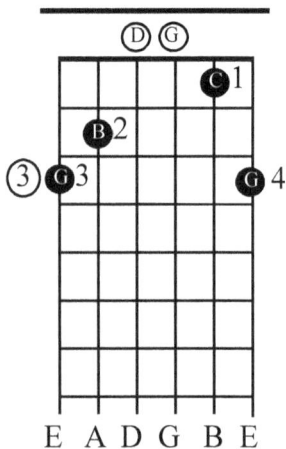

First, notice that the fingering has changed for this technique. In this example we will add the note C into our G chord. This note will feel like it wants to resolve. Therefore, you might strum the G chord once, then the G chord with the C added, and then back to the G chord. You will probably recognize this sound. You are adding in the avoid note for the G chord therefore it will feel like it wants to resolve. When you add the C to the G chord this chord is called a G add 4. You should try adding this 4th to each new chord you learn. I will give more examples as we move through other chords.

Applying Scale Addition to a Strummed Chord Progression

* Tensions are non chord tones that do not need to resolve. Therefore, they can be played at the same time as the chord.

**Avoid notes are notes that feel like they want to resolve. Each chord and scale type has it's own set of avoid note(s).

Sight Reading Exercise 2

See page 29 for an explanation on understanding the sight reading example.

Chapter Three

Music Theory Larger Intervals

The F Major Scale

The F Major Chord

Larger Intervals

If we continue past the octave, intervals are given new names to show that they are more than an octave apart (See example below). The larger intervals exercise on page 46 covers these intervals.

9th	10th	11th	12th	13th
14 half steps	16 half steps	17 half steps	19 half steps	21 half steps

An augmented interval may be written in different ways. A (+) may appear before the number, or a (♯) or (aug). If the interval is flatted it is usually indicated with a flat. The example below shows some of the common interval names you will need to know.

♭9th	♯9th	♯11th	♭13th	♭15th
13 half steps	15 half steps	18 half steps	20 half steps	23 half steps

Directions for Larger Intervals Excercise

The following page gives you 32 larger interval exercises to help you understand larger intervals on your instrument and in written notation. Each exercise gives you a note on the staff and an interval written above the staff. In example 1 which has already been done for you, the note was C and the interval was an octave. The note C was written on the third space of the staff an octave above C. On the guitar fretboard C and C are written to represent the same notes an octave apart on the guitar. For each example first write the given interval on the staff then write the same notes on the guitar fretboard.

Larger Interval Excerises

Example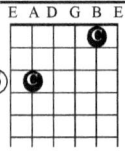

octave   major 9   minor 9   11th

♭9   ♯9   9th   11th

11th   9th   ♭13   ♯11

10th   10th   ♭15th   minor 9th

♭13   ♯11   octave   major 9

13th   minor 9   11th   ♭9

♯9   ♭9th   11th   ♯11th

9th   ♭13   ♯11   10th

F Major Scale Theory

Chromatic Scale Starting on F on Guitar Fretboard

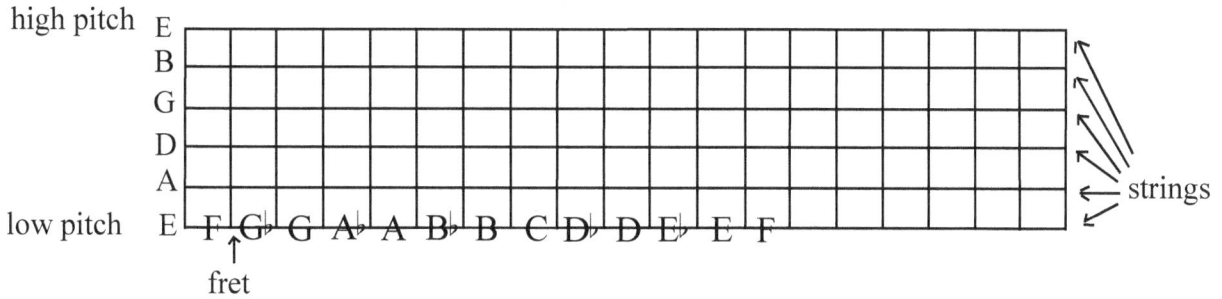

Extracting an F Major Scale from a Chromatic Scale

Though the chromatic scale represents all 12 notes, much of western music of the last few centuries has been based around only 7 tones. If we extract these 7 notes, as shown below. we end up with a major scale.

Major Scale Derived from Chromatic Scale

Chromatic Scale

Major Scale

Interval Relationships Found in a Major Scale

If we look at the distance in half steps between the notes of an F major scale we see a pattern; whole, whole, half, whole, whole, whole, half. **All major scales are based on these intervals.**

F Major Scale

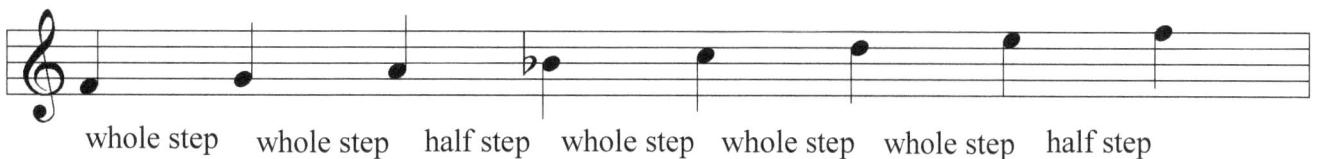

whole step   whole step   half step   whole step   whole step   whole step   half step

Seeing the F Major Scale on the Guitar

As previously discussed, if we apply this to the guitar fretboard, the information works out accordingly: start on any note on the guitar and move up on one string starting with a whole step (2 frets), whole step, half step (1 fret), whole step, whole step, whole step, half step. This is one way to play a major scale on the guitar.

Guitar Fretboard

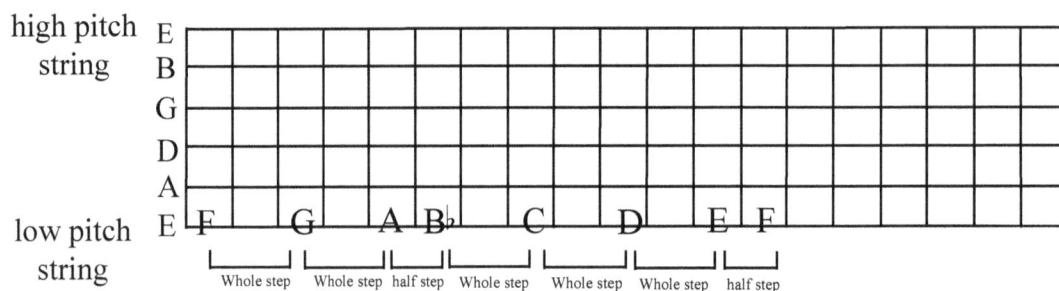

Another way to play this F major scale on the guitar is to play it in "open" position by using the open strings, and in this case, the first three frets of the guitar, as shown below.

Practical Way to Play an F Major Scale on the Guitar

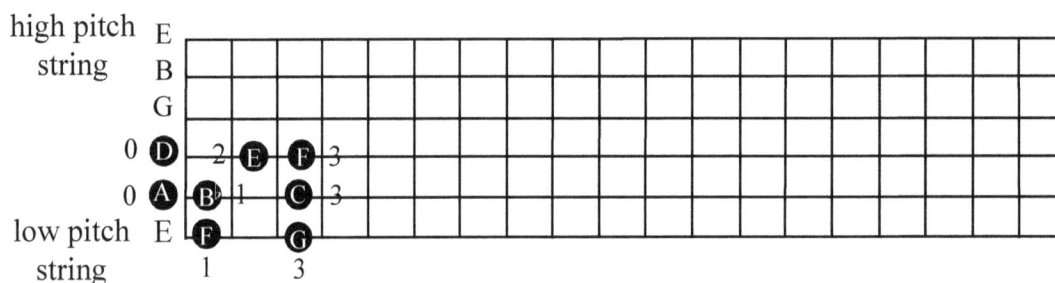

Building Chords

To review what you have learned so far, a chord can be a combination of any 3 or more notes played at the same time. Western music builds chords using a wide variety of intervals. One of the most common ways to build chords is to stack up diatonic 3rd intervals. For example, if we took F in the key of F and stacked up 3rds, we would get F, A, and C because all of those notes are in the key of F, and are a 3rd apart. **These structures built in thirds are commonly referred to as triads, and the F note is said to be the root of the chord.**

F Major Triad

Building an F Major Chord

The structure below, F, A, and C, form what is called a major chord. If we measure the distance or interval between each note using our chromatic scale we can find the formula for building major chords. Between F and A are 4 half steps or a major third. Between A and C are 3 half steps or a minor third. Therefore, to create a major chord we need to combine a major third on the bottom, and a minor third on the top.

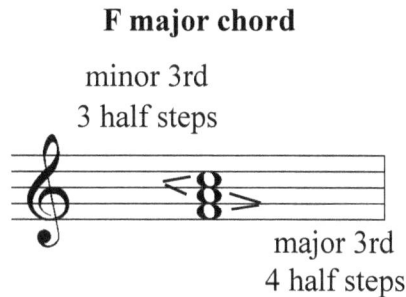

F major chord

minor 3rd
3 half steps

major 3rd
4 half steps

Playing an F Major Chord on the Guitar

The diagram below shows you how you would play this on the guitar. The tablature below shows fret location with the circled number, the fingering with the number next to the dots, and an X placed above to indicate which string is not played. Sometimes open circles will indicate that open strings are to be played (see example below). Index finger is 1, middle finger is 2, ring finger 3, little finger is 4.

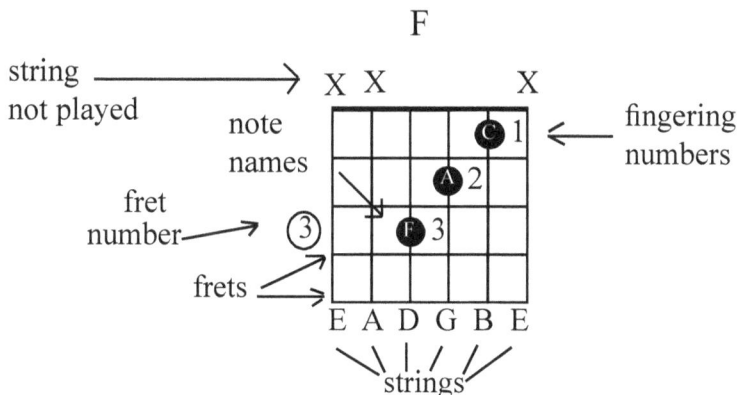

string not played → X X   X
                                          note names
                                                        fingering numbers
fret number → ③
frets

E A D G B E
strings

Understanding a Chord Voicing

Although the chord above will work fine for an F major chord, it is common that guitarist double a few notes from the triad in order to make the chord sound more full. It is combined into a chord on the guitar which is both playable and has a good sound. So, there are many ways to play any given chord depending on how many notes of the chord you use, and how many notes are doubled. **Each of these different combinations of notes is called a chord voicing.**

Common chord voicing for an F major.

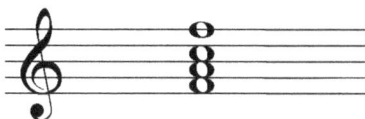

This is how you would play these notes on the guitar.

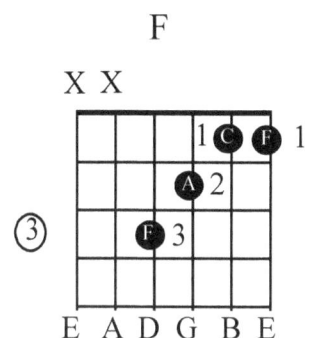

F

X X

③

E A D G B E

49

Root Position Major Chords Continued

Possible chord tones for major
1,3,5

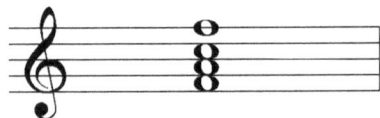

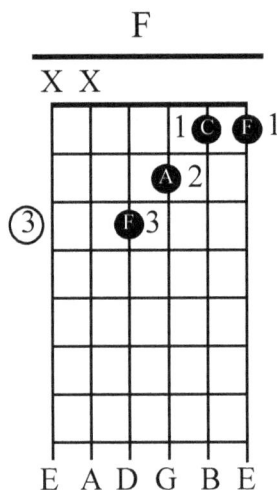

F

E A D G B E

The F chord is usually quite difficult for a beginner. The main problem comes with placing your 1st finger across two strings at once while at the same time reaching the F and A notes with your 2nd and 3rd fingers. (See photo 13) Give yourself a good couple of weeks with this chord. With the F chord and any chord you have problems with, practicing it many times a day for a few short moments will go a long way toward mastering the chord. Don't worry if it sounds good, just finger the chord and play it. Over time your fingers will gain strength and agility.

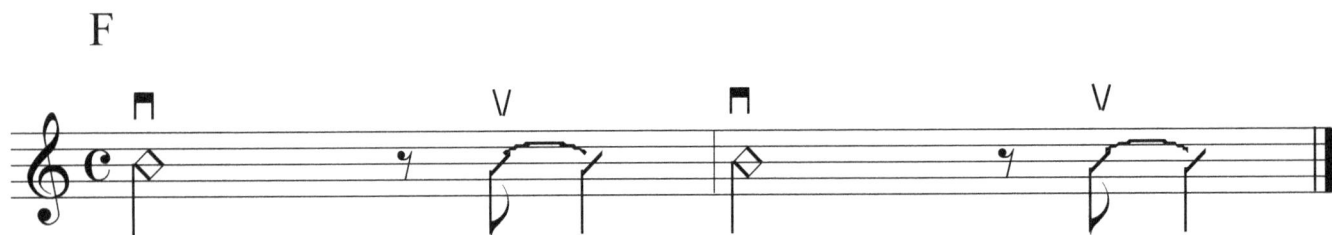

F

Explanation of Strumming Symbols

The following symbols are used to indicate an up or down stroke.

⊓ = Strum with a downward motion

V = Strum with an upward motion

Additional Techniques

As previously discussed, there are three ways to apply scales to chords. The example below shows you how to add the ninth/second scale degree to an F major chord.

Example of Applying Scales to Chords

Fadd9

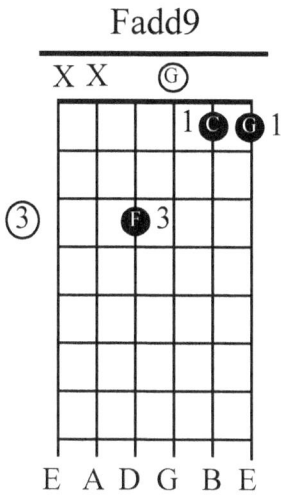

In this example we will add the note G into our F chord. This note will feel like it wants to resolve. Therefore, you might strum the F chord once, then the F chord with the G added, and the back to the F chord. You will probably recognize this sound. You are adding in the ninth for the F chord. When you add the G to the F chord this chord can be called either F add 9 or F add 2. You should try adding this 9th/2nd to each new chord you learn.

Applying Scale Addition to a Strummed Chord Progression

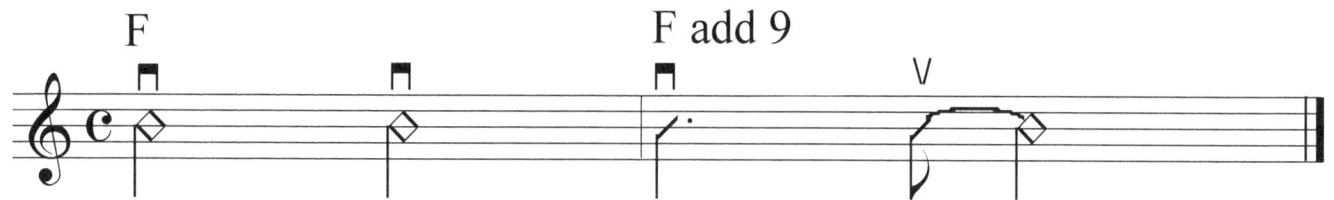

Sight Reading Exercise 3

See page 29 for an explanation on understanding the sight reading example.

Chapter Four

Music Theory Triads

The D Major Scale

The D Major Chord

Triads

The knowledge of the chromatic and major scale and the construction of intervals is a crucial tool to understanding the internal structure of chords. The process of learning all this information will take some time to memorize. Be patient with yourself. Through a combination of rereading these theory pages and working on the exercises you will find your theoretical knowledge will improve.

So far we have discussed 2 note intervals, sometimes called diads. When we add one more note to our 2 note interval we create a chord. A chord can be a combination of any 3 or more notes played at the same time. Western music can build chords using a wide variety of intervals. One of the most common ways to build chords is to stack up diatonic 3rd intervals. For example, if we took C in the key of C, and stacked up 3rds, we would get C, E, and G, because all of those notes are in the key of C, and are a 3rd apart (See example below). **These structures built in thirds are commonly referred to as triads and the C note is said to be the root of the chord**.

C Major Triad

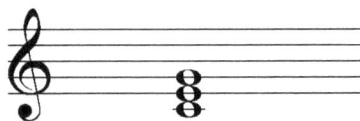

If we continue this process and build up diatonic triads above all the notes of C major we get the following 3 note structures

Triads Derived From Stacking 3rds Above a C Major Scale

These seven chords structures have a certain internal structure. The first structure C, E, and G form what is called a major chord. If we measure the distance or interval between each note using our chromatic scale, we can find the formula for building major chords. Between C and E are 4 half steps or a major third. Between E and G are 3 half steps or a minor third (See example on the following page). Therefore, to create a major chord we need to combine a major third on the bottom and a minor third on the top. You will notice that the chord starting on F and on G are also major chords. The exercise on page 7 covers major triads.

C Major Chord

minor 3rd
3 half steps

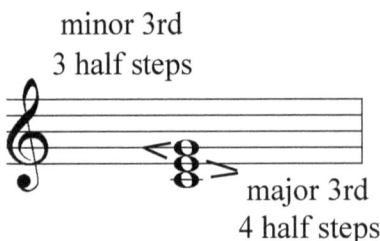

major 3rd
4 half steps

Major Triad Exercises

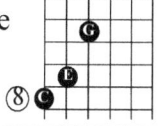

Example

D Major Scale Theory

Chromatic Scale Starting on D on Guitar Fretboard

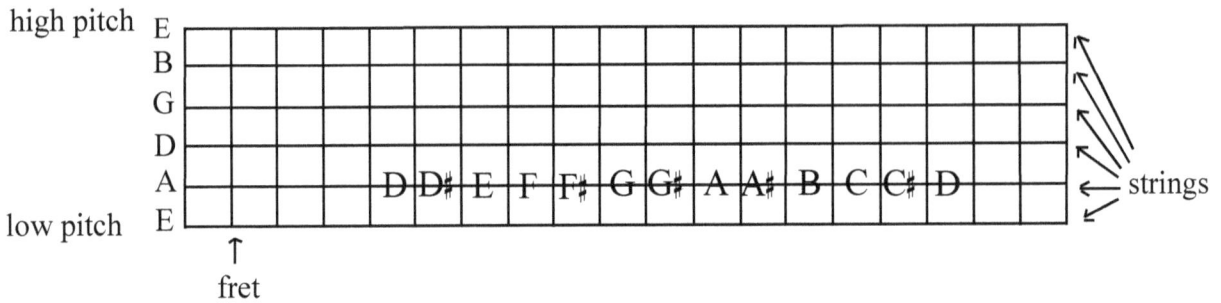

Extracting a D Major Scale from a Chromatic Scale

Though the chromatic scale represents all 12 notes, much of western music of the last few centuries has been based around only 7 tones. If we extract these 7 notes, as shown below, we end up with a major scale.

Major Scale Derived from Chromatic Scale

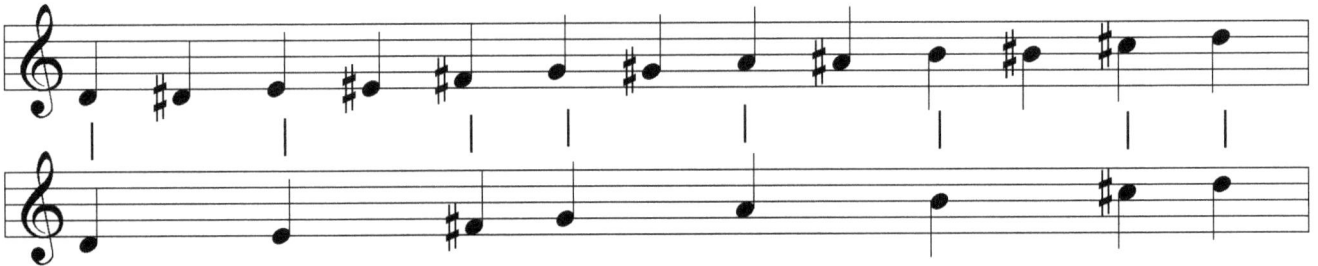

Interval Relationships Found in a Major Scale

If we look at the distance in half steps between the notes of a D major scale we see a pattern; whole, whole, half, whole, whole, whole, half. **All major scales are based on these intervals.**

D Major Scale

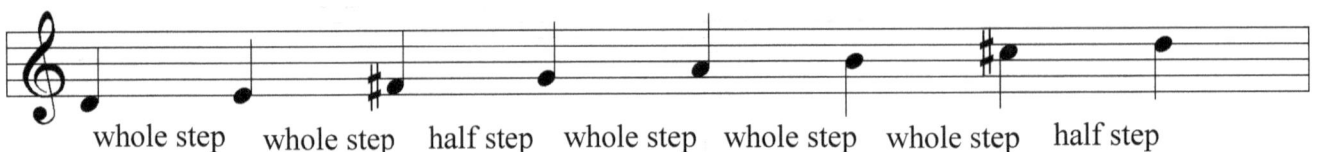

Seeing the D Major Scale on the Guitar

If we apply this to the guitar fretboard the information works out accordingly: start on any note on the guitar and move up on one string starting with a whole step (2 frets), whole step, half step (1 fret), whole step, whole step, whole step, half step. This is one way to play a major scale on the guitar.

Guitar Fretboard

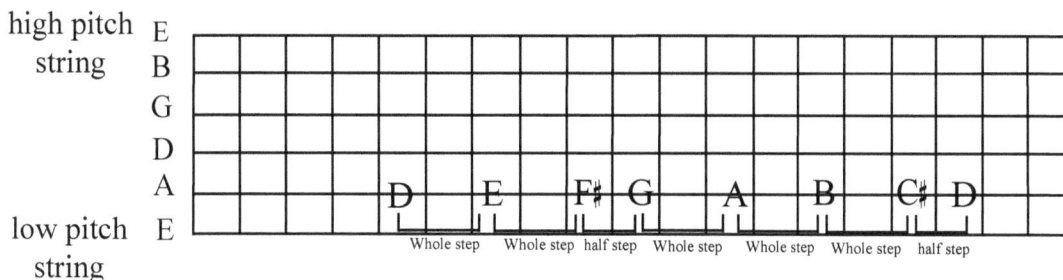

Another way to play this D Major scale on the guitar is to play it in "open" position by using the open strings, and in this case, the first four frets of the guitar, as shown below.

Practical Way to Play a D Major Scale on the Guitar

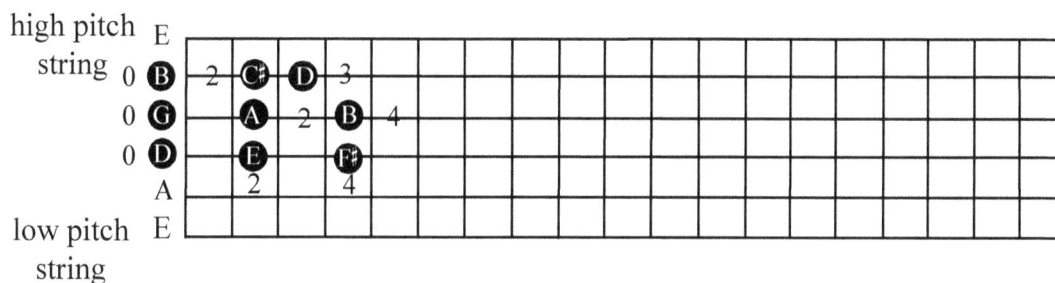

Building Chords

To review what you have learned so far a chord can be a combination of any 3 or more notes played at the same time. Western music builds chords using a wide variety of intervals. One of the most common ways to build chords is to stack up diatonic 3rd intervals. For example, if we took D in the key of D and stacked up 3rds we would get D, F#, and A because all of those notes are in the key of D, and are a 3rd apart. **These structures built in thirds are commonly referred to as triads and the D note is said to be the root of the chord.**

D Major Triad

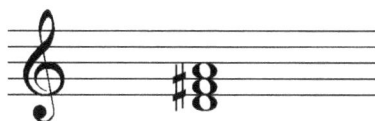

Building a D Major Chord

The structure below, D, F♯, and A form what is called a major chord. If we measure the distance or interval between each note using our chromatic scale we can find the formula for building major chords. Between D and F♯ is 4 half steps or a major third. Between F♯ and A is 3 half steps or a minor third. Therefore, to create a major chord we need to combine a major third on the bottom and a minor third on the top.

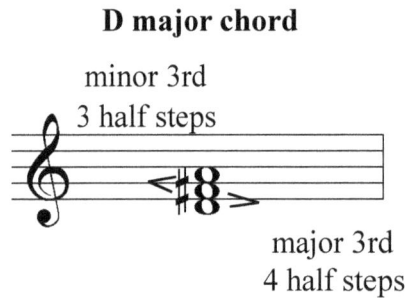

D major chord

minor 3rd
3 half steps

major 3rd
4 half steps

Playing a D Major Chord on the Guitar

The diagram below shows you how you would play this on the guitar. The tablature below shows fret location with the circled number, the fingering with the number next to the dots, and an X placed above to indicate which string is not played. Sometimes open circles will indicate that open strings are to be played (see example below). Index finger is 1, middle finger is 2, ring finger 3, little finger is 4.

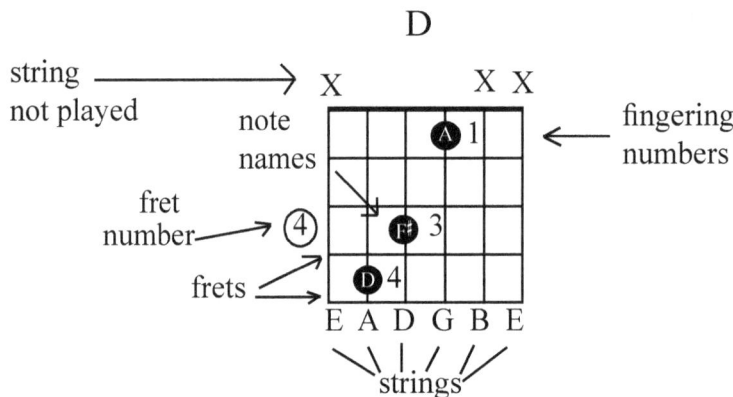

D

string not played → X   X X

note names   Ⓐ 1   fingering numbers ←

fret number → ④   F♯ 3

frets   Ⓓ 4

E A D G B E

strings

Understanding a Chord Voicing

Although the chord above will work fine for a D major chord it is common for guitarists to double a few notes from the triad in order to make the chord sound fuller. They are combined into a chord on the guitar which is both playable and has a good sound. So there are many ways to play any given chord depending on how many notes of the chord you use, and how many notes are doubled. **Each of these different combinations of notes is called a chord voicing.**

Common chord voicing for a D major.

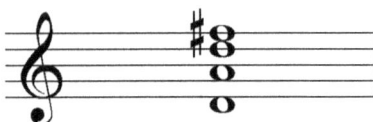

This is how you would play these notes on the guitar.

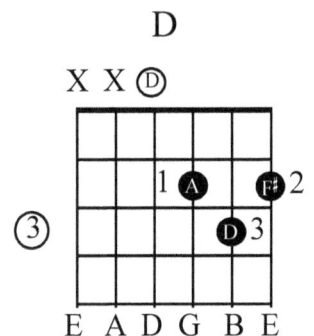

D

X X Ⓓ

③   1 Ⓐ   F♯ 2

Ⓓ 3

E A D G B E

Root Position Major Chords Continued

Possible chord tones for major
1,3,5

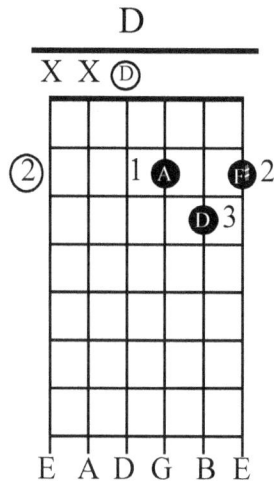

D

This is one of the easiest chords on the guitar. Watch out when strumming the chord that you only play the top 4 strings. You will sometimes hear people strumming the open A string with this chord. This will all depend on whether it works with the song in question.

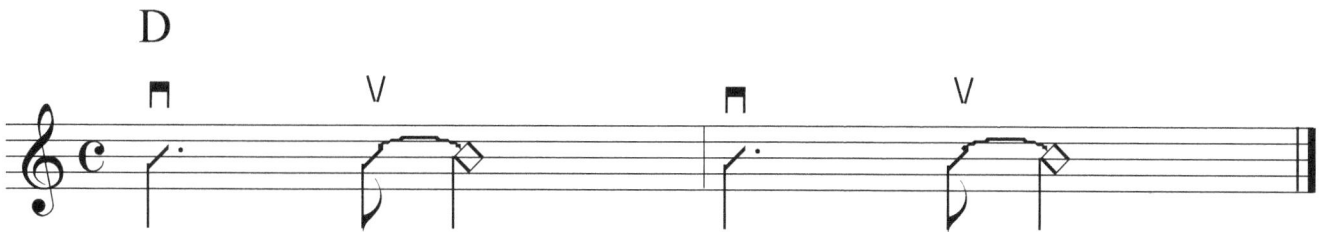

D

Explanation of Strumming Symbols

The following symbols are used to indicate an up or down stroke.

⊓ = Strum with a downward motion

V = Strum with an upward motion

Additional Techniques

As previously discussed there are three ways to apply scales to chords. The example below shows you how to add the 6th scale degree to a D major chord.

Example of Applying Scales to Chords

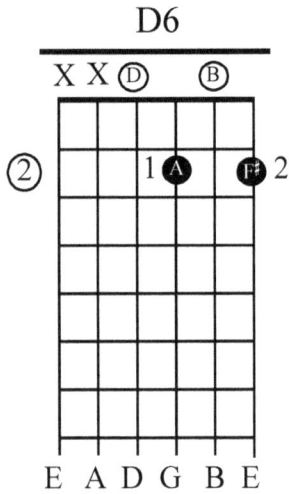

D6

In this example we will add the note B into our D chord. This note will feel like it wants to resolve. Therefore, you might strum the D chord once, then the D chord with the B added, and then back to the D chord. You will probably recognize this sound. You are adding in the sixth for the D chord. When you add the B to the D chord this chord is called D6. You should try adding this 6th to each new chord you learn.

E A D G B E

Applying Scale Addition to a Strummed Chord Progression

D   D6

Sight Reading Exercise 4

MacDougal St.

♩=120   SWING

Composer Bruce Arnold

To A for solos
Solo Form AAB

See page 29 for an explanation on understanding the sight reading example.

Chapter Five

Music Theory Minor Triads

The A Major Scale

The A Major Chord

Minor Triads

The second diatonic triad structure of the major scale D, F, and A form what is called a minor chord. Using the chromatic scale, once again we can find the formula for building minor chords. Between D and F is 3 half steps or a minor third. Between F and A is 4 half steps or a major third (See example below). Therefore, to create a minor chord we need to combine a minor third on the bottom and a major third on the top. The exercises on the following page cover minor triads.

D Minor Chord

major 3rd
4 half steps

minor 3rd
3 half steps

Minor Triad Exercises

Example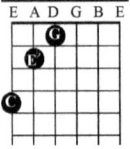

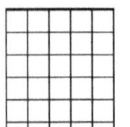

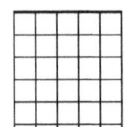

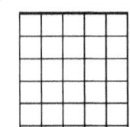

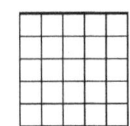

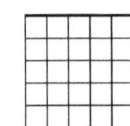

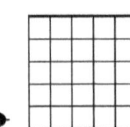

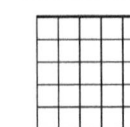

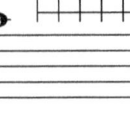

A Major Scale Theory

Chromatic Scale Starting on A on Guitar Fretboard

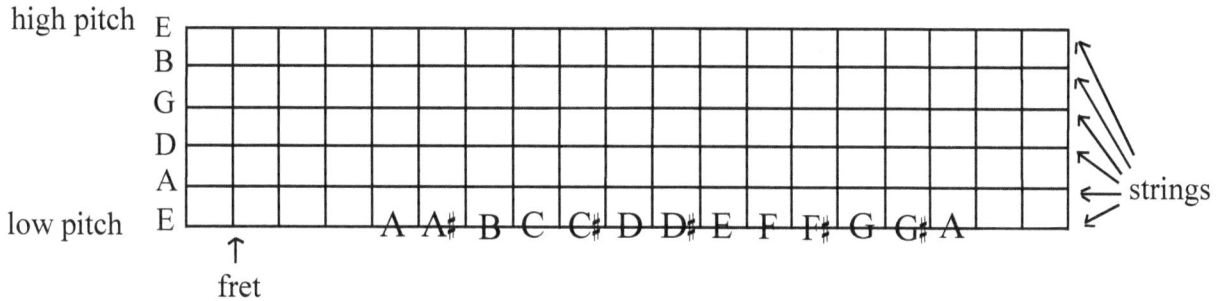

Extracting an A Major Scale from a Chromatic Scale

Though the chromatic scale represents all 12 notes, much of western music of the last few centuries has been based around only 7 tones. If we extract these 7 notes, as shown below, we end up with a major scale.

Major Scale Derived from Chromatic Scale

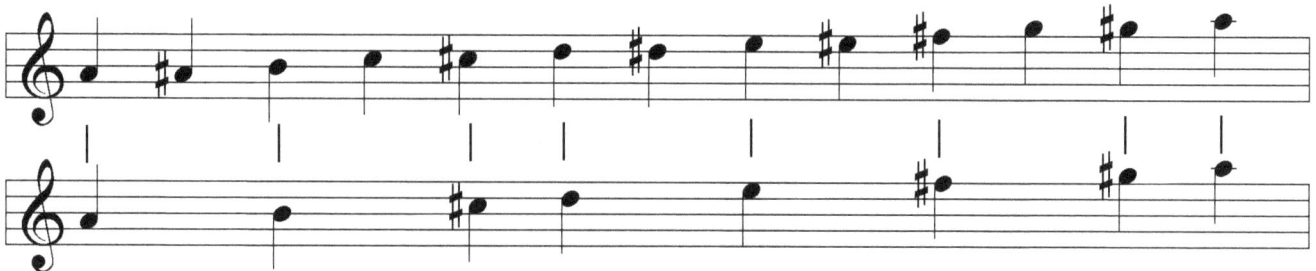

Interval Relationships Found in a Major Scale

If we look at the distance in half steps between the notes of an A major scale we see a pattern; whole, whole, half, whole, whole, whole, half. **All major scales are based on these intervals.**

A Major Scale

whole step   whole step   half step   whole step   whole step   whole step   half step

Seeing the A Major Scale on the Guitar

   If we apply this to the guitar fretboard the information works out accordingly: start on any note on the guitar and move up on one string starting with a whole step (2 frets), whole step, half step (1 fret), whole step, whole step, whole step, half step. This is one way to play a major scale on the guitar.

Guitar Fretboard

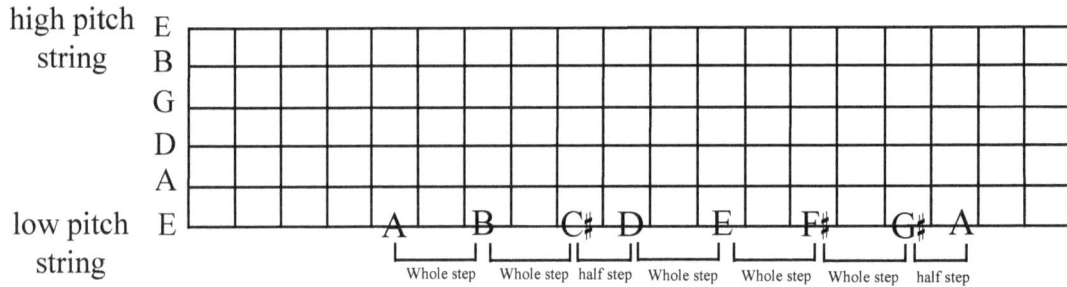

   Another way to play this A major scale on the guitar is to play it in "open" position by using the open strings, and in this case, the first four frets of the guitar, as shown below.

Practical Way to Play an A Major Scale on the Guitar

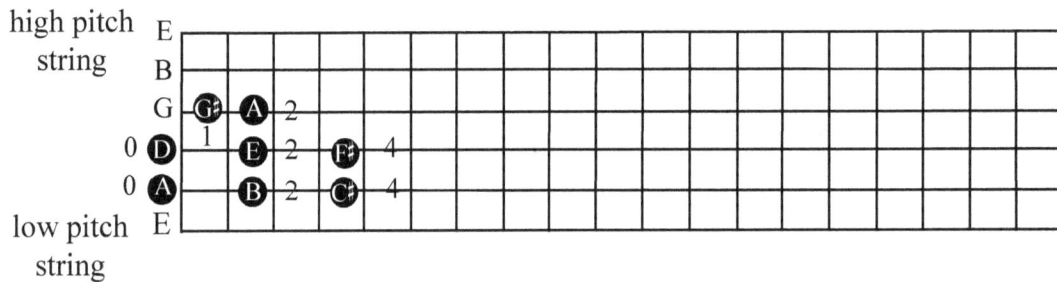

Building Chords

   To review what you have learned so far a chord can be a combination of any 3 or more notes played at the same time. Western music builds chords using a wide variety of intervals. One of the most common ways to build chords is to stack up diatonic 3rd intervals. For example, if we took A in the key of A and stacked up 3rds we would get A, C# and E because all of those notes are in the key of A, and are a 3rd apart. **These structures built in thirds are commonly referred to as triads, and the A note is said to be the root of the chord**.

A Major Triad

Building an A Major Chord

The structure below, A, C♯, and E form what is called a major chord. If we measure the distance or interval between each note using our chromatic scale, we can find the formula for building major chords. Between A and C♯ is 4 half steps or a major third. Between C♯ and E is 3 half steps or a minor third. Therefore, to create a major chord we need to combine a major third on the bottom and a minor third on the top.

A major chord

minor 3rd
3 half steps

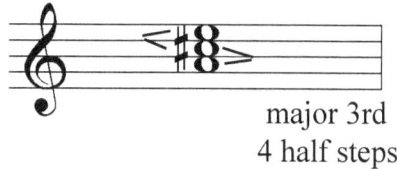

major 3rd
4 half steps

Playing an A Major Chord on the Guitar

The diagram below shows you how you would play this on the guitar. The tablature below shows fret location with the circled number, the fingering with the number next to the dots, and an X placed above to indicate which string is not played. Sometimes open circles will indicate that open strings are to be played (see example below). Index finger is 1, middle finger is 2, ring finger 3, little finger is 4.

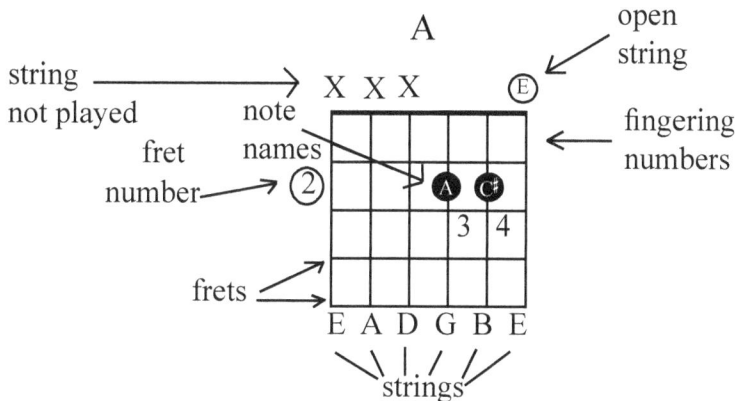

A

string not played → X X X

open string

note names

fret number → ②

fingering numbers

frets

E A D G B E

strings

Understanding a Chord Voicing

Although the chord above will work fine for an A major chord it is common for guitarists to double a few notes from the triad in order to make the chord sound fuller. It is combined into a chord on the guitar which is both playable, and has a good sound. So there are many ways to play any given chord depending on how many notes of the chord you use, and how many notes are doubled. **Each of these different combinations of notes is called a chord voicing.**

Common chord voicing for an A major.

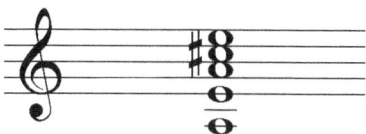

This is how you would play these notes on the guitar.

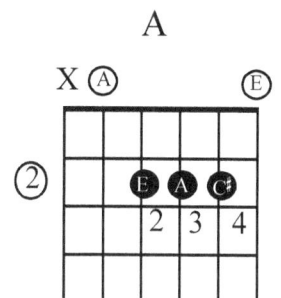

A

X Ⓐ   Ⓔ

②   Ⓔ Ⓐ C♯

2 3 4

67

Root Position Major Chords Continued

Possible chord tones for major
1,3,5

A

This chord can also be fingered with your 1st, 2nd, and 3rd finger where your 1st finger would be on the E on the D strings, 2nd finger on the A on the G string and your 3rd finger on the C# on the B string.

A

Explanation of Strumming Symbols

The following symbols are used to indicate an up or down stroke.

⊓ = Strum with a downward motion

V = Strum with an upward motion

Additional Techniques

As previously discussed there are three ways to apply scales to chords. The example below shows you how to add the seventh scale degree to an A major chord.

Example of Applying Scales to Chords

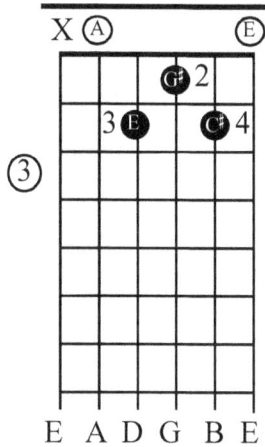

In this example we will add the note G♯ into our A chord. This note will feel like it wants to resolve. Therefore, you might strum the A chord once, then the A chord with the G♯ added, and then back to the A chord. You will probably recognize this sound. You are adding in the seventh for the A chord. When you add the G♯ to the A chord this chord is called A Major 7. You should try adding this seventh to each new chord you learn.

Applying Scale Addition to a Strummed Chord Progression

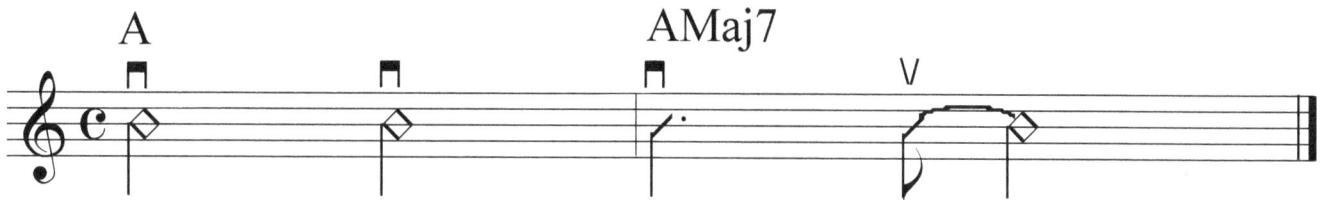

Sight Reading Exercise 5

See page 29 for an explanation on understanding the sight reading example.

Chapter Six

Music Theory: Diminished Triads

The E Major Scale

The E Major Chord

Diminished Triads

The last structure diatonic to a major scale, B, D, F form what is called a diminished chord. Using the same method we find that the distance between B and D is 3 half steps or a minor third. Between D and F is also 3 half steps or a minor third (See example below). Therefore, to create a diminished chord we need to combine a minor third on the bottom and a minor third on the top. The exercises on the following page will cover diminished triads.

B Diminished Chord

minor 3rd
3 half steps

minor 3rd
3 half steps

Diminished Triad Exercises

Example

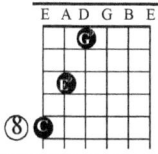

73

E Major Scale Theory

Chromatic Scale Starting on E on Guitar Fretboard

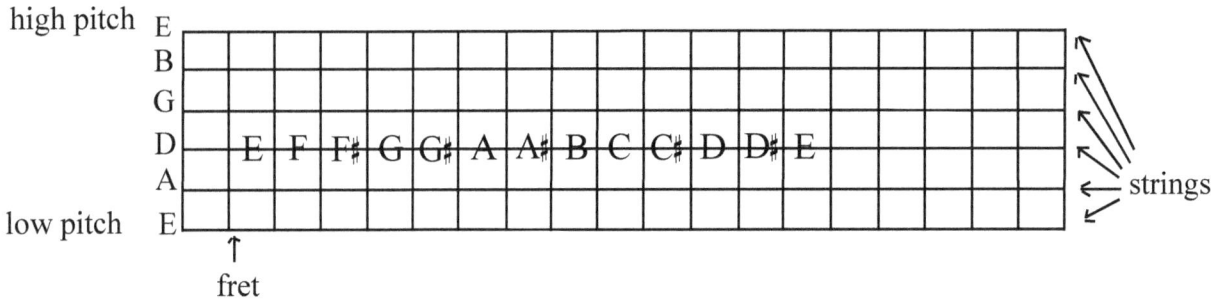

Extracting an E Major Scale from a Chromatic Scale

Though the chromatic scale represents all 12 notes, much of western music of the last few centuries has been based around only 7 tones. If we extract these 7 notes, as shown below, we end up with a major scale.

Major Scale Derived from Chromatic Scale

Chromatic Scale

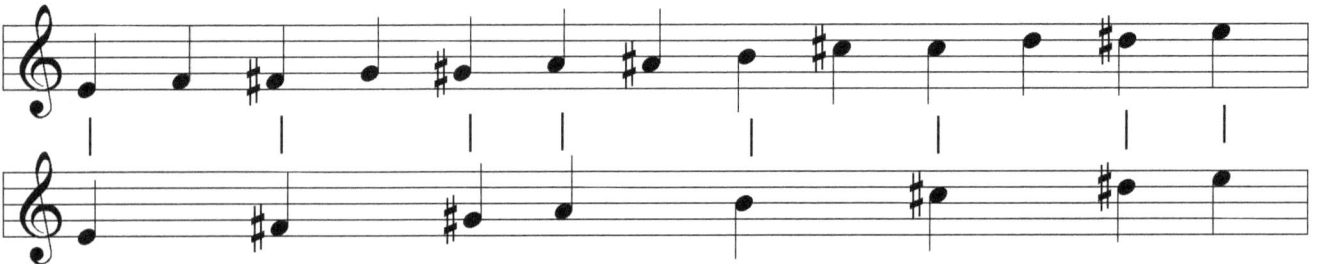

Major Scale

Interval Relationships Found in a Major Scale

If we look at the distance in half steps between the notes of an E major scale we see a pattern; whole, whole, half, whole, whole, whole, half. **All major scales are based on these intervals.**

E Major Scale

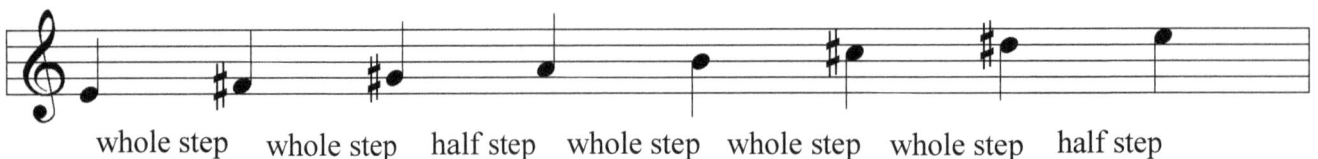

whole step   whole step   half step   whole step   whole step   whole step   half step

Seeing the E Major Scale on the Guitar

If we apply this to the guitar fretboard the information works out accordingly: start on any note on the guitar and move up on one string starting with a whole step (2 frets), whole step, half step (1 fret), whole step, whole step, whole step, half step. This is one way to play a major scale on the guitar.

Guitar Fretboard

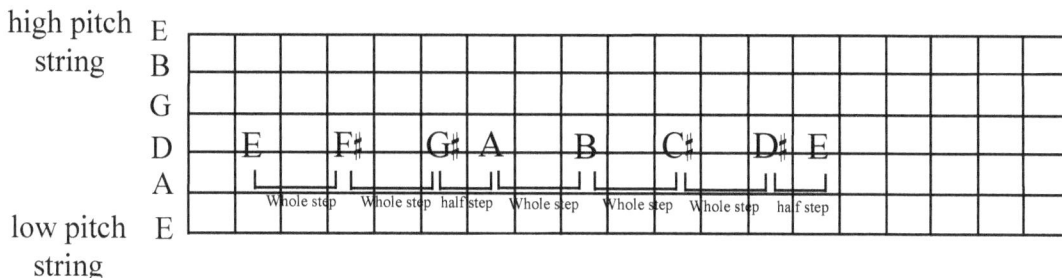

Another way to play this E major scale on the guitar is to play it in "open" position by using the open strings, and in this case, the first four frets of the guitar as shown below.

Practical Way to Play an E Major Scale on the Guitar

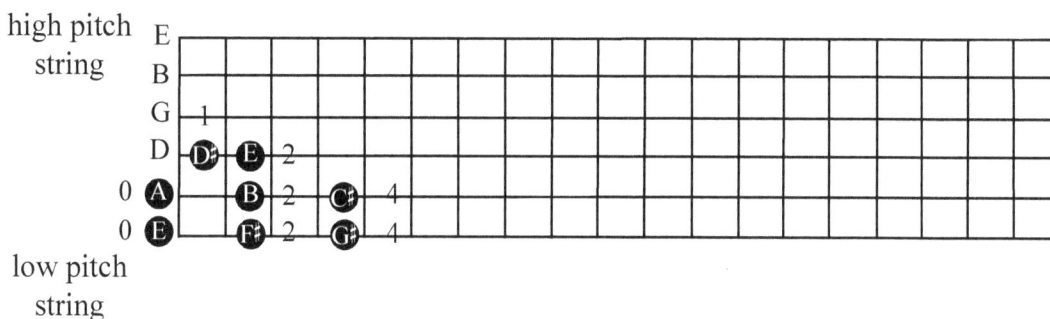

Building Chords

To review what you have learned so far, a chord can be a combination of any 3 or more notes played at the same time. Western music builds chords using a wide variety of intervals. One of the most common ways to build chords is to stack up diatonic 3rd intervals. For example, if we took E in the key of E, and stacked up 3rds we would get E, G♯ and B because all of those notes are in the key of E, and are a 3rd apart. **These structures built in thirds are commonly referred to as triads, and the E note is said to be the root of the chord.**

E Major Triad

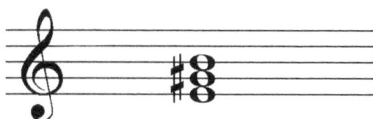

Building an E Major Chord

The structure below, E, G♯, and B form what is called a major chord. If we measure the distance or interval between each note using our chromatic scale we can find the formula for building major chords. Between E and G♯ is 4 half steps or a major third. Between G♯ and B is 3 half steps or a minor third. Therefore, to create a major chord we need to combine a major third on the bottom and a minor third on the top.

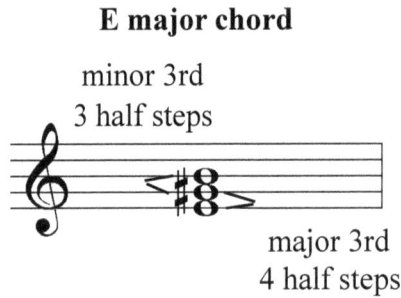

E major chord

minor 3rd
3 half steps

major 3rd
4 half steps

Playing an E Major Chord on the Guitar

The diagram below shows you how you would play this on the guitar. The tablature below shows fret location with the circled number, the fingering with the number next to the dots, and an X placed above to indicate which string is not played. Sometimes open circles will indicate that open strings are to be played (see example below). Index finger is 1, middle finger is 2, ring finger 3, little finger is 4.

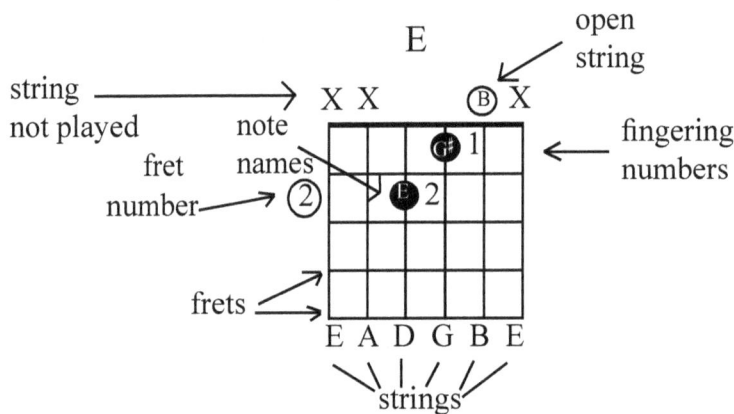

Understanding a Chord Voicing

Although the chord above will work fine for an E major chord, it is common for guitarists to double a few notes from the triad in order to make the chord sound fuller. They are combined into a chord on the guitar which is both playable and has a good sound. So there are many ways to play any given chord depending on how many notes of the chord you use, and how many notes are doubled. **Each of these different combinations of notes is called a chord voicing.**

Common chord voicing for an E major.

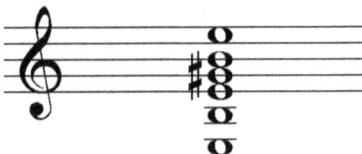

This is how you would play these notes on the guitar.

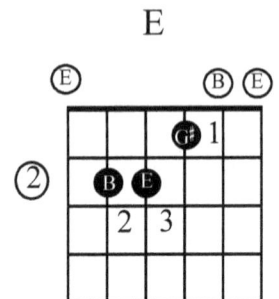

Root Position Major Chords Continued

Possible chord tones for major
1,3,5

E

E A D G B E

This is yet another easy chord on the guitar and by strumming all 6 strings you get a nice big sound on your guitar. Everyone loves "E!"

E

Explanation of Strumming Symbols

The following symbols are used to indicate an up or down stroke.

⊓ = Strum with a downward motion

V = Strum with an upward motion

Additional Techniques

Example of Applying Scales to Chords

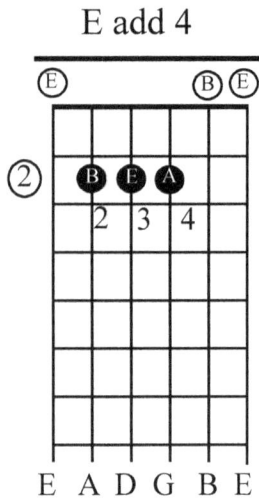

E add 4

In this example we will add the note A into our E chord. This note will feel like it wants to resolve. Therefore, you might strum the E chord once, then the E chord with the A added, and then back to the E chord. You will probably recognize this sound. You are adding in the fourth to the E chord. When you add the A to the E chord this chord is called E add 4 or E sus 4. You should try adding this fourth to each new chord you learn.

Applying Scale Addition to a Strummed Chord Progression

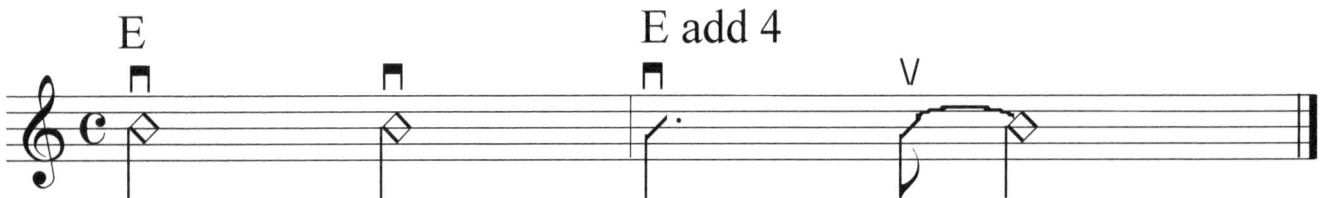

Sight Reading Exercise 6

Did I Tell You

ballad

Composer Bruce Arnold

See page 29 for an explanation on understanding the sight reading example.

Chapter Seven

Music Theory: Augmented Triads

The A Dorian Scale

The A Minor Chord

Augmented Triads

If we take the three types of chords learned so far and write them out we get the following: with C as the root we come up with C, E, G for a C major chord which is a major third stacked below a minor third. C, E♭, G form a C minor chord which has just the opposite interval combination; a minor third stacked below a major third. C, E♭, G♭ form a diminished chord which is two minor third intervals. You may notice that we have not yet discussed the combination of a major third and major third. This is shown in C, E, G♯. This combination is called an augmented chord and is written as follows: C augmented, C aug, C+.

C major

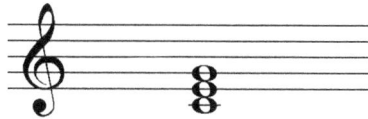

C minor

C diminished

C augmented

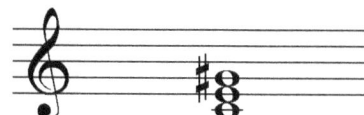

Augmented Triads Exercise

Example

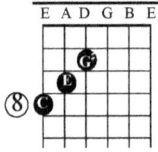 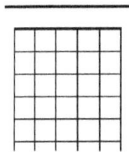 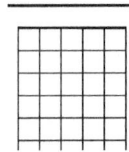 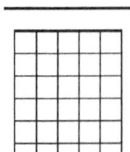

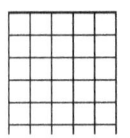 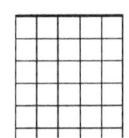 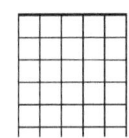 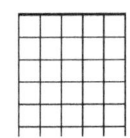

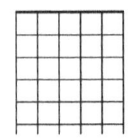 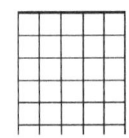 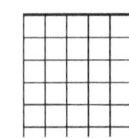 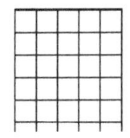

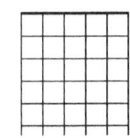 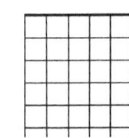 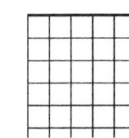 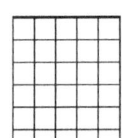

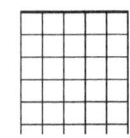 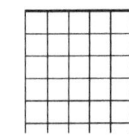 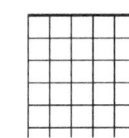 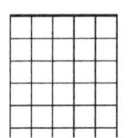

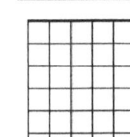 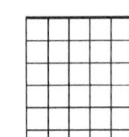 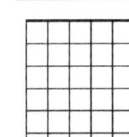 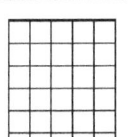

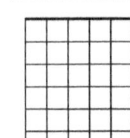 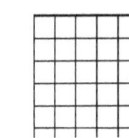 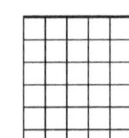 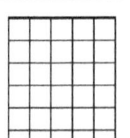

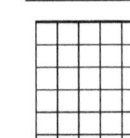 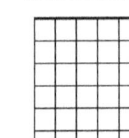 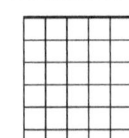 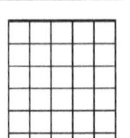

A Dorian Scale Theory

Chromatic Scale Starting on A on Guitar Fretboard

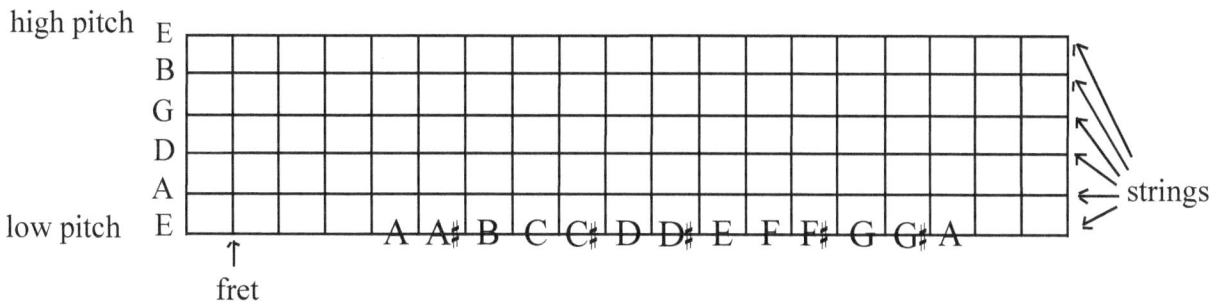

Extracting an A Dorian Scale from a Chromatic Scale

In the diagram above we can see all 12 notes again, which represent the chromatic scale. If we use the same process we did with the major scale and extract 7 notes, as shown below, we end up with a dorian scale. It is sometimes easier to think of the dorian scale as a major scale where the 3rd and the 7th have been flatted rather than memorizing the interval pattern. It should also be pointed out that if we play a G major scale starting on the 2nd degree (A) we will be playing an A dorian scale (A,B,C,D,E,F♯,G,A).

Dorian Scale Derived from Chromatic Scale

Chromatic Scale

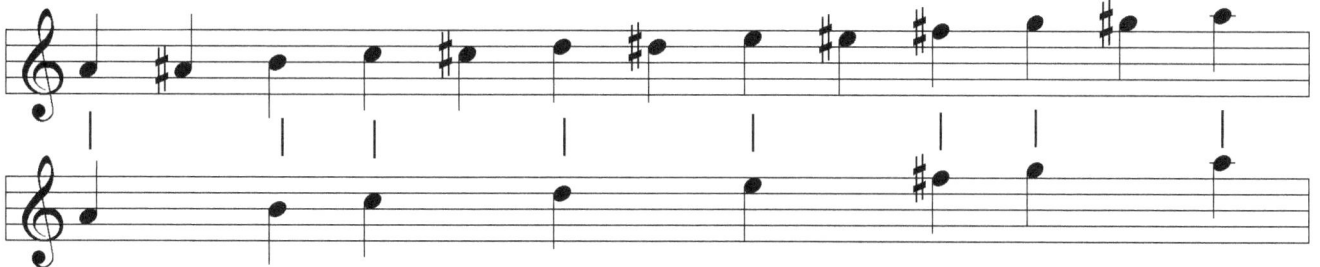

Dorian Scale

Interval Relationships Found in a Dorian Scale

If we look at the distance in half steps between the notes of an A dorian scale we see a pattern; whole, half, whole, whole, whole, half, whole.   **All dorian scales are based on these intervals.**

A Dorian Scale

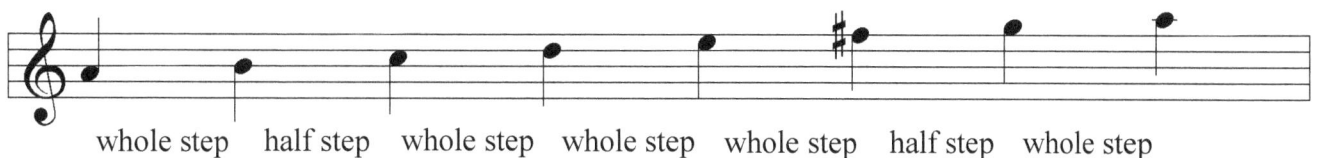

whole step   half step   whole step   whole step   whole step   half step   whole step

Seeing the A Dorian Scale on the Guitar

If we apply this to the guitar fretboard the information works out accordingly: start on any note on the guitar and move up on one string starting with a whole step (2 frets), half step (1 fret), whole step, whole step, whole step, half step, whole step. This is one way to play a dorian scale on the guitar.

Guitar Fretboard

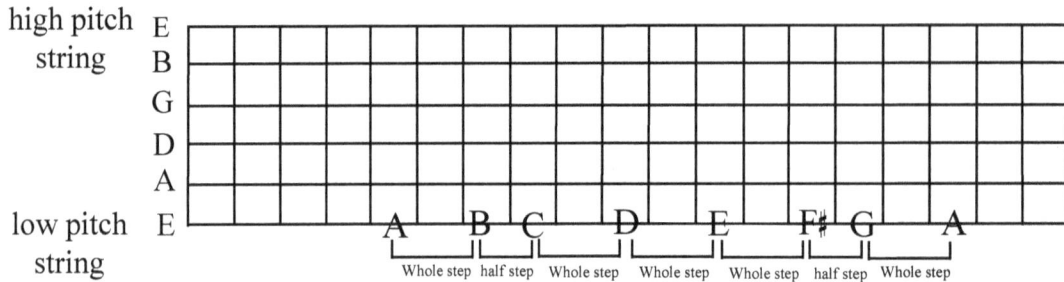

Another way to play this A Dorian scale on the guitar is to play it in "open" position by using the open strings, and in this case, the first four frets of the guitar as shown below.

Practical Way to Play an A Dorian Scale on the Guitar

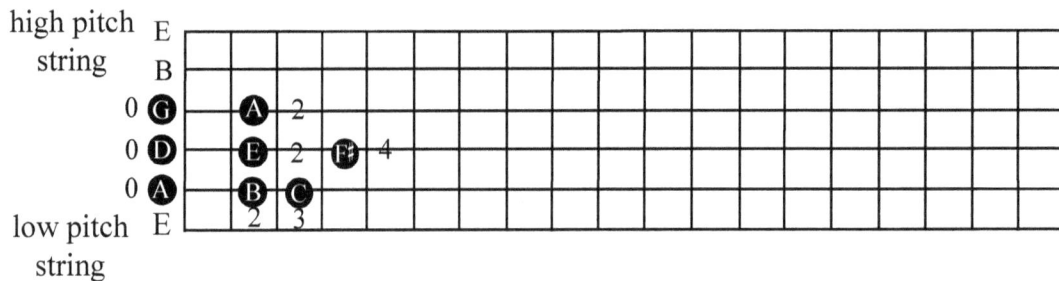

Building Chords

To review what you have learned so far a chord can be a combination of any 3 or more notes played at the same time. Western music builds chords using a wide variety of intervals. One of the most common ways to build chords is to stack up diatonic 3rd intervals. For example, if we took A in the key of A dorian and stacked up 3rds we would get A, C and E because all of those notes are in the key of A dorian, and are a 3rd apart. **These structures built in thirds are commonly referred to as triads and the A note is said to be the root of the chord.**

A Minor Triad

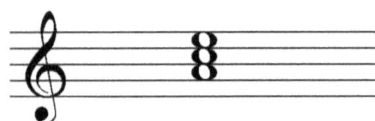

Building an A Minor Chord

The structure below, A, C and E form what is called a minor chord. If we measure the distance or interval between each note using our chromatic scale we can find the formula for building minor chords. Between A and C is 3 half steps or a minor third. Between C and E is 4 half steps or a major third. Therefore, to create a minor chord we need to combine a minor third on the bottom and a major third on the top.

A minor chord

major 3rd
4 half steps

minor 3rd
3 half steps

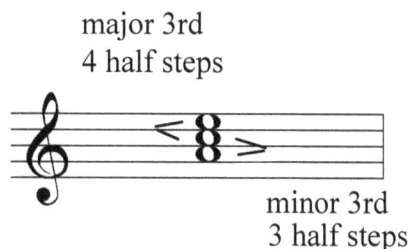

Playing an A Minor Chord on the Guitar

The diagram below shows you how you would play this on the guitar. The tablature below shows fret location with the circled number, the fingering with the number next to the dots, and an X placed above to indicate which string is not played. Sometimes open circles will indicate that open strings are to be played (see example below). Index finger is 1, middle finger is 2, ring finger 3, little finger is 4.

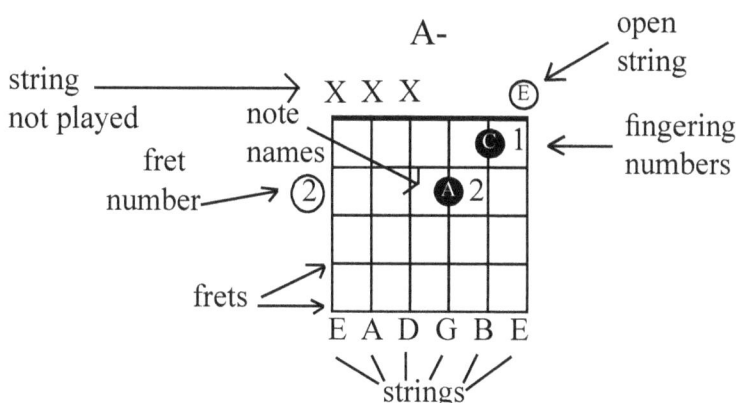

A-

open string

string not played

note names

fret number

fingering numbers

X X X

E

C 1

② A 2

frets

E A D G B E

strings

Understanding a Chord Voicing

Although the chord above will work fine for an A minor chord it is common for guitarists to double a few notes from the triad in order to make the chord sound fuller. They are combined into a chord on the guitar which is both playable and has a good sound. So there are many ways to play any given chord depending on how many notes of the chord you use, and how many notes are doubled. **Each of these different combinations of notes is called a chord voicing.**

Common chord voicing for an A minor.

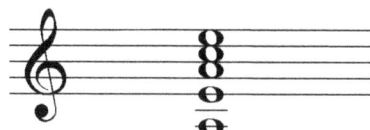

This is how you would play these notes on the guitar.

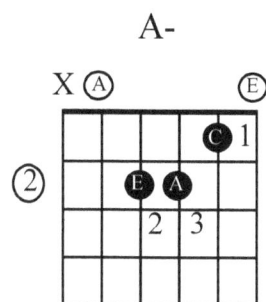

A-

X A

E

C 1

② E A

2 3

85

Root Position Minor Chords

Possible chord tones for minor
1,♭3,5

A-

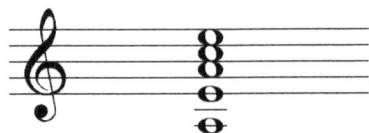

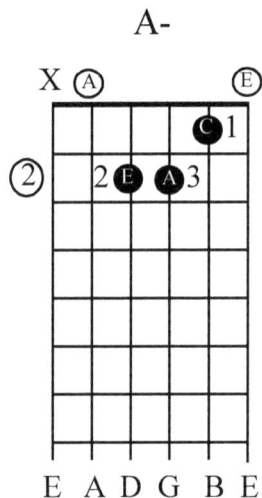

There are now three more chord progressions you can play with the chords learned so far. See pages 160, 162 and 163. You should first check page 159 for directions for how to practice the chord progressions. If you have problems with the rhythm in the chord progressions see pages 153-57.

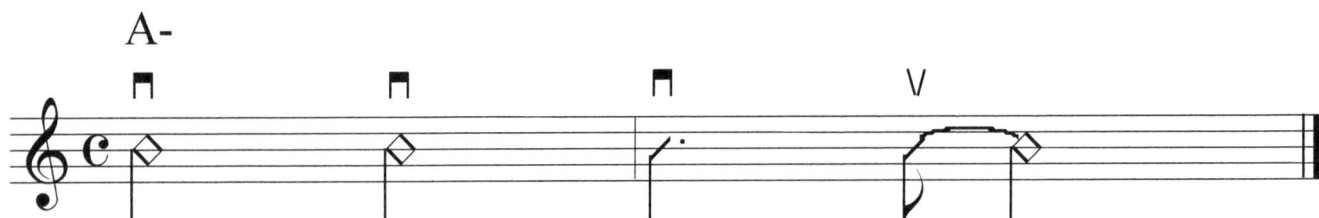

A-

Explanation of Strumming Symbols

The following symbols are used to indicate an up or down stroke.

⊓ = Strum with a downward motion

V = Strum with an upward motion

Additional Techniques

As previously discussed there are three ways to apply scales to chords. The example below shows you how to add the seventh scale degree to an A minor chord.

Example of Applying Scales to Chords

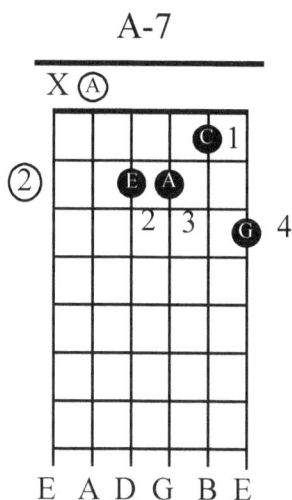

A-7

In this example we will add the note G into our A minor chord. This note will feel like it wants to resolve. Therefore, you might strum the A minor chord once, then the A Minor chord with the G added, and the back to the A minor chord. You will probably recognize this sound. You are adding in the seventh to the A minor chord. When you add the G to the A minor chord this chord is called A minor 7. You should try adding this seventh to each new chord you learn.

E A D G B E

Applying Scale Addition to a Strummed Chord Progression

Sight Reading Exercise 7

See page 29 for an explanation on understanding the sight reading example.

Chapter Eight

Music Theory: Sus4 Triads

The D Dorian Scale

The D Minor Chord

Suspended 4th Triads

There are two more triad chord structures that are commonly found in contemporary music; the suspended 4th chord (sus 4, see example below) and the add 9th (add 9 chords will be discussed in the following chapter). The sus 4 is a triad in which the 4th has replaced the 3rd. This creates an unusual structure of 5 half steps or a 4th and 2 half steps or a major 2nd. The suspended chord can be a diatonic chord built on the 1st, 2nd, 3rd, 5th, or 6th degrees. It is common to see the suspended chord written as C4, C sus or C sus 4. The exercises on the following page covers sus 4.

Csus4

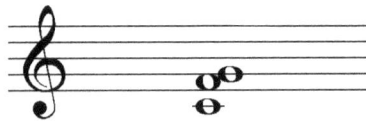

Suspended 4th Triad Exercises

Example

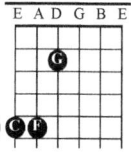 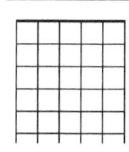 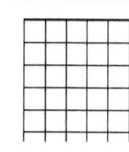 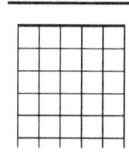

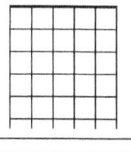 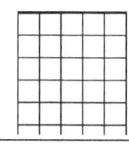 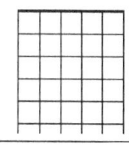 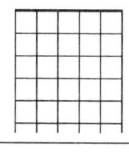

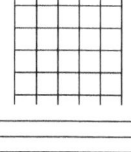 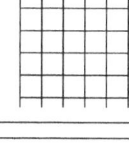 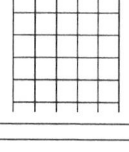 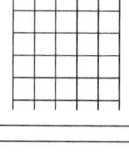

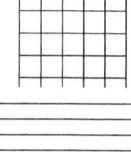 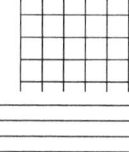 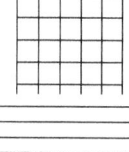 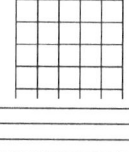

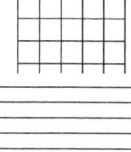 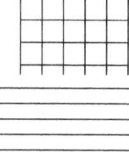 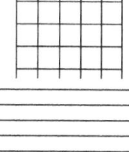 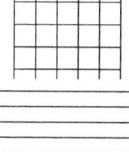

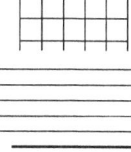   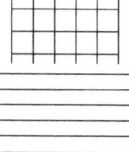

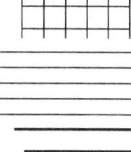 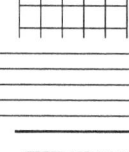 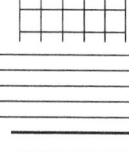 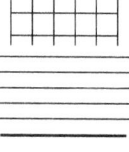

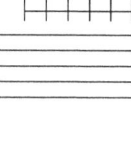 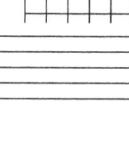 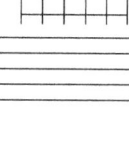 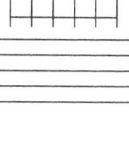

D Dorian Scale Theory

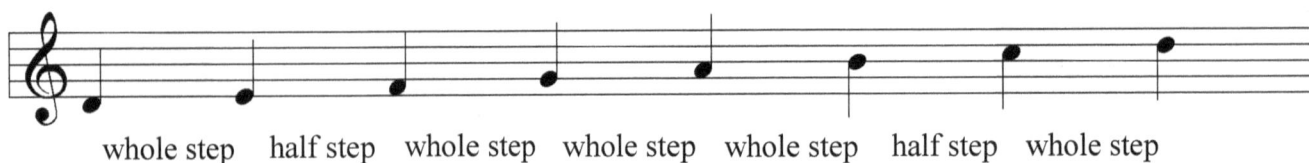

Chromatic Scale Starting on D on Guitar Fretboard

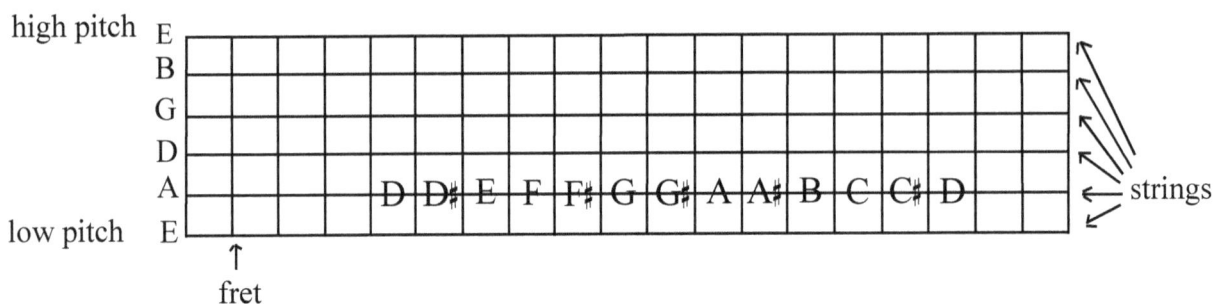

high pitch E
B
G
D
A   D D♯ E F F♯ G G♯ A A♯ B C C♯ D   ← strings
low pitch E

↑
fret

Extracting a D Dorian Scale from a Chromatic Scale

In the diagram above we can see all 12 notes again, which represent the chromatic scale. If we use the same process we did with the major scale and extract 7 notes, as shown below, we end up with a dorian scale. It is sometimes easier to think of the dorian scale as a major scale where the 3rd and the 7th have been flatted rather than memorizing the interval pattern. It should also be pointed out that if we play a C major scale starting on the 2nd degree (D) we will be playing a D dorian scale (D,E,F,G,A,B,C,D).

Dorian Scale Derived from Chromatic Scale

Chromatic Scale

Dorian Scale

Interval Relationships Found in a Dorian Scale

If we look at the distance in half steps between the notes of a D dorian scale we see a pattern; whole, half, whole, whole, whole, half, whole. **All dorian scales are based on these intervals.**

D Dorian Scale

whole step   half step   whole step   whole step   whole step   half step   whole step

Seeing the D Dorian Scale on the Guitar

If we apply this to the guitar fretboard the information works out accordingly: start on any note on the guitar and move up on one string starting with a whole step (2 frets), half step (1 fret), whole step, whole step, whole step, half step, whole step. This is one way to play a dorian scale on the guitar.

Guitar Fretboard

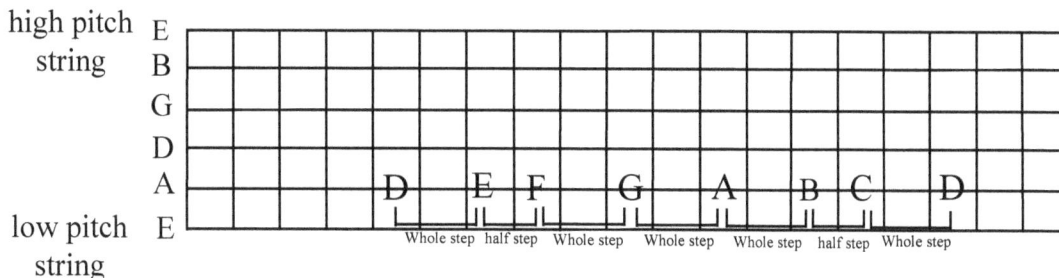

Another way to play this D Dorian scale on the guitar is to play it in "open" position by using the open strings, and in this case, the first three frets of the guitar as shown below.

Practical Way to Play a D Dorian Scale on the Guitar

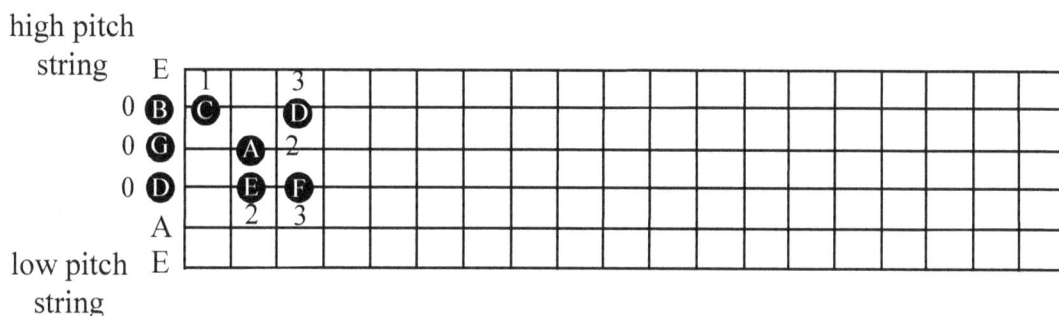

Building Chords

To review what you have learned so far a chord can be a combination of any 3 or more notes played at the same time. Western music builds chords using a wide variety of intervals. One of the most common ways to build chords is to stack up diatonic 3rd intervals. For example, if we took D in the key of D dorian and stacked up 3rds we would get D, F, and A because all of those notes are in the key of D dorian, and are a 3rd apart. **These structures built in thirds are commonly referred to as triads and the D note is said to be the root of the chord.**

D Minor Triad

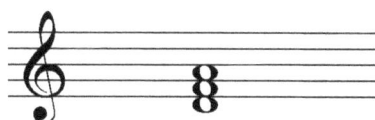

Building a D Minor Chord

The structure below, A, C, and E form what is called a minor chord. If we measure the distance or interval between each note using our chromatic scale we can find the formula for building minor chords. Between A and C is 3 half steps or a minor third. Between C and E is 4 half steps or a major third. Therefore, to create a minor chord we need to combine a minor third on the bottom and a major third on the top.

A minor chord

major 3rd
4 half steps

minor 3rd
3 half steps

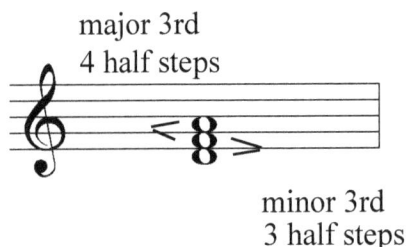

Playing a D Minor Chord on the Guitar

The diagram below shows you how you would play this on the guitar. The tablature below shows fret location with the circled number, the fingering with the number next to the dots, and an X placed above to indicate which string is not played. Sometimes open circles will indicate that open strings are to be played (see example below). Index finger is 1, middle finger is 2, ring finger 3, little finger is 4.

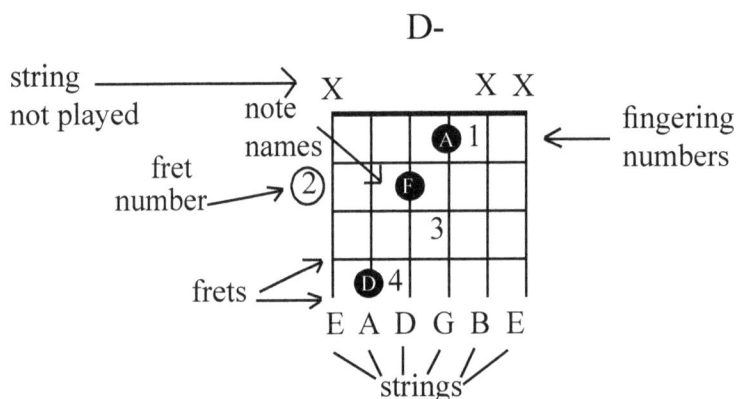

D-

string not played

note names

fret number

frets

fingering numbers

E A D G B E

strings

Understanding a Chord Voicing

Although the chord above will work fine for a D minor chord it is common for guitarists to double a few notes from the triad in order to make the chord sound fuller. They are combined into a chord on the guitar which is both playable and has a good sound. So, there are many ways to play any given chord, depending on how many notes of the chord you use, and how many notes are doubled. **Each of these different combinations of notes is called a chord voicing.**

D-

Common chord voicing for a D minor.

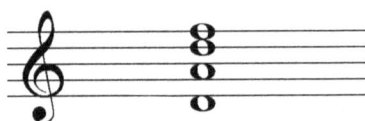

This is how you would play these notes on the guitar.

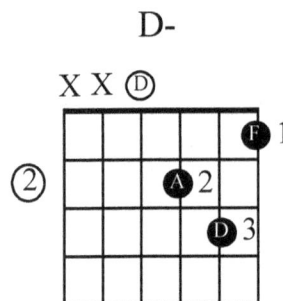

94

Root Position Minor Chords

Possible chord tones for minor
1,♭3,5

D-

D-

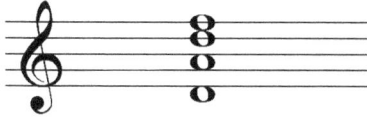

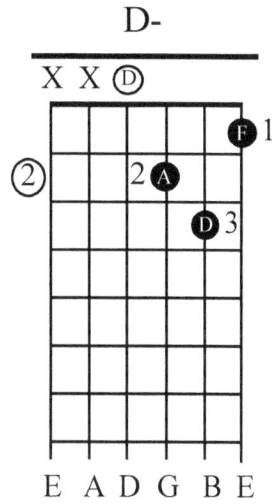

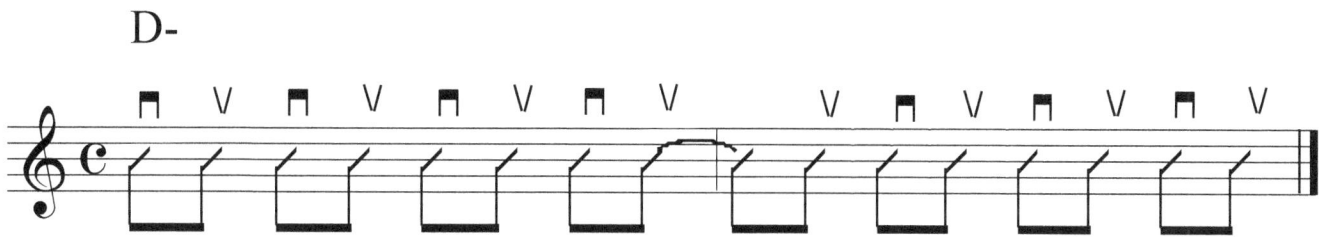

Explanation of Strumming Symbols

The following symbols are used to indicate an up or down stroke.

⊓ = Strum with a downward motion

V = Strum with an upward motion

Additional Techniques

As previously discussed there are three ways to apply scales to chords. The example below shows you how to add the fourth scale degree to a D minor chord.

Example of Applying Scales to Chords

Dsus4

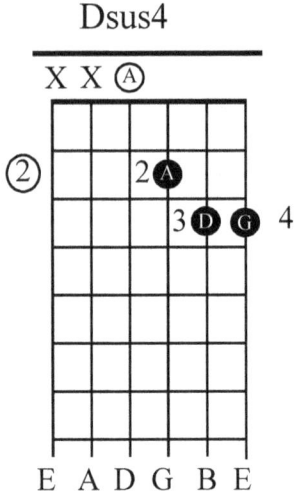

In this example we will add the note G into our D minor chord. This note will feel like it wants to resolve. Therefore, you might strum the D minor chord once, then the D Minor chord with the G added, and then back to the D minor chord. You will probably recognize this sound. You are adding in the fourth to the D minor chord. When you add the G to the D minor chord this chord is called Dsus4. You should try adding this fourth to each new chord you learn.

Applying Scale Addition to a Strummed Chord Progression

Sight Reading Exercise 8

See page 29 for an explanation on understanding the sight reading example.

Chapter Nine

Music Theory: Add9 Triads

The E Dorian Scale

The E Minor Chord

Add 9 Triads

The add 9 replaces the 3rd of a major triad with the second. The interval structure of this chord would be 2 half steps or a major 2nd, and 5 half steps or a perfect 4th. The add 9 chord can be a diatonic chord built on the 1st, 2nd, 4th 5th or 6th degrees of the scale. The exercises on the following page covers the add 9 triads.

C add 9

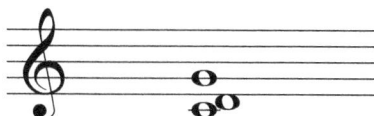

Add 9 Triad Exercises

E Dorian Scale Theory

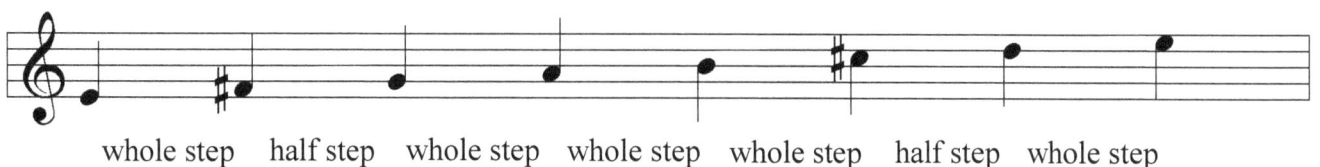

Chromatic Scale Starting on E on Guitar Fretboard

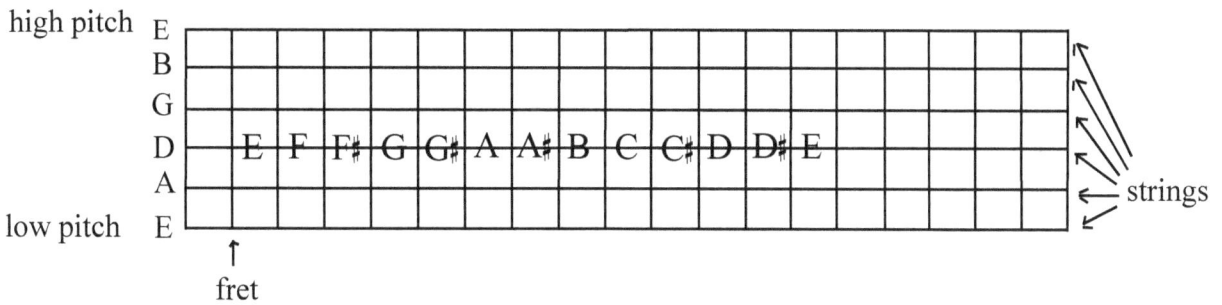

high pitch

E
B
G
D   E F F♯ G G♯ A A♯ B C C♯ D D♯ E
A
low pitch E

← strings

↑
fret

Extracting an E Dorian Scale from a Chromatic Scale

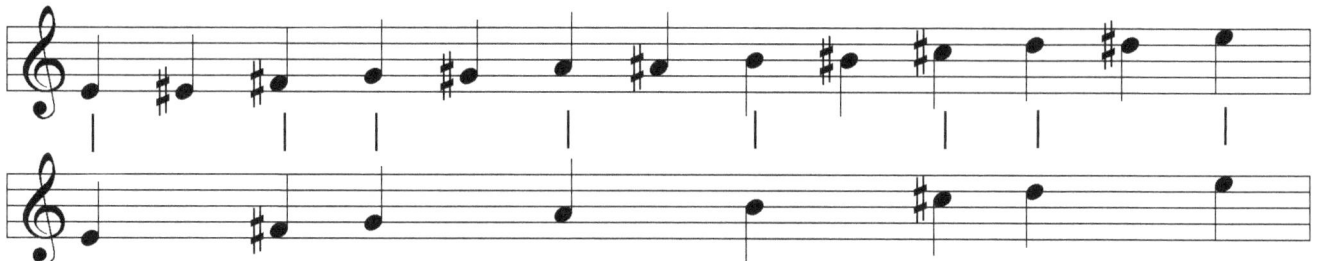

In the diagram above we can see all 12 notes again, which represent the chromatic scale. If we use the same process we did with the major scale and extract 7 notes, as shown below, we end up with a dorian scale. It is sometimes easier to think of the dorian scale as a major scale where the 3rd and the 7th have been flatted rather than memorizing the interval pattern. It should also be pointed out that if we play a D major scale starting on the 2nd degree (E) we will be playing an E dorian scale (E,F♯,G,A,B,C,D,E).

Dorian Scale Derived from Chromatic Scale

Chromatic Scale

Dorian Scale

Interval Relationships Found in a Dorian Scale

If we look at the distance in half steps between the notes of an E dorian scale we see a pattern; whole, half, whole, whole, whole, half, whole. **All dorian scales are based on these intervals.**

E Dorian Scale

whole step   half step   whole step   whole step   whole step   half step   whole step

Seeing the E Dorian Scale on the Guitar

If we apply this to the guitar fretboard the information works out accordingly: start on any note on the guitar and move up on one string starting with a whole step (2 frets), half step (1 fret), whole step, whole step, whole step, half step, whole step. This is one way to play a dorian scale on the guitar.

Guitar Fretboard

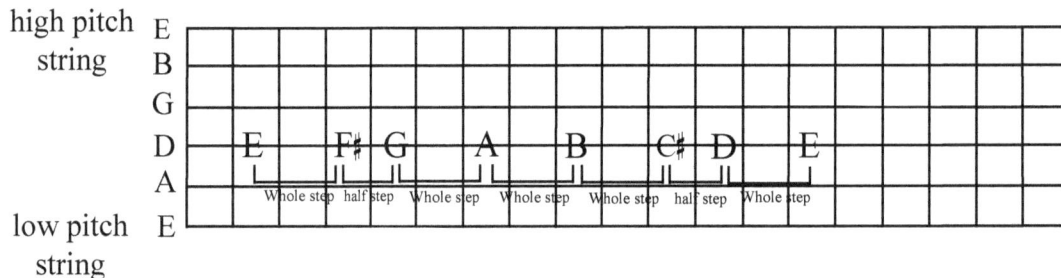

Another way to play this E dorian scale on the guitar is to play it in "open" position by using the open strings, and in this case, the first four frets of the guitar as shown below.

Practical Way to Play an E Dorian Scale on the Guitar

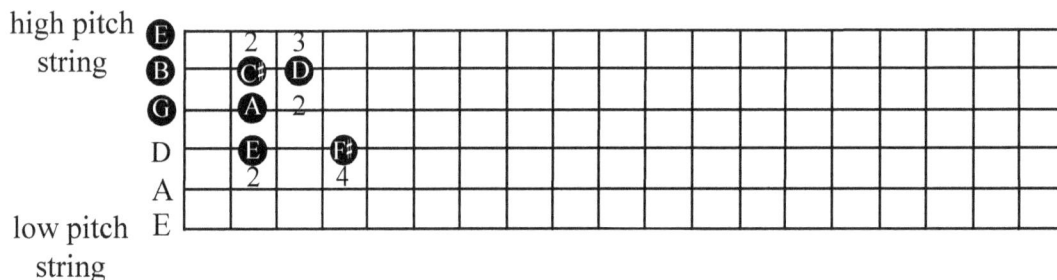

Building Chords

To review what you have learned so far a chord can be a combination of any 3 or more notes played at the same time. Western music builds chords using a wide variety of intervals. One of the most common ways to build chords is to stack up diatonic 3rd intervals. For example, if we took E in the key of E dorian and stacked up 3rds, we would get E, G and B because all of those notes are in the key of E dorian, and are a 3rd apart. **These structures built in thirds are commonly referred to as triads and the E note is said to be the root of the chord.**

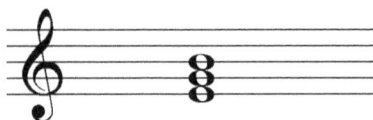

Building an E Minor Chord

The structure below, E, G, and B form what is called a minor chord. If we measure the distance or interval between each note using our chromatic scale we can find the formula for building minor chords. Between E and G is 3 half steps or a minor third. Between G and B is 4 half steps or a major third. Therefore to create a minor chord we need to combine a minor third on the bottom and a major third on the top.

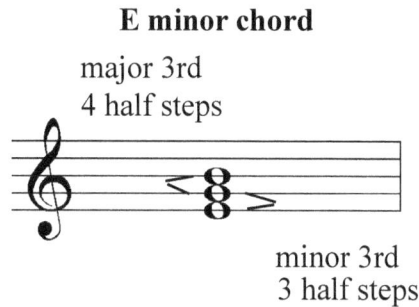

E minor chord

major 3rd
4 half steps

minor 3rd
3 half steps

Playing an E Minor Chord on the Guitar

The diagram below shows you how you would play this on the guitar. The tablature below shows fret location with the circled number, the fingering with the number next to the dots, and an X placed above to indicate which string is not played. Sometimes open circles will indicate that open strings are to be played (see example below). Index finger is 1, middle finger is 2, ring finger 3, little finger is 4.

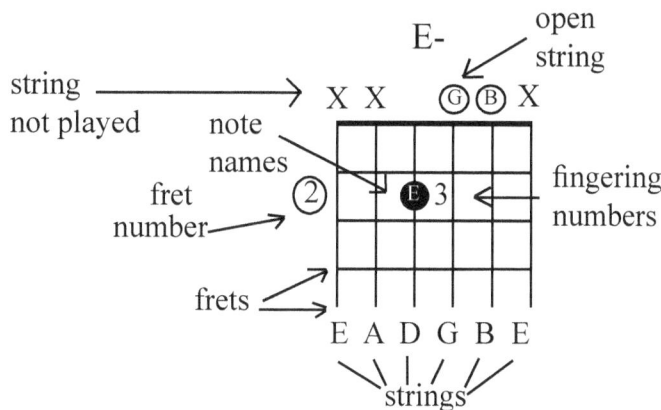

string not played → X X   Ⓖ Ⓑ X   open string

E-

note names

fret number

② Ⓔ 3   fingering numbers

frets

E A D G B E

strings

Understanding a Chord Voicing

Although the chord above will work fine for an E minor chord it is common for guitarists to double a few notes from the triad in order to make the chord sound fuller. They are combined into a chord on the guitar which is both playable and has a good sound. So there are many ways to play any given chord depending on how many notes of the chord you use and how many notes are doubled. **Each of these different combinations of notes is called a chord voicing.**

Common chord voicing for an E minor.

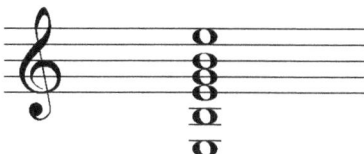

This is how you would play these notes on the guitar.

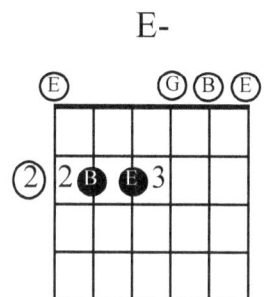

E-

Ⓔ   Ⓖ Ⓑ Ⓔ

② 2 Ⓑ Ⓔ 3

Root Position Minor Chords

Possible chord tones for minor
1,♭3,5

E-

E A D G B E

E-

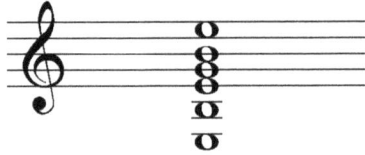

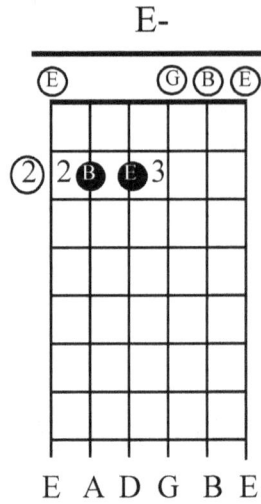

Explanation of Strumming Symbols

The following symbols are used to indicate an up or down stroke.

⊓ = Strum with a downward motion

V = Strum with an upward motion

Additional Techniques

As previously discussed there are three ways to apply scales to chords. The example below shows you how to add the sixth scale degree to an E minor chord.

Example of Applying Scales to Chords

E-6

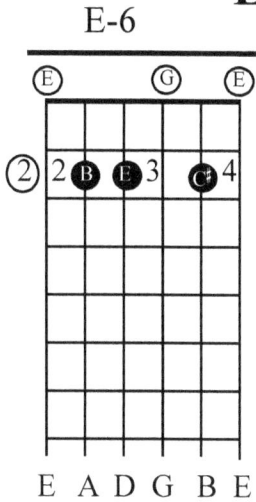

E A D G B E

In this example we will add the note C♯ into our E minor chord. This note will feel like it wants to resolve. Therefore, you might strum the E minor chord once, then the E Minor chord with the C♯ added, and then back to the E minor chord. You will probably recognize this sound. You are adding in the sixth to the E minor chord. When you add the C♯ to the E minor chord this chord is called E minor 6. You should try adding this sixth to each new chord you learn.

Applying Scale Addition to a Strummed Chord Progression

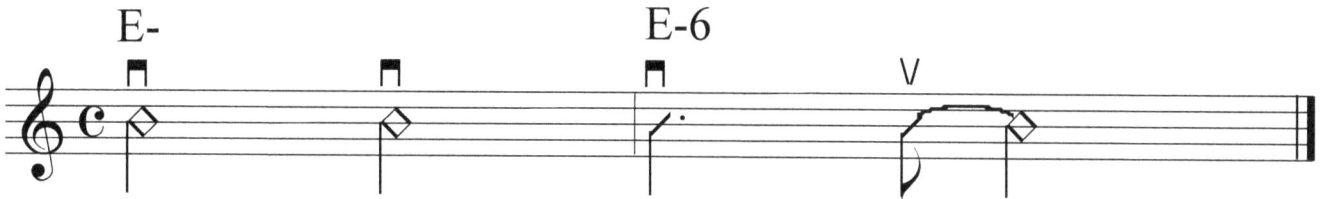

Sight Reading Exercise 9

Cara a Cara
(Face to Face)

Composer Bruce Arnold

latin
6/8 feel

* The tempo given for each piece is the suggested tempo and should be looked at as a goal tempo to work up to over time.

See page 29 for an explanation on understanding the sight reading example.

Chapter Ten

Music Theory: Diatonic Triads

The F Dorian Scale

The F Minor Chord

Diatonic Chords

The example below shows a list of all the diatonic triads and their chord names found in the key of C major. These chords are referred to as the diatonic triad or chords of a major key. You will see each of these chords labeled in many ways. C major could be shown as: C major, CMaj, C, CM. D minor could be shown as: D minor, Dmin, D-, Dm. B diminished could be shown as: B diminished, B dim, or B°.

They are also numbered sequentially which allows someone to refer to the D minor chord in the key of C, as a "II chord". Because many contemporary tunes are written using only the diatonic chords of a key, it is a very common practice among musicians to learn the diatonic chords of every key using numbers and letters. This helps aid in the memorization and quick learning of new songs.

Diatonic Chords of C Major

At this point many students wonder why all this information is so important. Let me give you one quick example. If you have followed this whole theory discussion up to this point you now know how most songs are written. If you were to write a song in C major, 90 percent of the time you would only use the diatonic chords of the key of C. Therefore, learning the diatonic chords of each key helps you to write music and also to understand why certain chords are used in your favorite tunes. Try analyzing some of the progressions found in this book. Most of them only use the diatonic chords of a key.

As each chord is introduced in this book the chord tones are shown in staff notation along with a list of the notes contained in the chord. Remember that memorizing the notes contained in each chord presented, along with knowing what notes you are playing, will open up a whole new world on the guitar. The example below shows how each chord type will appear.

Chord Tones for a C Major Chord

Diatonic Triad Exercises

To complete your knowledge of triad theory fill in the worksheet below with the diatonic triads for all twelve keys.

Recap of What You Have Learned so Far

Thus far we have discussed all the basic triads commonly used in music. There is one other chord we will be using that we should have a short discussion about. To first recap a little, the notes of each chord are called the chord tones. For example, the chord tones of a C major chord are C, E, and G.

It is possible to build chords that contain more notes. The next most common chord type found in music is a four note structure which is commonly referred to as a 7th chord. To build a 7th chord you add a note a third above the triads we have just discussed. If we add a minor third above our C major triad we get C, E, G, B♭.

This new structure C, E, G and B♭ forms a dominant 7th chord. Using the chromatic scale we can find the formula for building dominant 7th chords. Between C and E is 4 half steps or a major third, between E and G is 3 half steps or a minor third, between G and B♭ is 3 half steps or a minor third. **Therefore, to create a dominant 7th chord we need to combine a major third on the bottom, a minor third in the middle, and a minor third on the top.**

F Dorian Scale Theory

Chromatic Scale Starting on F on Guitar Fretboard

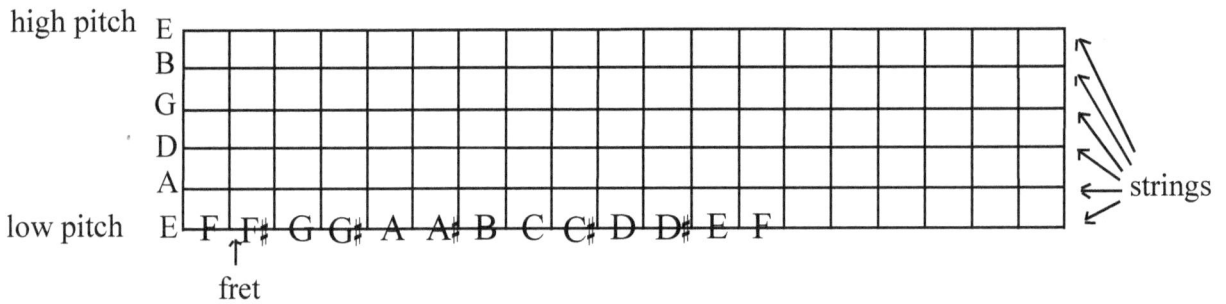

Extracting an F Dorian Scale from a Chromatic Scale

In the diagram above we can see all 12 notes again, which represent the chromatic scale. If we use the same process we did with the major scale and extract 7 notes, as shown below, we end up with a Dorian scale. It is sometimes easier to think of the Dorian scale as a major scale where the 3rd and the 7th have been flatted rather than memorizing the interval pattern. It should also be pointed out that if we play an Eb major scale starting on the 2nd degree (F) we will be playing an F Dorian scale (F,G,A♭,B♭,C,D,E♭,F).

Dorian Scale Derived from Chromatic Scale

Chromatic Scale

Dorian Scale

Interval Relationships Found in a Dorian Scale

If we look at the distance in half steps between the notes of an F Dorian scale we see a pattern; whole, half, whole, whole, whole, half, whole. **All Dorian scales are based on these intervals.**

F Dorian Scale

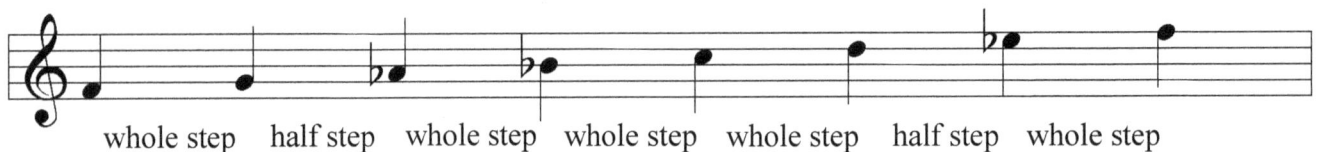

whole step   half step   whole step   whole step   whole step   half step   whole step

110

Seeing the F Dorian Scale on the Guitar

If we apply this to the guitar fretboard the information works out accordingly: start on any note on the guitar and move up on one string starting with a whole step (2 frets), half step (1 fret), whole step, whole step, whole step, half step, whole step,. This is one way to play a Dorian scale on the guitar.

Guitar Fretboard

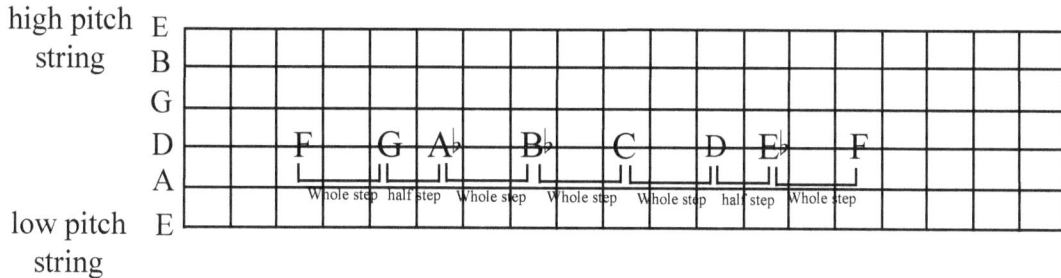

Another way to play this F Dorian scale on the guitar is to play it in "open" position by using the open strings, and in this case, the first four frets of the guitar as shown below.

Practical Way to Play an F Dorian Scale on the Guitar

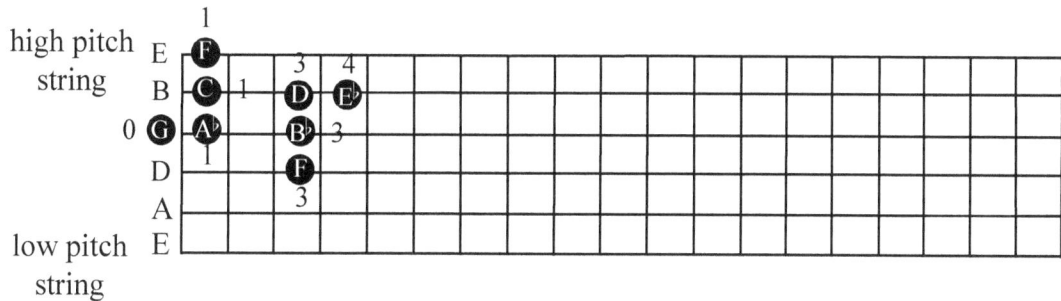

Building Chords

To review what you have learned so far a chord can be a combination of any 3 or more notes played at the same time. Western music builds chords using a wide variety of intervals. One of the most common ways to build chords is to stack up diatonic 3rd intervals. For example if we took F in the key of F Dorian and stacked up 3rds we would get F, A♭, and C because all of those notes are in the key of F Dorian and are a 3rd apart. **These structures built in thirds are commonly referred to as triads and the F note is said to be the root of the chord.**

F Minor Triad

Building an F Minor Chord

The structure below, F, A♭, and C form what is called a minor chord. If we measure the distance or interval between each note using our chromatic scale we can find the formula for building minor chords. Between F and A♭ is 3 half steps or a minor third. Between A♭ and C is 4 half steps or a major third. Therefore, to create a minor chord we need to combine a minor third on the bottom and a major third on the top.

Playing an F Minor Chord on the Guitar

The diagram below shows you how you would play this on the guitar. The tablature below shows fret location with the circled number, the fingering with the number next to the dots, and an X placed above to indicate which string is not played. Sometimes open circles will indicate that open strings are to be played (see example below). Index finger is 1, middle finger is 2, ring finger 3, little finger is 4.

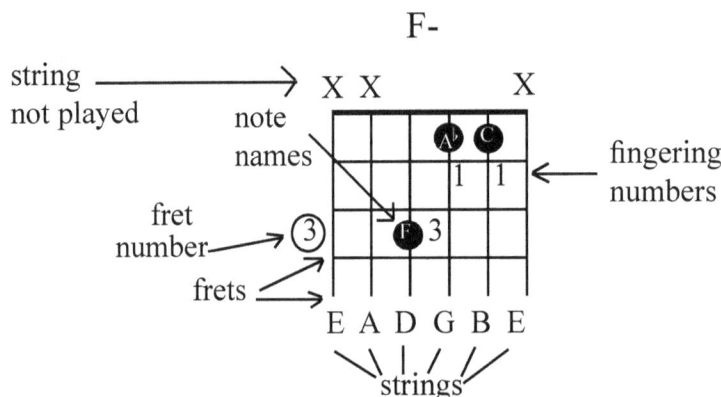

Understanding a Chord Voicing

Although the chord above will work fine for an F minor chord it is common for guitarists to double a few notes from the triad in order to make the chord sound fuller. They are combined into a chord on the guitar which is both playable and has a good sound. So there are many ways to play any given chord depending on how many notes of the chord you use and how many notes are doubled. **Each of these different combinations of notes is called a chord voicing.**

Common chord voicing for an F minor.

This is how you would play these notes on the guitar.

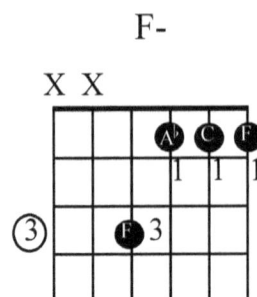

112

Root Position Minor Chords

Possible chord tones for minor
1,♭3,5

F-

E A D G B E

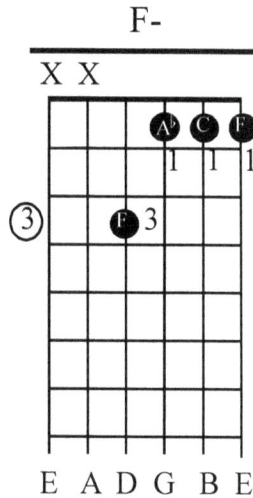

F minor presents the same problem that F major did. It is hard to place your 1st finger across three strings and then get your 3rd finger up to the F on the 3rd fret. I sometimes recommend playing this chord higher up on the guitar neck. The frets are closer together as you move up the neck so the stretch is not as difficult. Over time, you should practice moving the chord down until you can play it as indicated. Although the F minor chord isn't used in any of the chord progressions found in this book it is an important stepping stone to playing the "barre" chords starting on page 149. See photo 13 for a close look at playing the F minor chord.

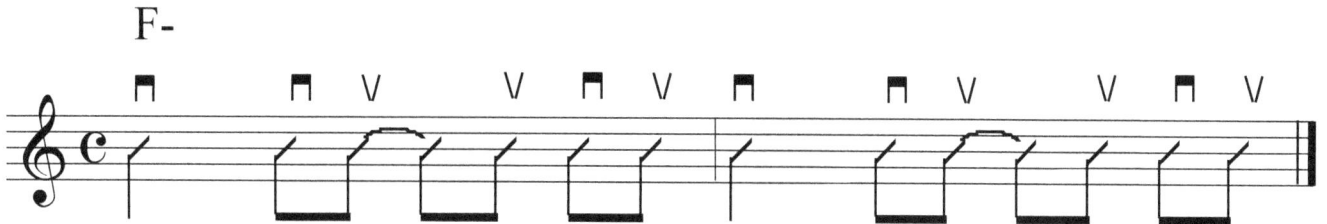

F-

Explanation of Strumming Symbols

The following symbols are used to indicate an up or down stroke.

⊓ = Strum with a downward motion
V = Strum with an upward motion

Additional Techniques

As previously discussed there are three ways to apply scales to chords. The example below shows you how to add the second scale degree to an F minor chord.

Example of Applying Scales to Chords

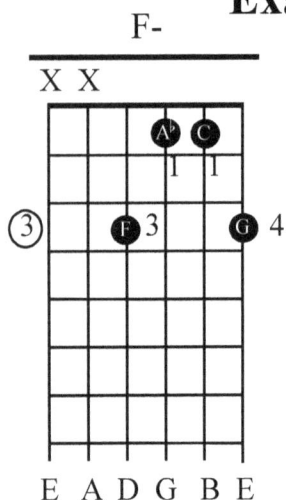

In this example we will add the note G into our F minor chord. This note will feel like it wants to resolve. Therefore, you might strum the F minor chord once, then the F Minor chord with the G added, and then back to the F minor chord. You will probably recognize this sound. You are adding in the second to the F minor chord. When you add the G to the F minor chord this chord is called F minor add 2 or F minor add 9. You should try adding the ninth to each new chord you learn.

Applying Scale Addition to a Strummed Chord Progression

Sight Reading Exercise 10

Two Blue

swing 16ths

Composer Bruce Arnold

See page 29 for an explanation on understanding the sight reading example.

Chapter Eleven

The C Mixolydian Scale

The C Dominant 7 Chord

C Mixolydian Scale Theory

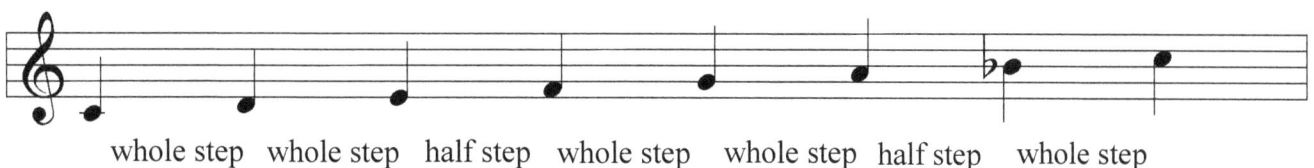

Chromatic Scale Starting on C on Guitar Fretboard

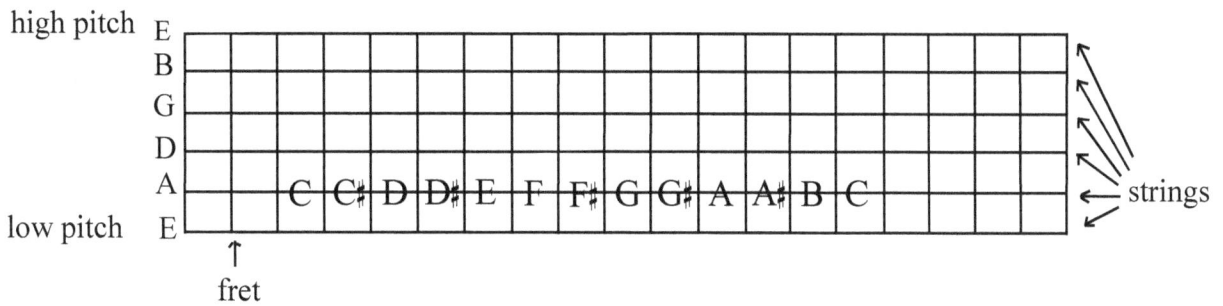

high pitch E
B
G
D
A C C♯ D D♯ E F F♯ G G♯ A A♯ B C ← strings
low pitch E

↑
fret

Extracting a C Mixolydian Scale from a Chromatic Scale

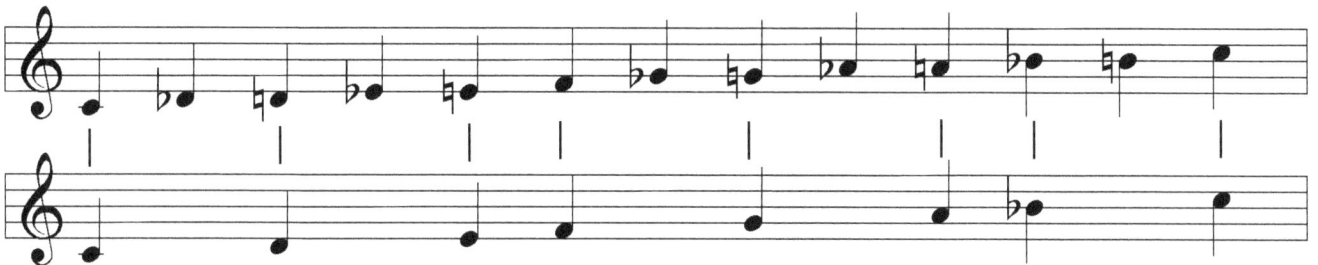

In the diagram above we can see all 12 notes again, which represent the chromatic scale. If we use the same process we did with the major scale and extract 7 notes, as shown below, we end up with a Mixolydian scale. It is sometimes easier to think of the Mixolydian scale as a major scale where the 7th have been flatted rather than memorizing the interval pattern. It should also be pointed out that if we play an F major scale starting on the 5th degree (C) we will be playing a C Mixolydian scale (C,D,E,F,G,A,B♭,C).

Mixolydian Scale Derived from Chromatic Scale

Chromatic Scale

Mixolydian Scale

Interval Relationships Found in a Mixolydian Scale

If we look at the distance in half steps between the notes of a Mixolydian scale we see a pattern; whole, whole, half, whole, whole, half, whole. **All Mixolydian scales are based on these intervals.**

C Mixolydian Scale

whole step whole step half step whole step whole step half step whole step

117

Seeing the C Mixolydian Scale on the Guitar

If we apply this to the guitar fretboard the information works out accordingly: start on any note on the guitar and move up on one string starting with a whole step (2 frets), whole step, half step (1 fret), whole step, whole step, half step, whole step. This is one way to play a Mixolydian scale on the guitar.

Guitar Fretboard

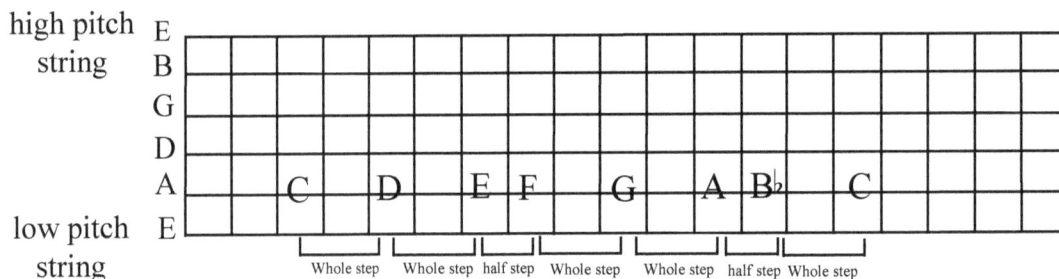

Another way to play this C Mixolydian scale on the guitar is to play it in "open" position by using the open strings, and in this case, the first three frets of the guitar as shown below.

Practical Way to Play a C Mixolydian Scale on the Guitar

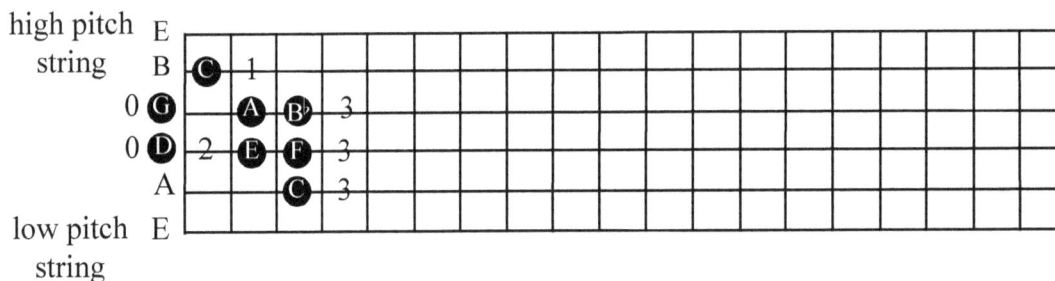

Building Seventh Chords

To review what you have learned so far, a chord can be a combination of any 3 or more notes, played at the same time. Western music builds chords using a wide variety of intervals. One of the most common ways to build chords is to stack up diatonic 3rd intervals. For example, if we took C in the key of C Mixolydian, and stacked up 3rds, we would get C, E, G, and B♭ because all of those notes are in the key of C Mixolydian, and are a 3rd apart. **These structures built in thirds are commonly referred to as seventh chords and the C note is said to be the root of the chord**.

C Dominant 7 Chord

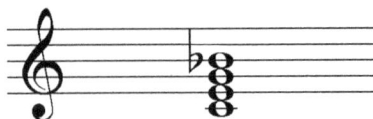

Building a C Dominant7 Chord

The structure below, C, E, G and B♭ form what is called a dominant7 chord. If we measure the distance or interval between each note using our chromatic scale we can find the formula for building dominant7 chords. Between C and E is 4 half steps or a major third. Between E and G is 3 half steps or a minor third. Between G and B♭ is 3 half steps or a minor third. Therefore to create a dominant7 chord we need to combine a major third on the bottom and a minor third in the middle and a minor third on the top.

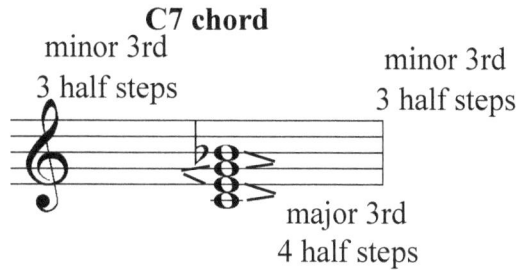

C7 chord

minor 3rd
3 half steps

minor 3rd
3 half steps

major 3rd
4 half steps

Playing a C Dominant7 Chord on the Guitar

It is possible to play the above dominant7 chord voicing on the guitar but it is very difficult. Because of this difficulty the dominant seventh chords in this book will be presented in the voicings that are easiest to play on the guitar.

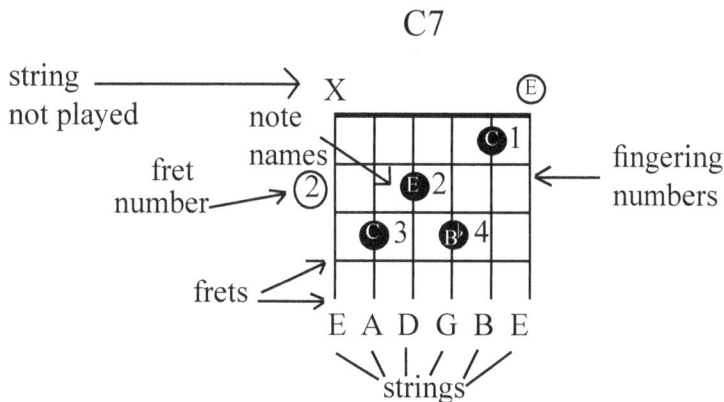

C7

string not played

note names

fret number

frets

fingering numbers

E A D G B E

strings

Understanding a Chord Voicing

Although the chord above will work fine for a C Dominant7 chord it is common for guitarists to double a few notes from the triad in order to make the chord sound fuller. They are combined into a chord on the guitar which is both playable and has a good sound. So, there are many ways to play any given chord depending on how many notes of the chord you use, and how many notes are doubled. **Each of these different combinations of notes is called a chord voicing.**

Common chord voicing for a C Dominant 7.

This is how you would play these notes on the guitar.

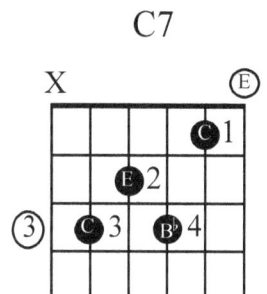

C7

Root Position Dominant 7th Chords

Possible chord tones for 7
1,3,5,♭7

C7

When you hear a dominant seventh chord, you will realize that it too, has been used in many of your favorite songs as a way to enhance the harmonic passages of a composition. The dominant has a special characteristic in that it feels like it wants to resolve. Understanding these tendencies can greatly aid you in applying this chord. Dominant chords are commonly used in a Blues progression. See pages 170-1 for an example.

C7

Explanation of Strumming Symbols

The following symbols are used to indicate an up or down stroke.

⊓ = Strum with a downward motion
V = Strum with an upward motion

Sight Reading Exercise 11

Composer Bruce Arnold

Reflection

See page 29 for an explanation on understanding the sight reading example.

Chapter Twelve

The D Mixolydian Scale

The D Dominant 7 Chord

D Mixolydian Scale Theory

Chromatic Scale Starting on D on Guitar Fretboard

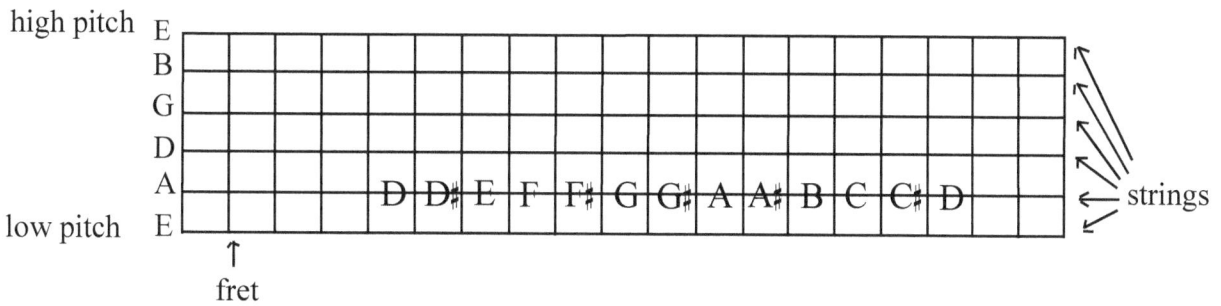

Extracting a D Mixolydian Scale from a Chromatic Scale

In the diagram above we can see all 12 notes again, which represent the chromatic scale. If we use the same process we did with the major scale and extract 7 notes, as shown below, we end up with a Mixolydian scale. It is sometimes easier to think of the Mixolydian scale as a major scale where the 7th has been flatted rather than memorizing the interval pattern. It should also be pointed out that if we play a G major scale starting on the 5th degree (D) we will be playing a D Mixolydian scale (D,E,F♯,G,A,B,C,D).

Mixolydian Scale Derived from Chromatic Scale

Chromatic Scale

Mixolydian Scale

Interval Relationships Found in a Mixolydian Scale

If we look at the distance in half steps between the notes of a Mixolydian scale we see a pattern; whole, whole, half, whole, whole, half, whole.   **All Mixolydian scales are based on these intervals.**

D Mixolydian Scale

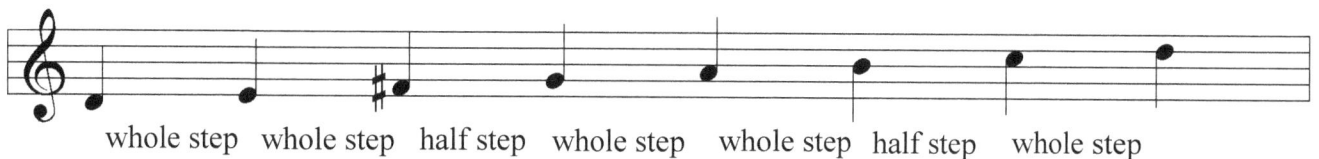

whole step   whole step   half step   whole step   whole step   half step   whole step

123

Seeing the D Mixolydian Scale on the Guitar

If we apply this to the guitar fretboard the information works out accordingly: start on any note on the guitar and move up on one string starting with a whole step (2 frets), whole step, half step (1 fret), whole step, whole step, half step, whole step. This is one way to play a Mixolydian scale on the guitar.

Guitar Fretboard

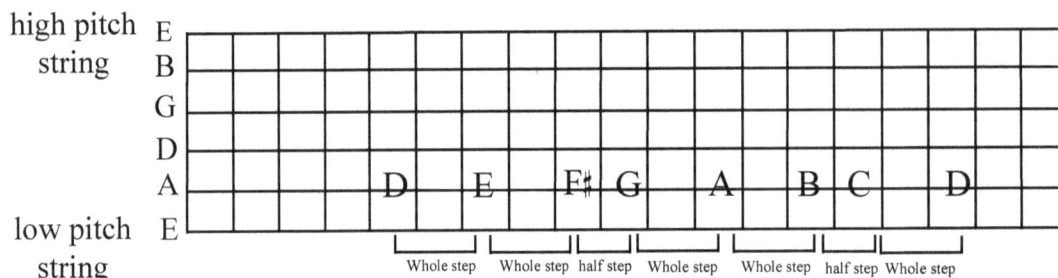

Another way to play this D Mixolydian scale on the guitar is to play it in "open" position by using the open strings, and in this case, the first four frets of the guitar as shown below.

Practical Way to Play a D Mixolydian Scale on the Guitar

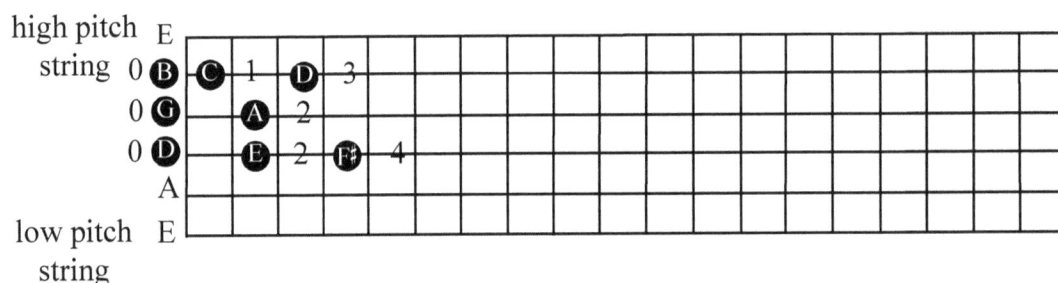

Building Seventh Chords

To review what you have learned so far, a chord can be a combination of any 3 or more notes played at the same time. Western music builds chords using a wide variety of intervals. One of the most common ways to build chords is to stack up diatonic 3rd intervals. For example, if we took D7 in the key of D Mixolyian, and stacked up 3rds, we would get D, F#, A, and C because all of those notes are in the key of D Mixolydian, and are a 3rd apart. **These four part structures built in thirds are commonly referred to as seventh chords, and the D note is said to be the root of the chord**.

D Dominant 7 Chord

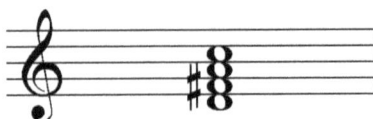

Building a D Dominant7 Chord

The structure below, D, F♯, A and C form what is called a dominant7 chord. If we measure the distance or interval between each note using our chromatic scale we can find the formula for building dominant7 chords. Between D and F♯ is 4 half steps or a major third. Between F♯ and A is 3 half steps or a minor third. Between A and C is 3 half steps or a minor third. Therefore to create a dominant7 chord we need to combine a major third on the bottom and a minor third in the middle and a minor third on the top.

D7 chord

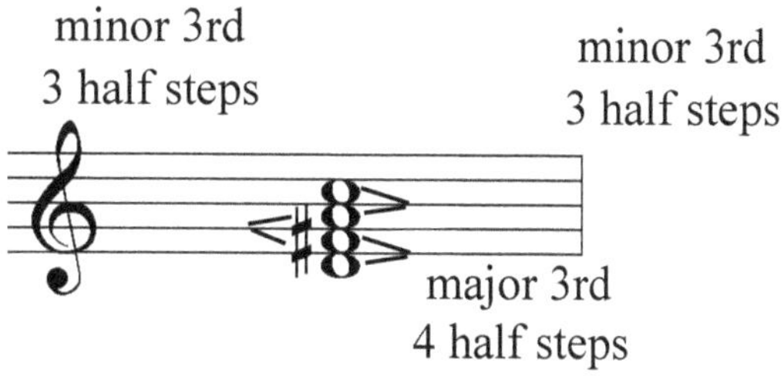

minor 3rd
3 half steps

minor 3rd
3 half steps

major 3rd
4 half steps

Playing a D Dominant7 Chord on the Guitar

It is possible to play the above dominant7 chord voicing on the guitar but it is very difficult. Because of this difficulty the dominant seventh chords in this book will be presented in the voicings that are easiest to play on the guitar.

D7

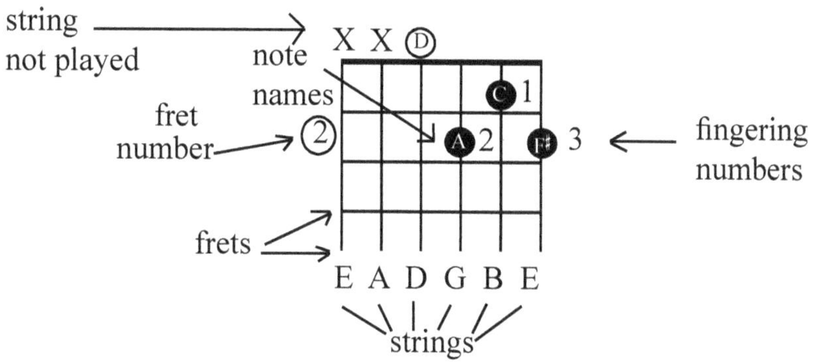

string
not played

note
names

fret
number

frets

fingering
numbers

E A D G B E

strings

Understanding a Chord Voicing

Although the chord above will work fine for a D Dominant7 chord it is common for guitarists to double a few notes from the triad in order to make the chord sound fuller. They are combined into a chord on the guitar which is both playable and has a good sound. So there are many ways to play any given chord depending on how many notes of the chord you use and how many notes are doubled. **Each of these different combinations of notes is called a chord voicing.**

**Common chord voicing
for a D Dominant7.**

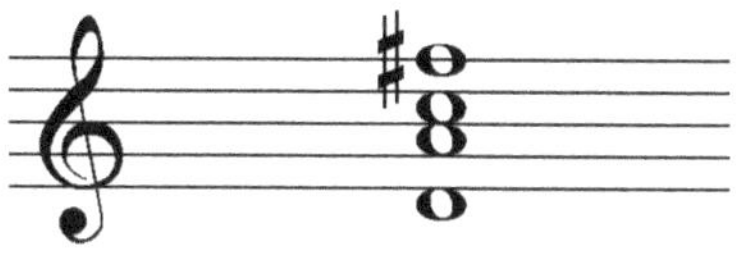

This is how you would play
these notes on the guitar.

D7

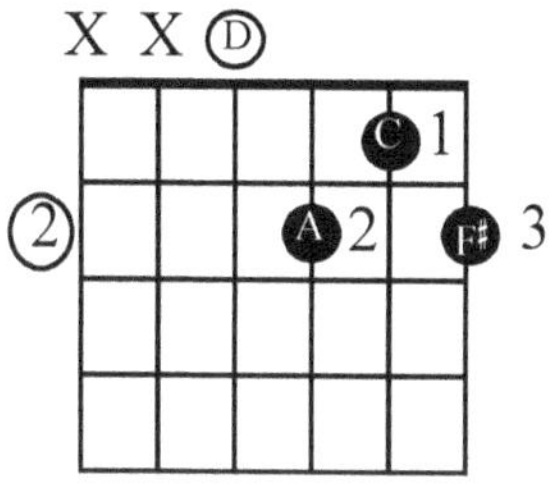

X X D

125

Root Position Dominant 7th Chords

Possible chord tones for 7

1,3,5,♭7

D7

E A D G B E

D7

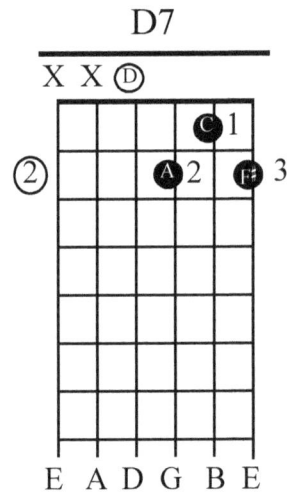

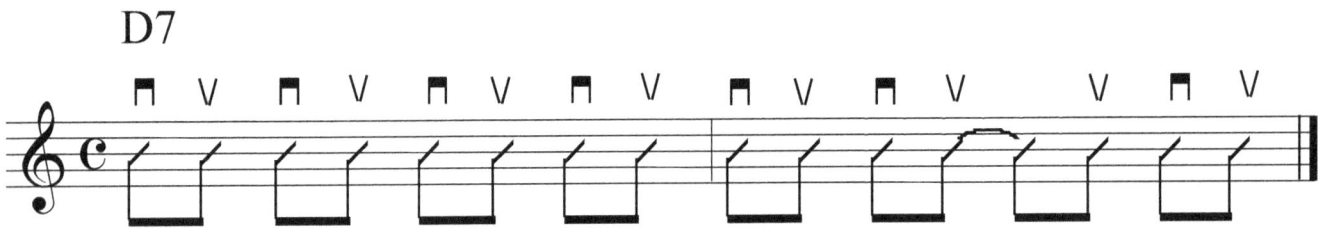

Explanation of Strumming Symbols

The following symbols are used to indicate an up or down stroke.

⊓ = Strum with a downward motion

V = Strum with an upward motion

Sight Reading Exercise 12

See page 29 for an explanation on understanding the sight reading example.

Chapter Thirteen

The E Mixolydian Scale

The E Dominant 7 Chord

E Mixolydian Scale Theory

Chromatic Scale Starting on E on Guitar Fretboard

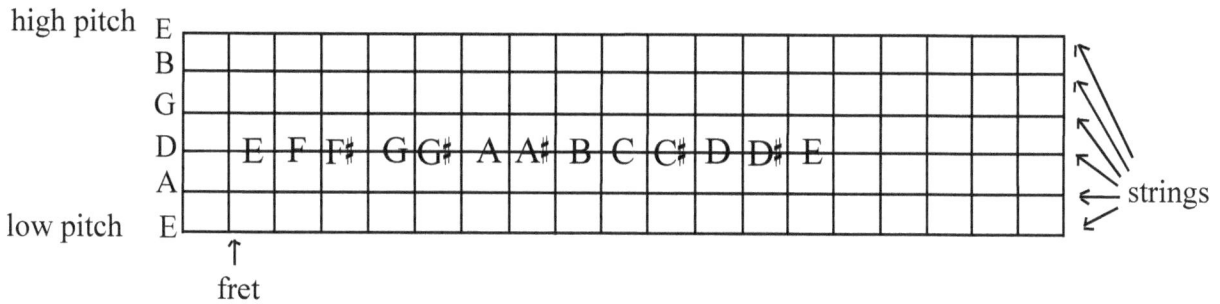

Extracting an E Mixolydian Scale from a Chromatic Scale

In the diagram above we can see all 12 notes again, which represent the chromatic scale. If we use the same process we did with the major scale and extract 7 notes, as shown below, we end up with a Mixolydian scale. It is sometimes easier to think of the Mixolydian scale as a major scale where the 7th have been flatted rather than memorizing the interval pattern. It should also be pointed out that if we play an A major scale starting on the 5th degree (E) we will be playing an E Mixolydian scale (E,F♯,G,G♯,A,B,C,D,E).

Mixolydian Scale Derived from Chromatic Scale

Chromatic Scale

Mixolydian Scale

Interval Relationships Found in a Mixolydian Scale

If we look at the distance in half steps between the notes of a Mixolydian scale we see a pattern; whole, whole, half, whole, whole, half, whole. **All Mixolydian scales are based on these intervals.**

E Mixolydian Scale

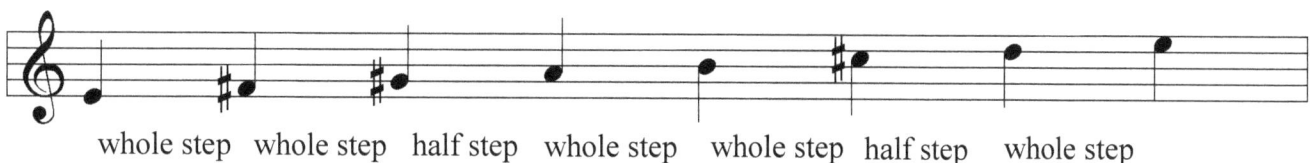

whole step   whole step   half step   whole step   whole step   half step   whole step

Seeing the E Mixolydian Scale on the Guitar

If we apply this to the guitar fretboard the information works out accordingly: start on any note on the guitar and move up on one string starting with a whole step (2 frets), whole step, half step (1 fret), whole step, whole step, half step, whole step. This is one way to play a Mixolydian scale on the guitar.

Guitar Fretboard

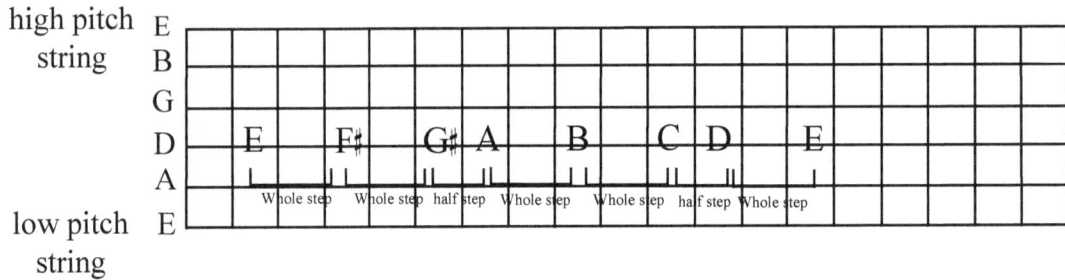

Another way to play this E Mixolydian scale on the guitar is to play it in "open" position by using the open strings, and in this case, the first four frets of the guitar as shown below.

Practical Way to Play an E Mixolydian Scale on the Guitar

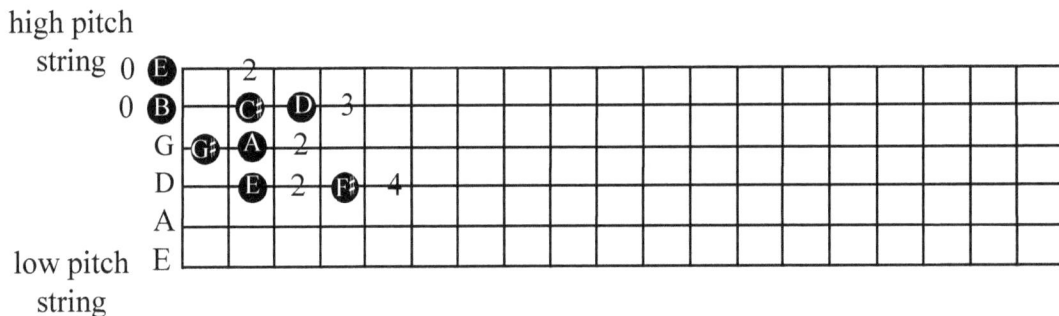

Building Seventh Chords

To review what you have learned so far, a chord can be a combination of any 3 or more notes played at the same time. Western music builds chords using a wide variety of intervals. One of the most common ways to build chords is to stack up diatonic 3rd intervals. For example, if we took E7 in the key of E Mixolyian and stacked up 3rds we would get E, G♯, B, and D because all of those notes are in the key of E Mixolydian and are a 3rd apart. **These four part structures built in thirds are commonly referred to as seventh chords and the E note is said to be the root of the chord**.

E Dominant 7 Chord

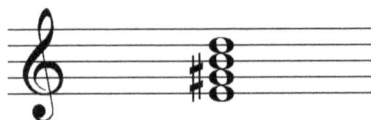

Building an E Dominant7 Chord

The structure below, E, G♯, B and D form what is called a dominant7 chord. If we measure the distance or interval between each note using our chromatic scale we can find the formula for building dominant7 chords. Between E and G♯ is 4 half steps or a major third. Between G♯ and B is 3 half steps or a minor third. Between B and D is 3 half steps or a minor third. Therefore to create a dominant7 chord we need to combine a major third on the bottom and a minor third in the middle and a minor third on the top.

E7 chord

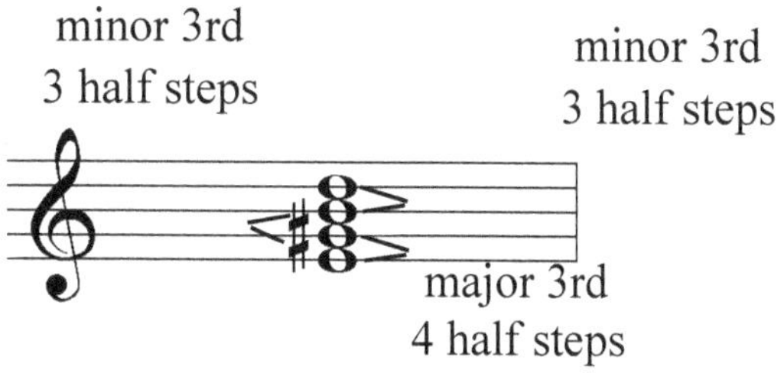

minor 3rd
3 half steps

minor 3rd
3 half steps

major 3rd
4 half steps

Playing an E Dominant7 Chord on the Guitar

It is possible to play the above dominant7 chord voicing on the guitar but it is very difficult. Because of this difficulty the dominant seventh chords in this book will be presented in the voicings that are easiest to play on the guitar.

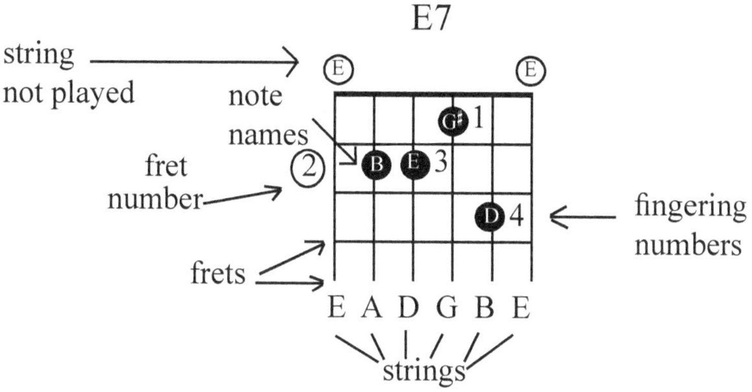

E7

string not played

note names

fret number

frets

fingering numbers

E A D G B E

strings

Understanding a Chord Voicing

Although the chord above will work fine for an E Dominant7 chord it is common for guitarists to double a few notes from the triad in order to make the chord sound fuller. They are combined into a chord on the guitar which is both playable and has a good sound. So there are many ways to play any given chord depending on how many notes of the chord you use and how many notes are doubled. **Each of these different combinations of notes is called a chord voicing.**

**Common chord voicing
for an E Dominant 7.**

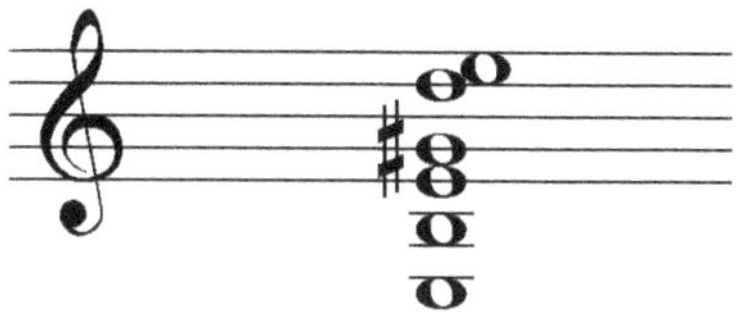

**This is how you would play
these notes on the guitar.**

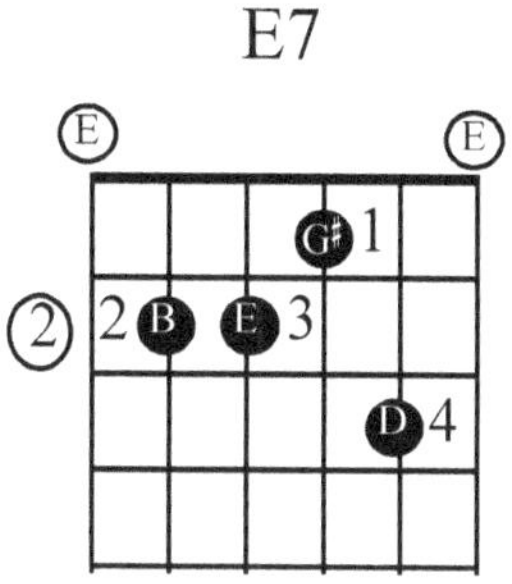

E7

131

Root Position Dominant 7th Chords

Possible chord tones for 7
1,3,5,♭7

E7

E7

Explanation of Strumming Symbols

The following symbols are used to indicate an up or down stroke.

⊓ = Strum with a downward motion
V = Strum with an upward motion

Sight Reading Exercise 13

See page 29 for an explanation on understanding the sight reading example.

Chapter Fourteen

The F Mixolydian Scale

The F Dominant 7 Chord

F Mixolydian Scale Theory

Chromatic Scale Starting on F on Guitar Fretboard

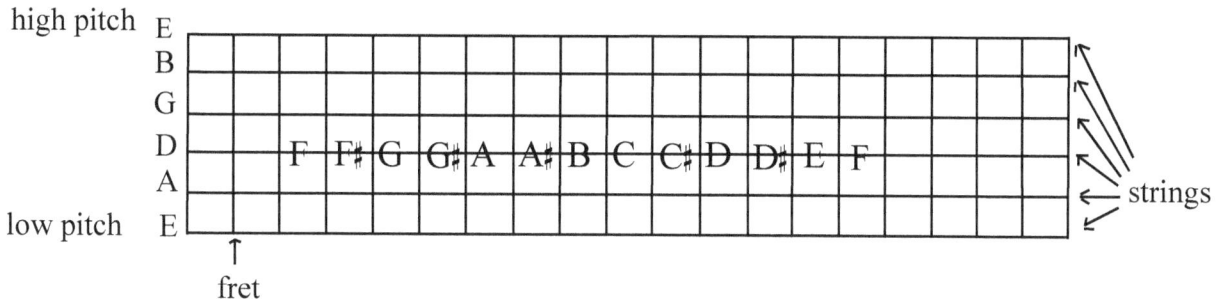

Extracting an F Mixolydian Scale from a Chromatic Scale

In the diagram above we can see all 12 notes again, which represent the chromatic scale. If we use the same process we did with the major scale and extract 7 notes, as shown below, we end up with a Mixolydian scale. It is sometimes easier to think of the Mixolydian scale as a major scale where the 7th have been flatted rather than memorizing the interval pattern. It should also be pointed out that if we play a B♭ major scale starting on the 5th degree (F) we will be playing an F Mixolydian scale (F,G,A,B♭,C,D,Eb,F).

Mixolydian Scale Derived from Chromatic scale

Chromatic Scale

Mixolydian Scale

Interval Relationships Found in a Mixolydian Scale

If we look at the distance in half steps between the notes of a Mixolydian scale we see a pattern; whole, whole, half, whole, whole, half, whole. **All Mixolydian scales are based on these intervals.**

F Mixolydian Scale

whole step   whole step   half step   whole step   whole step   half step   whole step

Seeing the F Mixolydian Scale on the Guitar

If we apply this to the guitar fretboard the information works out accordingly: start on any note on the guitar and move up on one string starting with a whole step (2 frets), whole step, half step (1 fret), whole step, whole step, half step, whole step. This is one way to play a Mixolydian scale on the guitar.

Guitar Fretboard

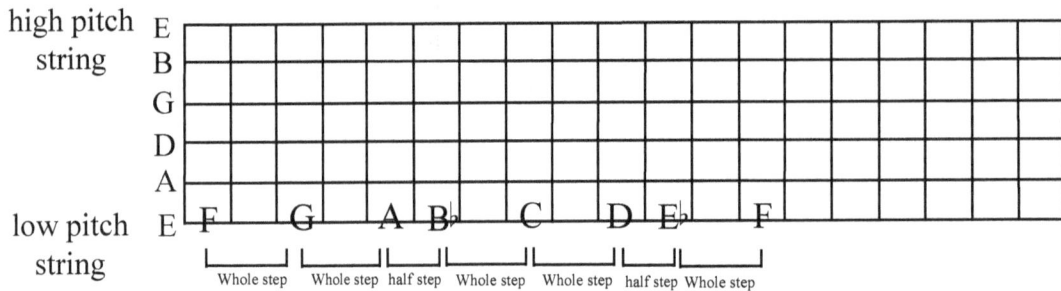

high pitch string | low pitch string

E
B
G
D
A
E — F   G   A B♭   C   D E♭   F

Whole step Whole step half step Whole step Whole step half step Whole step

Another way to play this F Mixolydian scale on the guitar is to play it in "open" position by using the open strings, and in this case, the first four frets of the guitar as shown below.

Practical Way to Play an F Mixolydian Scale on the Guitar

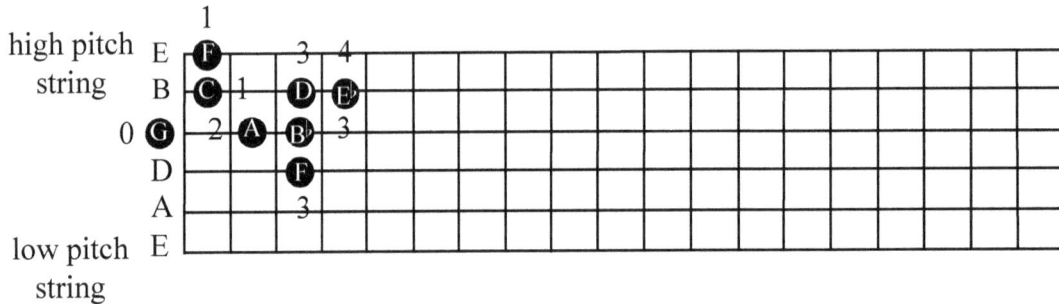

high pitch string | low pitch string

Building Seventh Chords

To review what you have learned so far a chord can be a combination of any 3 or more notes played at the same time. Western music builds chords using a wide variety of intervals. One of the most common ways to build chords is to stack up diatonic 3rd intervals. For example if we took F7 in the key of F Mixolyian and stacked up 3rds we would get F, A, C, and E♭ because all of those notes are in the key of F Mixolydian and are a 3rd apart. **These four part structures built in thirds are commonly referred to as seventh chords and the F note is said to be the root of the chord.**

F Dominant7 Chord

Building an F Dominant7 Chord

The structure below, F, A, C and E♭ form what is called a dominant7 chord. If we measure the distance or interval between each note using our chromatic scale we can find the formula for building dominant7 chords. Between F and A is 4 half steps or a major third. Between A and C is 3 half steps or a minor third. Between C and E♭ is 3 half steps or a minor third. Therefore to create a dominant7 chord we need to combine a major third on the bottom and a minor third in the middle

F7 chord

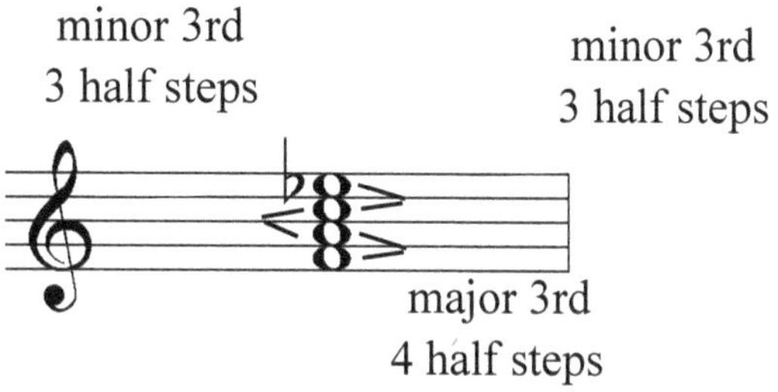

minor 3rd
3 half steps

minor 3rd
3 half steps

major 3rd
4 half steps

Playing an F Dominant7 Chord on the Guitar

It is possible to play the above dominant7 chord voicing on the guitar but it is very difficult. Because of this difficulty the dominant seventh chords in this book will be presented in the voicings that are easiest to play on the guitar.

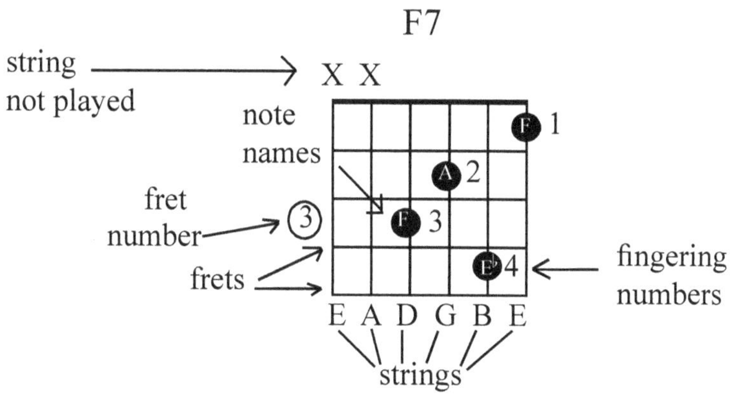

F7

string not played

note names

fret number

frets

fingering numbers

E A D G B E

strings

Understanding a Chord Voicing

Although the chord above will work fine for an F Dominant7 chord it is common for guitarists to double a few notes from the triad in order to make the chord sound fuller. They are combined into a chord on the guitar which is both playable and has a good sound. So there are many ways to play any given chord depending on how many notes of the chord you use and how many notes are doubled. **Each of these different combinations of notes is called a chord voicing.**

Common chord voicing for an F Dominant7.

This is how you would play these notes on the guitar.

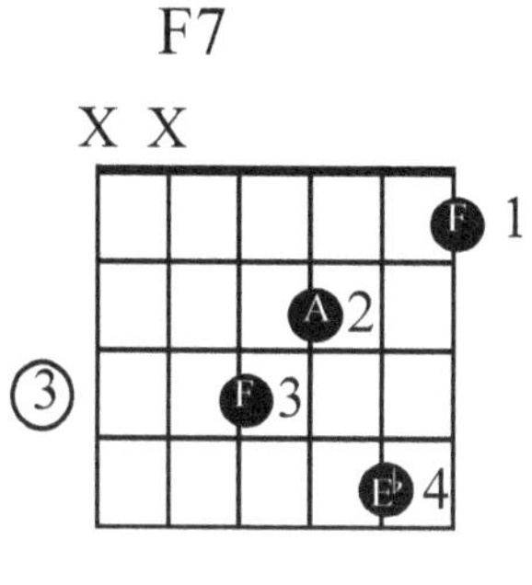

F7

X X

137

Root Position Dominant 7th Chords

Possible chord tones for 7
1,3,5,♭7

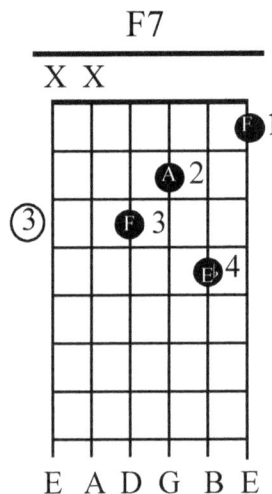

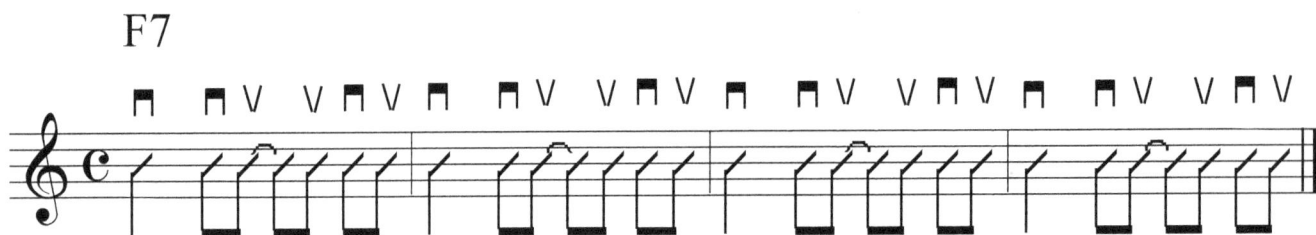

F7

E A D G B E

F7

Explanation of Strumming Symbols

The following symbols are used to indicate an up or down stroke.

⊓ = Strum with a downward motion

V = Strum with an upward motion

Ballad ♩=**84**

Bruce Arnold

See page 29 for an explanation on understanding the sight reading example.

Chapter Fifteen

The G Mixolydian Scale

The G Dominant 7 Chord

G Mixolydian Scale Theory

Chromatic Scale Starting on G on Guitar Fretboard

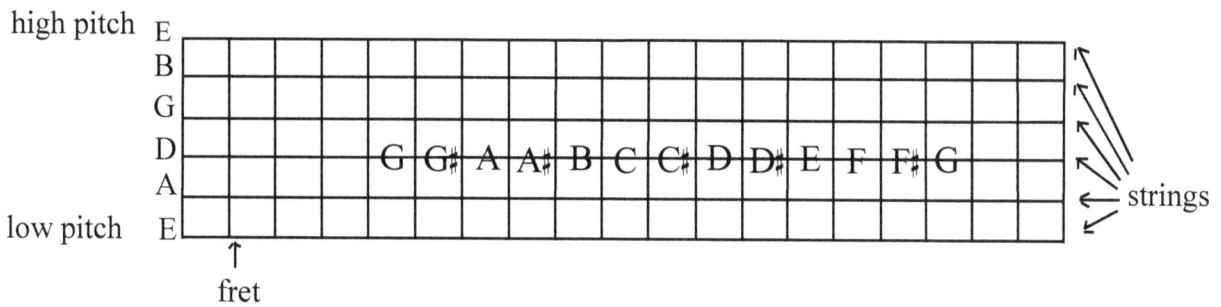

Extracting a G Mixolydian Scale from a Chromatic Scale

In the diagram above we can see all 12 notes again, which represent the chromatic scale. If we use the same process we did with the major scale and extract 7 notes, as shown below, we end up with a Mixolydian scale. It is sometimes easier to think of the Mixolydian scale as a major scale where the 7th have been flatted rather than memorizing the interval pattern. It should also be pointed out that if we play a C major scale starting on the 5th degree (G) we will be playing an G Mixolydian scale (G,A,B,C,D,E,F,G).

Mixolydian Scale Derived from Chromatic Scale

Chromatic Scale

Mixolydian Scale

Interval Relationships Found in a Mixolydian Scale

If we look at the distance in half steps between the notes of a Mixolydian scale we see a pattern; whole, whole, half, whole, whole, half, whole. **All Mixolydian scales are based on these intervals.**

G Mixolydian Scale

whole step   whole step   half step   whole step   whole step   half step   whole step

Seeing the G Mixolydian Scale on the Guitar

If we apply this to the guitar fretboard the information works out accordingly: start on any note on the guitar and move up on one string starting with a whole step (2 frets), whole step, half step (1 fret), whole step, whole step, half step, whole step. This is one way to play a Mixolydian scale on the guitar.

Guitar Fretboard

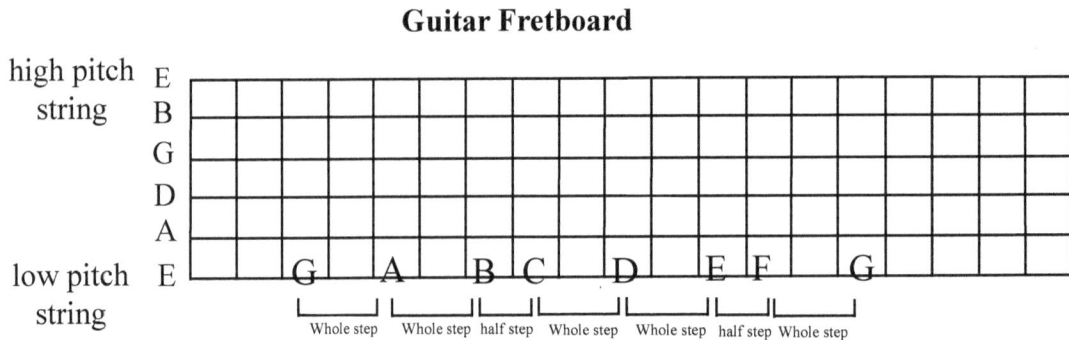

Another way to play this G Mixolydian scale on the guitar is to play it in "open" position by using the open strings, and in this case, the first three frets of the guitar as shown below.

Practical Way to Play a G Mixolydian Scale on the Guitar

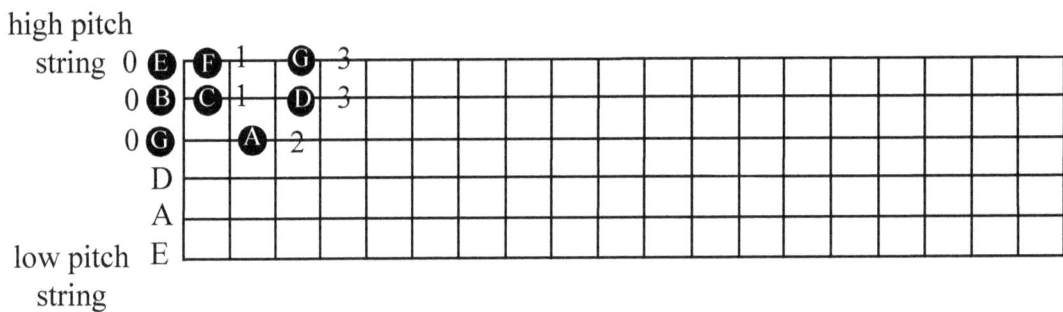

Building Seventh Chords

Western music builds chords using a wide variety of intervals. One of the most common ways to build chords is to stack up diatonic 3rd intervals. For example if we took G7 in the key of G Mixolyian and stacked up 3rds we would get G, B, D, and F because all of those notes are in the key of G Mixolydian and are a 3rd apart. **These four part structures built in thirds are commonly referred to as seventh chords and the F note is said to be the root of the chord**.

G Dominant7 Chord

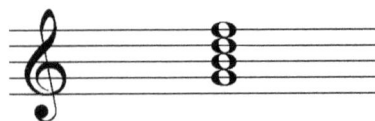

Building a G Dominant7 Chord

The structure below, G, B, D and F form what is called a dominant7 chord. If we measure the distance or interval between each note using our chromatic scale we can find the formula for building dominant7 chords. Between G and B is 4 half steps or a major third. Between B and D is 3 half steps or a minor third. Between D and F is 3 half steps or a minor third. Therefore, to create a dominant7 chord we need to combine a major third on the bottom and a minor third in the middle and a minor third on the top.

G7 chord

minor 3rd
3 half steps

minor 3rd
3 half steps

major 3rd
4 half steps

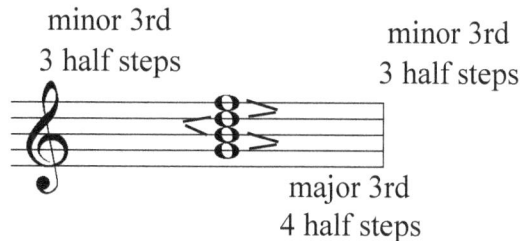

Playing a G Dominant7 Chord on the Guitar

It is possible to play the above dominant7 chord voicing on the guitar but it is very difficult. Because of this difficulty the dominant seventh chords in this book will be presented in the voicings that are easiest to play on the guitar.

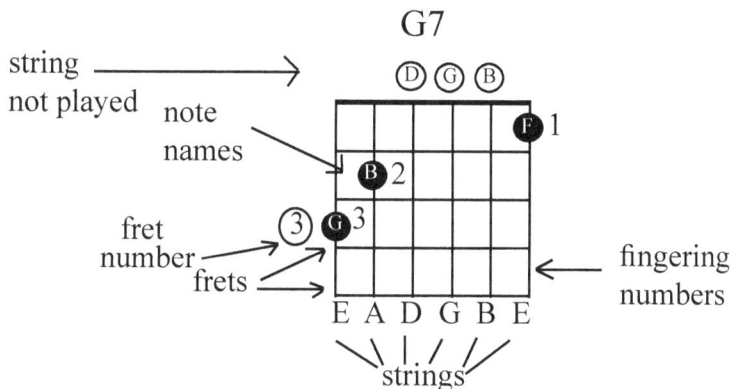

G7

string
not played

note
names

fret
number
frets

fingering
numbers

E A D G B E

strings

Understanding a Chord Voicing

Although the chord above will work fine for a G Dominant7 chord, it is common for guitarists to double a few notes from the triad in order to make the chord sound fuller. They are combined into a chord on the guitar which is both playable, and has a good sound. So there are many ways to play any given chord depending on how many notes of the chord you use and how many notes are doubled. **Each of these different combinations of notes is called a chord voicing.**

**Common chord voicing
for a G Dominant7.**

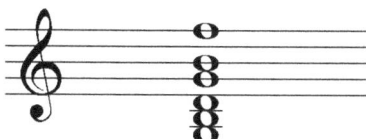

**This is how you would play
these notes on the guitar.**

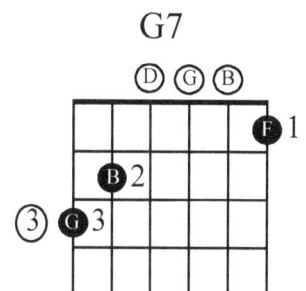

G7

143

Root Position Dominant 7th Chords

Possible chord tones for 7
1,3,5,♭7

G7

E A D G B E

Be careful when playing the G7 chord that all the "open" strings sound clear. Although neither of these chords are present in any of the chord progressions starting on page 160 they both are commonly found in popular tunes.

G7

Explanation of Strumming Symbols

The following symbols are used to indicate an up or down stroke.

⊓ = Strum with a downward motion
V = Strum with an upward motion

Sight Reading Exercise 15

See page 29 for an explanation on understanding the sight reading example.

Chapter Sixteen

Explanation of Barre Chords

Leaving Out Notes in Chords

Adding Notes to Chords

Moveable Chord Forms

Cycle 5

Root Position Major Barre Chords

Barre Chords

The next chords we will look at are the "Barre Chords" (pronounced "bar".) These chords are the same chords we have already learned but we are going to play them in a different way. As previously discussed, there is more than one way to play any chord. This is accomplished by doubling or leaving out certain notes.

These barre chords are some of the most commonly played chord voicings on the guitar. In general, you will find that the "open" voiced chords you have just learned are used more in folk music, while the barre chords are found more in rock.

Barre chords are not easy for a beginner (see picture 14.) It takes time to develop strength in your index finger to hold down more that one string at a time. You will find the practice suggestion on the next page to be a great way to learn these barre chords. The cool thing about these chords is that you can slide them around the neck to play other chords of the same type. When you start to practice these chords don't worry so much about how they sound, just form the chord and play it. Over time the chords will start to sound better as your hand strengthens and is able to play each note clearly. If you find these chords to be quite difficult and frustrating I recommend you play a barre chord, and then play each string, adjusting your hand to make each note sound. You will probably find you are unable to make all the notes sound clearly together. However, if you use the technique of playing each note and adjusting your hand, you will find eventually the barre chord starts sounding better and better.

I can't over emphasize the importance of practicing the barre chords using the technique on the next page. Barre chords allow you to play one fingering pattern and then move it around the neck to play all the possible types of that chord. For instance, once you learn the major chord presented on the next page you can move this voicing around the neck to play ANY major chord. You just need to memorize what the "root note" or bottom note of the chord is and instantly you have learned all the major chords. This is one of the great things about a guitar. It allows you to move barre chords around to different frets so that you can play all possible chords using the same position.

Give yourself a few weeks, if not a month, on these chords. They are very hard on your hand at first and require time for your hand to adjust. The chord progressions in the back of this book will also help you to apply and develop these chords until they sound clear and distinct.

Leaving Out Notes in Chords

It is common to leave out certain notes of a chord when playing barre chords but you will also find this happening with other chords as you explore music more in-depth. There is a hierarchy of which notes are left out more often. The 5th of a chord is the first note to be left out. This is because it is the note that least defines the sound of any chord. The (1) or the root is the next to go. This is because usually the bass player in a group is playing the root so you don't need to double it.

Adding Notes to Chords

As we have discussed in the previous chapters in this book, it is also common to add notes to chords. It is beyond the scope of this book to explain all the theory and occurrences of this phenomenon. Added notes can create a great effect in music, giving the chords inner life and movement. So that you have a general idea of the process of adding notes, here is a very cursory explanation. The notes that are most commonly added are the passing tones of the scale that is used for the chord you are playing. Another process that is also used is the addition of the available tensions for any chord. Both processes overlap each other and can add great color and movement for your chord progressions. This topic will be discussed in greater detail in further volumes of this series.

Moveable Chord Forms

The chords that follow allow you to learn a chord form and then move it around the neck to get that chord type for every degree of a chromatic scale. All the notated examples of chords should be practiced "cycle 5". Cycle 5 is a way to play all 12 chromatic notes by moving in a pattern of 5ths (or 7 half steps) down from the previous chord. Therefore, C moves to F, then B♭, E♭, A♭, D♭, G♭, B, E, A, D, G. On the guitar for example, this means you would play the first C major chord at the 3rd fret as indicated, and then play the same fingering at the 8th fret on the 5th string to get F major, then the 1st fret for B♭ major, 6th fret for E♭ major etc. The example below shows you how to proceed.

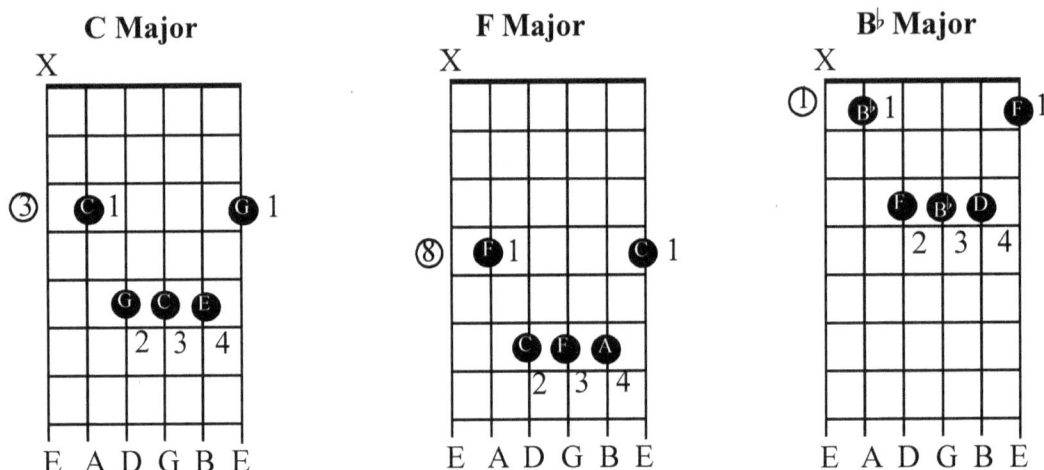

C Major   **F Major**   **B♭ Major**

E A D G B E   E A D G B E   E A D G B E

Don't just memorize the position of each of these chords without thinking of what chord you are playing. Memorize the shape, so you can recognize the chord type, then memorize the bottom of each chord to tell you which chord you are playing as you move through the cycle 5 progression. Remember, all examples in this book have the root as the lowest note of each chord voicing, so by memorizing the bottom note as you move cycle 5 you will be memorizing the notes on the E and A strings. When you have memorized the notes on the E and A strings you only need to memorize the new chord type as you move through this book.

Cycle 5 is one of the most common chord movements in music. Therefore, practicing chords cycle 5 is excellent preparation for playing music.

Cycle 5 Progression or the Circle of Fifths

C, F, B♭, E♭, A♭, D♭, G♭, B, E, A, D, G

It is also a good idea to go through the cycle in a couple of ways. For example, when you get to G♭ think F♯ instead. G♭ and F♯ are said to be enharmonic keys because their pitches are the same on the guitar but their names are different. Refer back to your list of keys to find other enharmonic keys to practice.

Try not to count down a certain number of frets to find the next chord. Memorizing the pitches of each fret will be much better in the long run. All moveable chord forms found in this book should be practiced using the cycle 5 movement. Remember, when practicing, always think what note you are playing rather than memorizing the position.

Root Position Major Chords

Possible chord tones for C major

1,3,5

C Major

X

E A D G B E

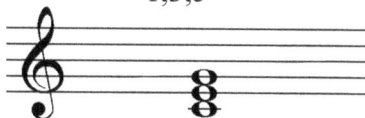

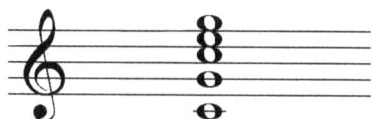

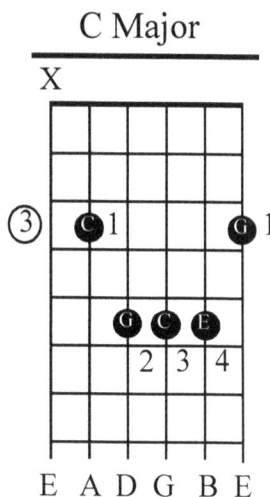

It is also possible to finger this chord by replacing your 2nd, 3rd, and 4th finger with your 3rd finger and pressing down across the aforementioned notes. This requires flexibility in the 1st joint of your **3rd** finger. Photo 11 shows this flexibility using the 1st finger for demonstration.

With the C major barre chord and a working knowledge of how to play it in any key as shown on page 148 it is suggested that you also check out the chord progression on page 165 and also check page 159 for directions for how to practice the chord progressions. If you have problems with the rhythm in the chord progressions see pages 153-57

Please note: Your first finger essentially presses down all the way across the neck, but your 2nd, 3rd and 4th fingers are creating higher notes on the A, D and G strings.

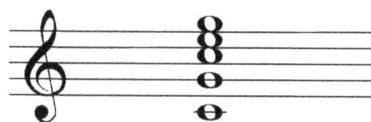

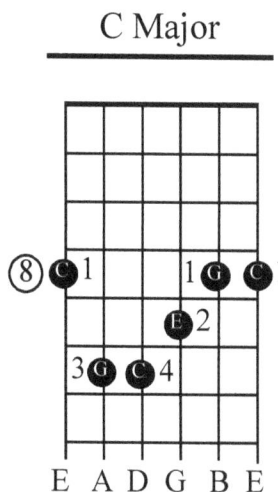

C Major

E A D G B E

This is one of the most popular barre chords. Make sure to play this chord through the exercises on page 148. This will help you to memorize all the notes on the low E string and prepare you for the chord progression found on page 160. See photo 14 for a close up look at this chord.

Root Position Minor Chords

Possible chord tones for C-

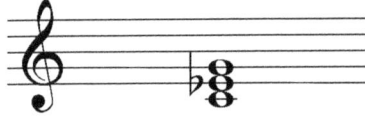

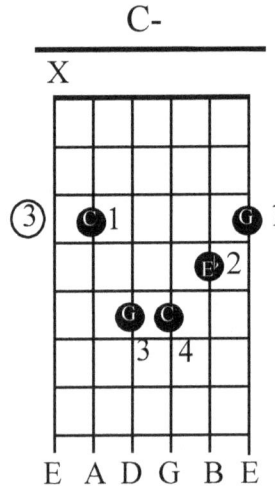

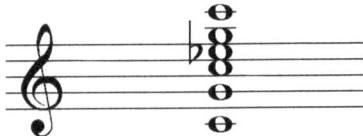

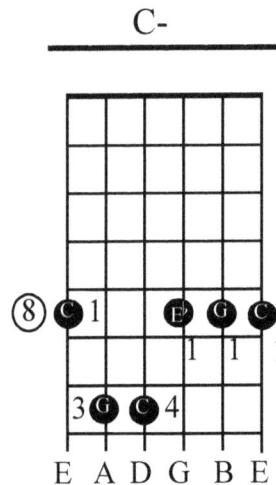

1,♭3,5

Once again play these chords through the exercise found on page 148 After you feel like you know the minor chords in all keys, try the chord progressions on pages 160-71. You should first check page 159 for directions on how to practice the chord progressions. If you have problems with the rhythm in the chord progressions see pages 153-57.

Congratulations for making it this far!

Believe it or not you have now learned most of the chords you will commonly find in rock and folk. Although we still have a few more chords to present, your palette of chord possibilities is now at a point where you should be able to buy music books of your favorite artists' songs and feel familiar with the chords.

Root Position Dominant 7th Chords

Possible chord tones for C7

1,3,5,♭7

C7

Make sure the G string sounds with this chord to give it the proper sound.

C7

C7

Make sure the D string sounds with this chord to give it the proper sound. You should play these chords once again through the exercise on page 148. You can then play the blues chord progression found on pages 170-71.

Chapter Seventeen

Rhythm

Understanding Rhythm

One of the most overlooked aspects of learning to play an instrument is rhythm. You can learn all the chords in the world, play all the scales, and understand all the theory, but if you don't have a basic understanding of rhythm none of it will sound like music. Rhythm is the heart beat of music and you need to understand it at least at a rudimentary level in order to play any piece of music.

The following pages will present you with a simple discussion of how rhythm is notated in music. This will help you considerably in understanding the rhythms in the chord progression. Furthermore, it will also help you with any piece of music you come across. Audio examples in the form of midifiles are available on the muse-eek.com website, so you can hear what each rhythm sounds like. Each file will give you a one bar count off (4 ticks) and then play the example. Using these help files will greatly speed up your understanding of rhythm.

The Nuts and Bolts of Rhythm

The rhythm in a piece of music is presented in overall units call "measures." These measures are further divided up into beats. (More on this in a moment) Example One shows you one "measure" of music. There are many different symbols in a measure of music. These symbols show how to play the music. To the far left there is always a clef sign. This tells the reader what pitch level the notes will be on the staff. The clef sign used here is the treble clef sign. Therefore, the 4 notes presented in this measure would be four C's. The next symbol is the time signature. This tells you how the measure will be divided rhythmically. In this case the time signature is 4/4. The top 4 tells you how many beats are in a measure. In this case the measure has 4 beats in it. The bottom 4 tells you what unit of measure will be used to show those 4 beats. In this case the 4 represents a quarter note. So this whole measure is divided up into 4 quarters and these 4 quarters are each represented by a note called a quarter note. A quarter note would be held for one beat. A line is placed at the end of each measure to show where the end of each measure is.

Example 1

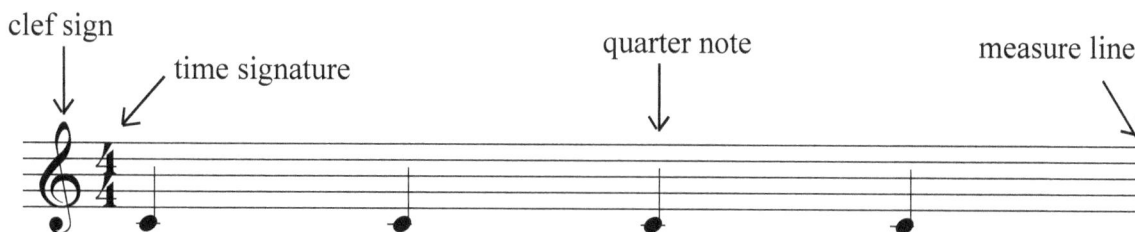

You can use the suggested midifiles to play any of the examples found here or you can use a metronome to help you maintain a steady pulse. A metronome plays a steady clicking sound at a user selectable rate. This can help you maintain a steady pulse as you work on the exercises. Metronomes can be purchased at any music store but you can also find many electronic metronomes on the Internet that will work on your computer.

Rhythm can of course be much more or less complicated than example 1. In example 2 we still have a 4/4 measure and it still has only 4 beats in the measure but we have only one note which happens on beat one. This note takes up all four beats of the measure so you would sustain the sound for four beats. This note is called a whole note. Example 3 shows a measure that has been divided up into two equal parts. These notes are called half notes and because we have a 4/4 measure there can only be 2 half notes in a measure because a half note gets 2 beats. The first note is played on beat one and the second note is played on beat 3.

Example 2

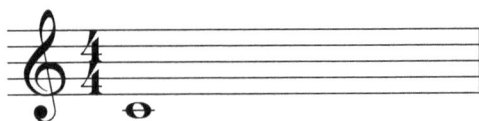

Example 3

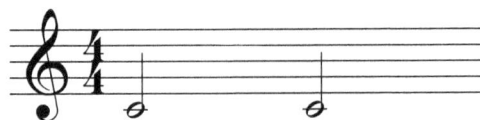

As I have said, rhythm can be much more complicated than the previous example. In example 4 we still have a 4/4 measure and it still has only 4 beats in the measure but each beat has been divided into equal divisions to form a new rhythm. Now rather than just four rhythmic hits in the measure there are eight. These new notes are referred to as eighth notes because it takes 8 eighth notes to make up one measure of 4/4. So for each beat you would play two notes equally dividing that beat into two parts.

Example 4

Rhythm can get even more complicated than these examples. We can also add in rest periods where you don't play anything. The next page will explain this process and how it is notated.

Rests

In each of the rhythms presented in the previous examples we could have left some notes out to create other rhythms. These left out notes are called rests and use the symbols shown in the examples below. During the rests you don't play anything. You will see in the forthcoming examples that when rests are placed into measures the rhythm can become quite complex. We will start with some simple examples.

Examples 5-7 show measures with three kinds of rests. In example 5 there is a whole note rest. Nothing would be played during this measure. Example 6 shows a half note rest. In this case nothing would be played for the first two beats of the measure. Example 7 shows a quarter note rest. In this case nothing would be played for beat 3 of this measure.

Example 5
whole note rest

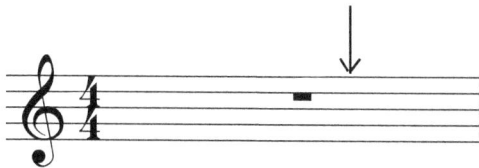

Example 6
half note rest

Example 7
quarter note rest

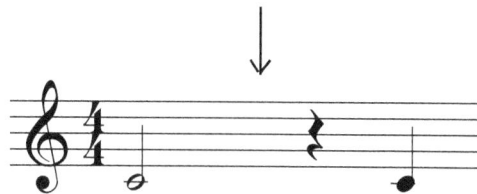

Examples 8 show a measure that is composed of eighth notes but in which one of the eighth notes has been left out.

Example 8
eighth note rest

155

Dots

A dot can be placed after a note or rest to lengthen its value. A dot adds 1/2 of the note's value. Therefore, in example 9 the dot placed after the quarter note adds a one eighth value so you hold this note for 3 eighths duration. (One quarter plus one eighth = 3 eighths) Example 10 shows the same situation but with a tie rather than a rest.

Example 9

Example 10

Ties

Ties can also be placed into music to lengthen a particular note. Example 11 shows two quarter notes tied together. Example 12 shows what this rhythm would sound like.

Example 11

Example 12

Although I don't recommend it as a long term habit, a beginner often needs a method to help count each beat and subdivision. Over time you should develop the ability to recognize any rhythm and know what it sounds like. However, if you are a beginner or you are having a problem with a rhythm, counting is a way to work it through. The follow examples give the counting method I recommend.

Rhythmic Notation
Slanted lines or Slashes

New York Guitar Method Primer Book 1 uses rhythmic notation which is commonly used in professional music to indicate the rhythm of a chord progression or to 'mark' time. Example A shows slanted lines or slashes "/" to indicate each beat in the measure. Example A is in 4/4 time which is also known as common time. This is why there is a "C" shown after the treble clef sign. The slashes are not telling you to play on every beat; they are used for your eye to quickly see how many beats are in each bar.

Example A

4/4 common time

B-   B-   A ⎯ One bar ⎯ A

treble clef sign   Slashes showing each beat

When playing a song you very often need to play chords. These chords will be played in a certain rhythm which will help give the song it's distinctive flavor or style. Professional musicians use a great system of rhythmic notation to indicate the rhythm needed for each chord. Example B shows each chord being played twice per measure and changing chord each measure. You need to play the chords once on the 1st beat and once on the 3rd beat. Rhythmic notation uses similiar types of notes to regular notation. (Please see the Member's Area for the help file on rhythm to understand each rhythmic value and how this is notated). You will notice that the diamond shapes with flags look a lot like half notes in regular notation and in fact they have the same value. So for each of the diamond shapes below you will strum the chord which will create two strums per bar on beats one and three.

Example B

G   D   A-   A-
diamond shapes   Beat one   Beat three

flags

All rhythms can be notated with rhythmic notation. Example C shows three of these rhythms. The first bar is a whole note written in rhythmic notation so you strum the chord once. The second measure has a dotted quarter written in rhythmic notation so you play the chord on one and hold it for a beat and half. Next you have an eighth tied to a half note written in rhythmic notation which means you will strum the B♭ chord on two "and," and hold it for 2 and one half beats.

Example C

D-   C   B♭   A

Whole Note   Eighth tied to a half equals
equals 4 beats   Dotted quarter equals   two and one half beats.
                     one beat and a half   157

Chapter Eighteen

Chord Progressions

Applying Your New Chords to Common Chord Progressions

The following pages contain chord progressions that will help you to apply the chords and the rhythm knowledge you have learned so far. There are many ways to approach these chord progressions. There are 10 progressions in total. The first eight chord progressions have been divided up into 3 levels of difficulty. Each level gets progressively harder so you can slowly master each aspect of changing chords, strumming and keeping time. The first level entitled "A," gives you just the chords with a simple strumming pattern. The second level "B," gives you the chord progression with a more complex strumming and rhythmic pattern. The third level entitled "C," gives you the actual way this progression would be played. By working your way through each level you should find that you progress quickly.

Many help files are available at the muse-eek.com website to enable a student to master each level and each progression. Again, it's not essential to use these files to learn the progression but they can make the process a lot more fun, and also help to point out problems that you might not be aware of. Whether you use the files or not, you should work on the progressions in the following manner.

How to Practice the Chord Progressions

1. Play each example (A, B, C) slowly, using a metronome or a help file, or count the correct number of beats for each.
2. Follow the picking directions (see bottom of page for explanation of picking symbols)
3. Speed up the example over a week of practice then proceed to the next level.

If You Have Problems There is More Help Online at muse-eek.com

You have two different types of files available to help you master each strumming exercise. The midifiles (played by downloading a midifile player from the muse-eek.com website) will play each example at whatever tempo you select.

This process of using audio and midifiles can really speed up your progress on the guitar. I urge you to take the time to set up your computer so you can take advantage of these help files. You will also notice that the midifile player allows you to speed up and slow down the audio so you can gradually play the chords faster and faster.

I know it is hard to remember all the chords we have looked at so far. Chord progressions are a great tool to help you remember all the chord voicings. I have only suggested one group of chords for each chord progression but as you have learned, there is more than one way to play each chord. (There are "open" voicings and "barre" chords.) After you have mastered these progressions try replacing the chords with alternate possibilities. This will help you to memorize more chords and give you more agility on the guitar. Remember to be patient with yourself. Some students can take months before this flows smoothly while others get it going within weeks. Don't dwell on what your inherent ability might be; just remember that perseverance pays off and is its own reward.

Explanation of Strumming Symbols

The following symbols are used to indicate an up or down stroke.

⊓ = Strum with a downward motion
V = Strum with an upward motion

Chord Progression 1

G — D G B — E A D G B E

D — X X D — E A D G B E

A- — X A ... E — E A D G B E

Example A

G   D   A-   A-

Example B

G   D   A-   A-

Example C

mm=112

G   D   A-   A-

Chord Progression 2

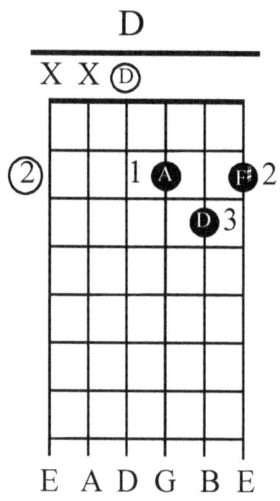
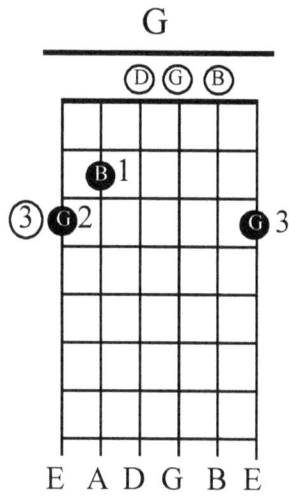
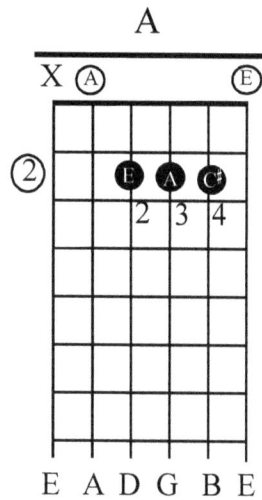
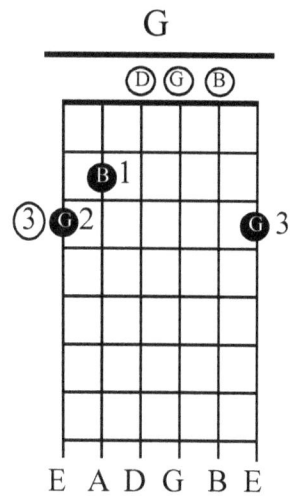

Example A

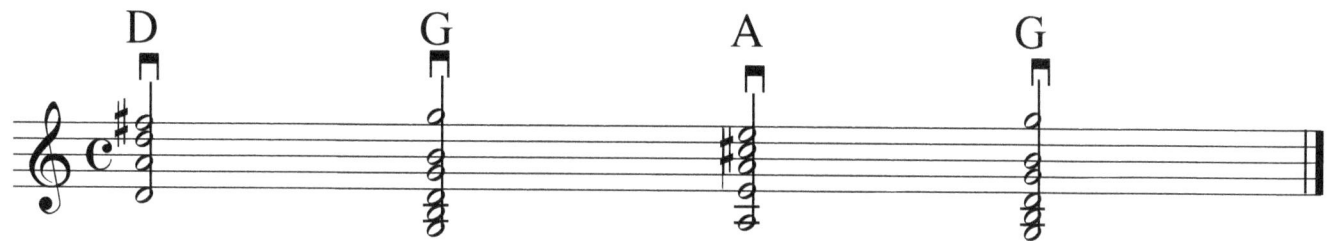

Example B

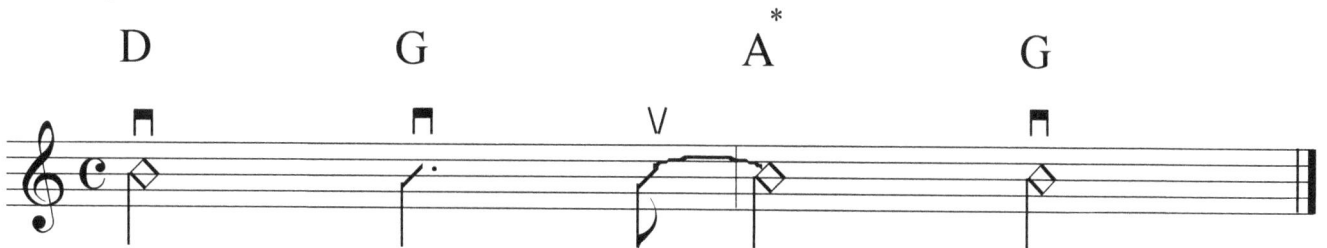

*When a chord is tied over from a previous measure the chord symbol is placed on the 1st beat of the following measure.

Example C

mm=120

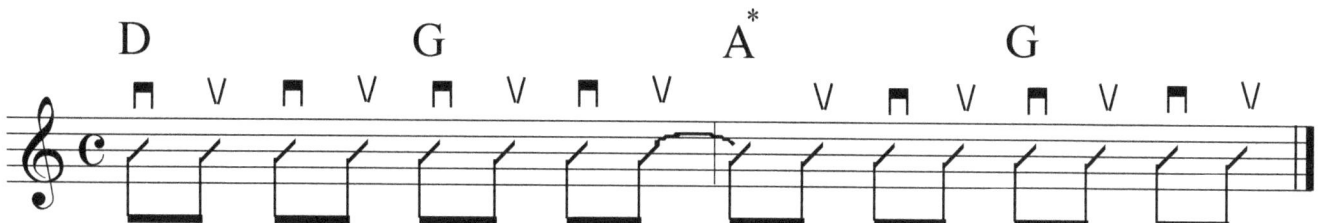

Chord Progression 3

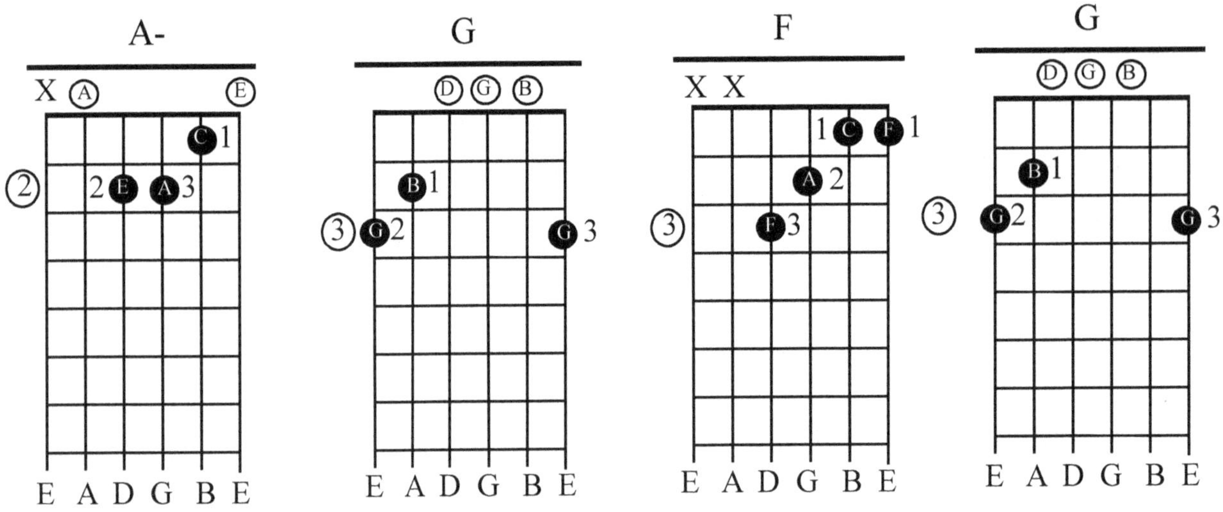

Example A

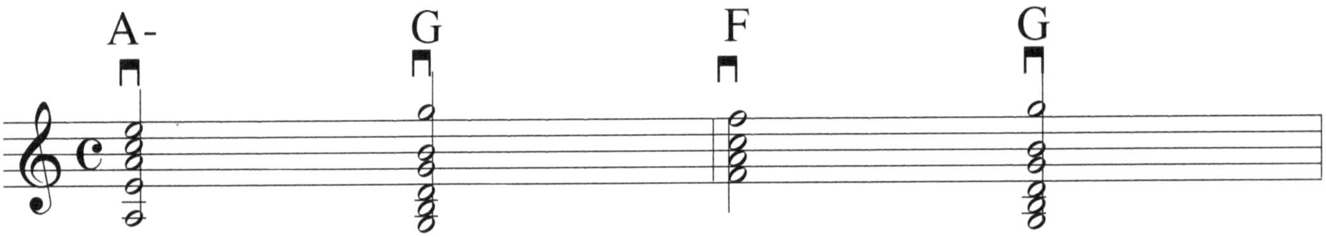

Example B

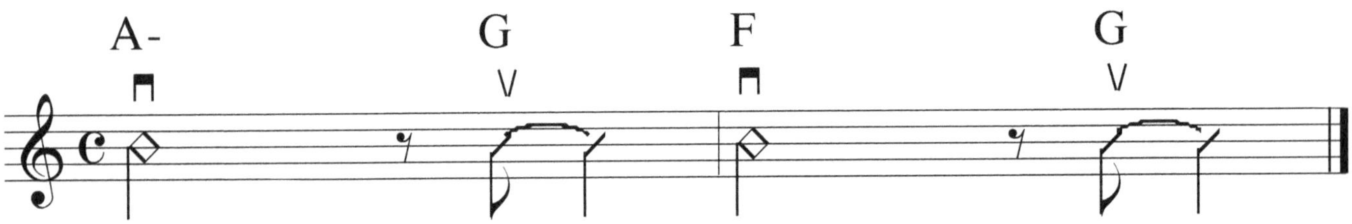

Example C

mm=88

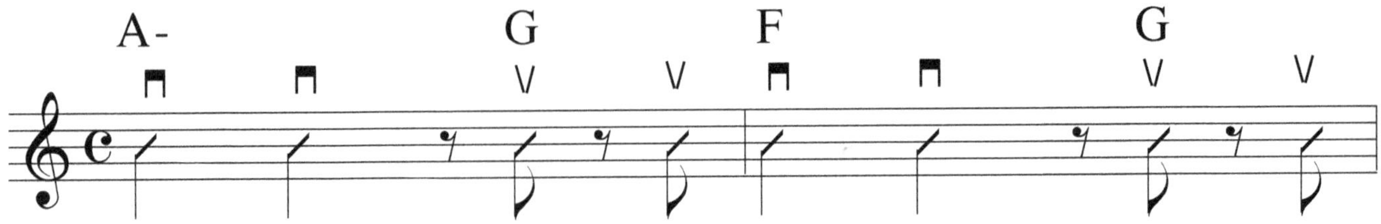

Chord Progression 4

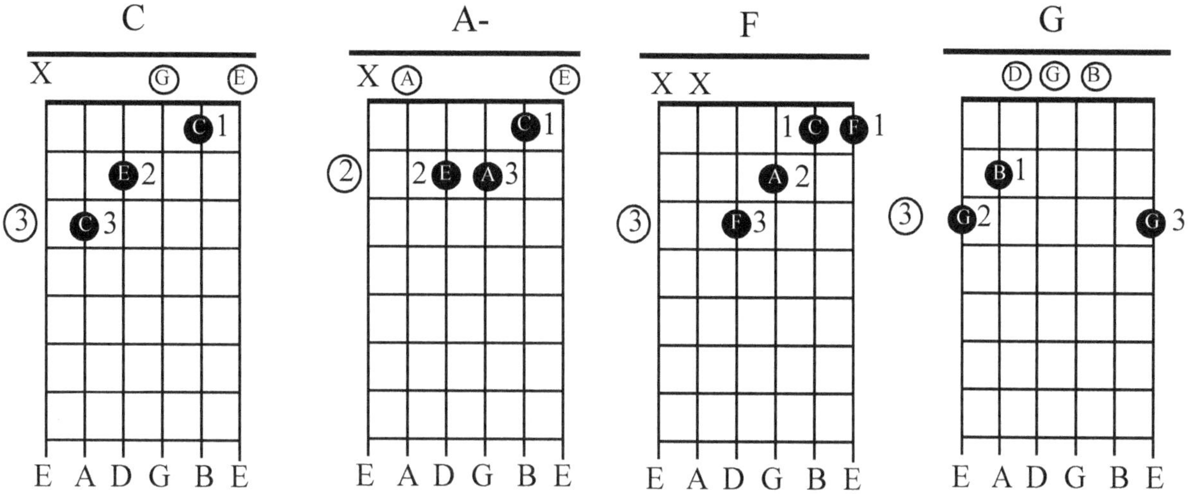

Example A

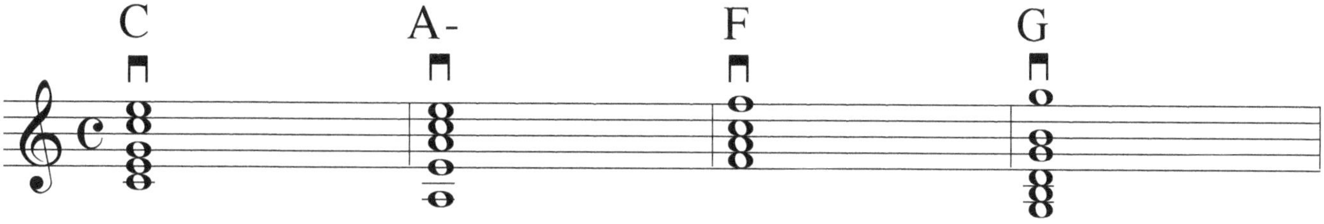

Example B

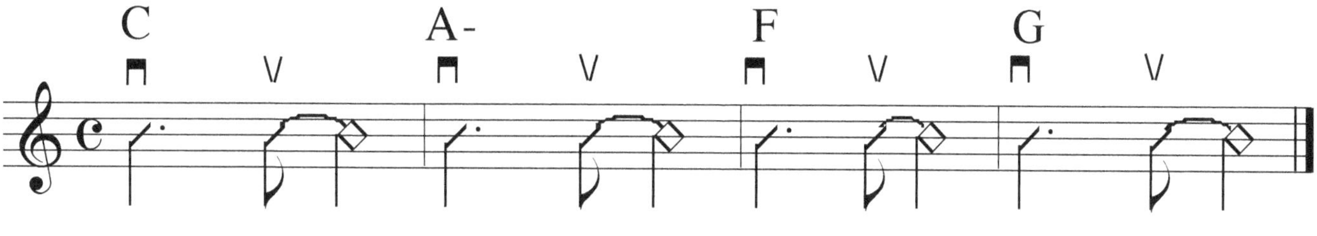

Example C

mm=88

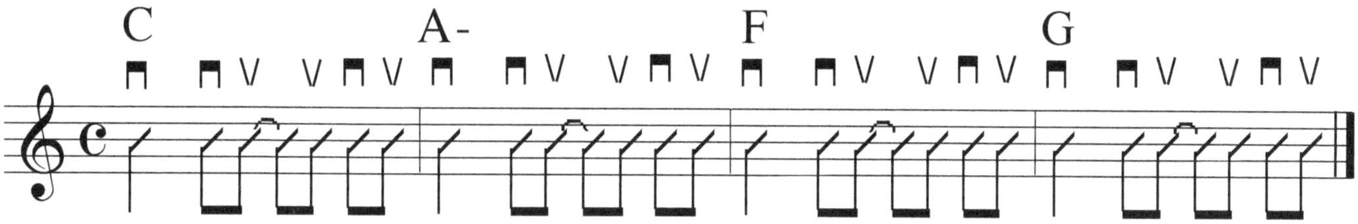

Chord Progression 5

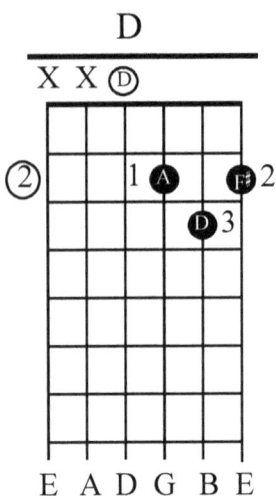

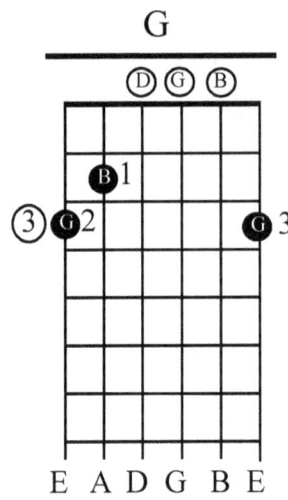

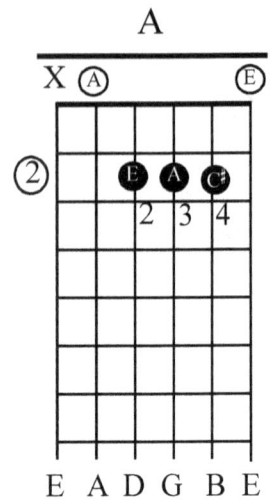

Example A

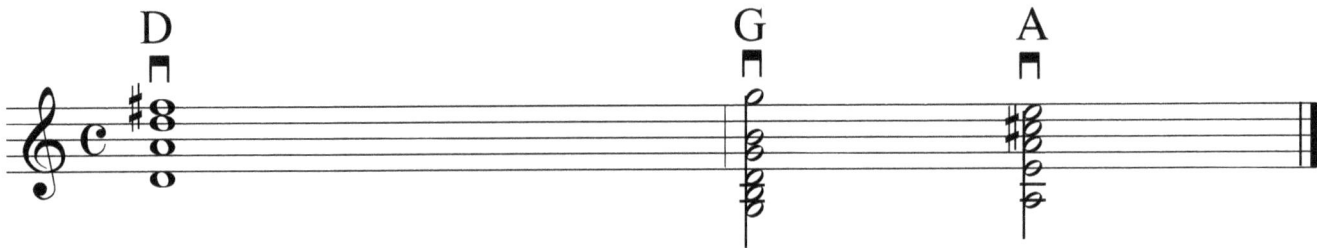

Example B

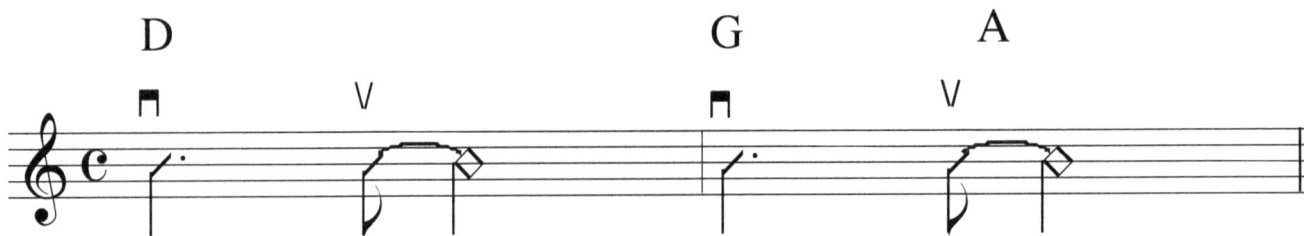

Example C

Chord Progression 6

mm=104

Chord Progression 7

Example A

Example B

Example C

mm=112

Chord Progression 8

C Major   **E♭ Major**   **D Major**   **F Major**

Example A

Example B

Example C

mm=100

For this type of progression and style it is common to just play the bottom 3 notes of each chord. This style of playing only the bottom 3 notes of a major or minor barre chord is frequently referred to as playing "power chords." Distortion is also a key element in the effectiveness of the "power chord" style. Distortion can be achieved by either turning your amp and guitar up very loud (hopefully when your neighbors are not around) or using a distortion box.

Chord Progression 9

This is our first 8 bar progression and our first progression using a dominant 7th chord. Work with this page until you can switch chords fluently. Then, try the progression with the rhythm found on the next page.

B-

A Major

B-   **B-**   **A**   **A**

E-

F♯7

E-   **E-**   **F♯7**   **F♯7**

Chord Progression 9

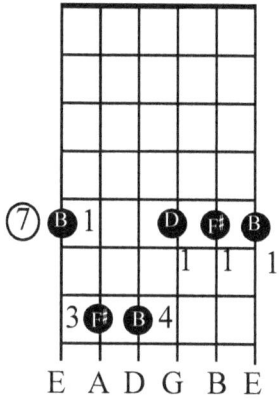

B-

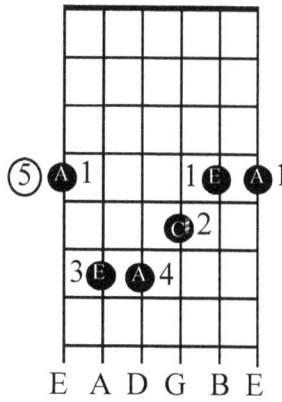

A Major

mm=160

B-   B-   A   A

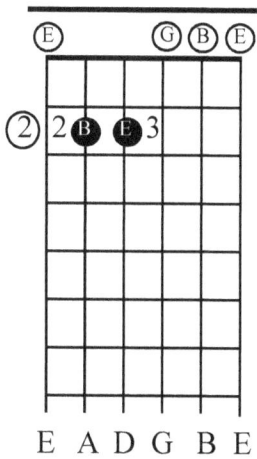

E-

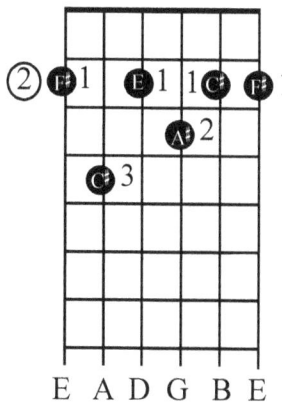

F♯7

E-   E-   F♯7   F♯7

Chord Progression 10
The Blues

G7

C7

G7

G7   **C7**   **G7**   **G7**

C7

G7

C7   **C7**   **G7**   **G7**

D7

C7

G7

D7

D7   **C7**   **G7**   **D7**

Chord Progression 10

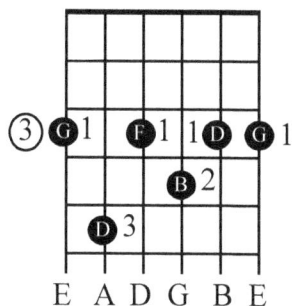

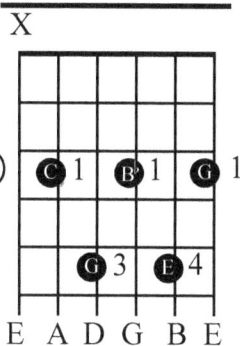

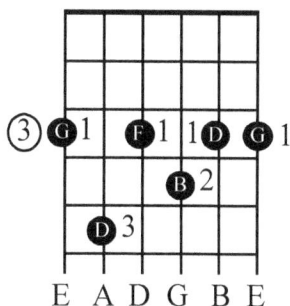

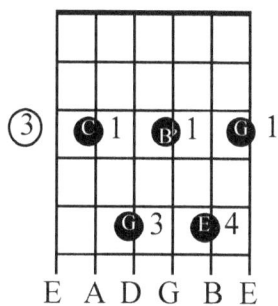

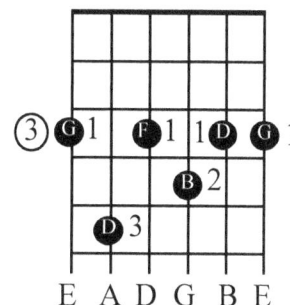

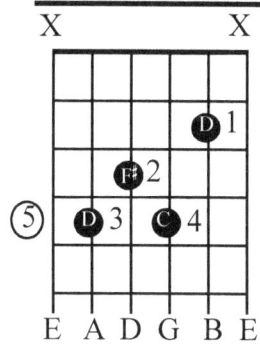

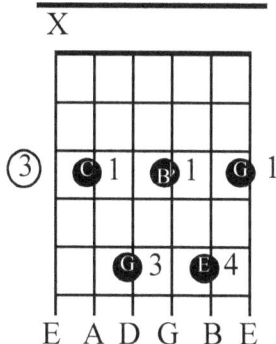

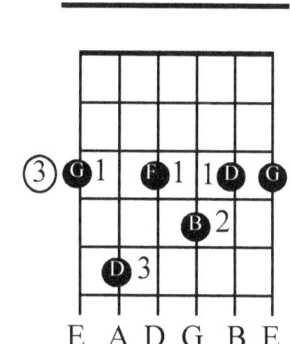

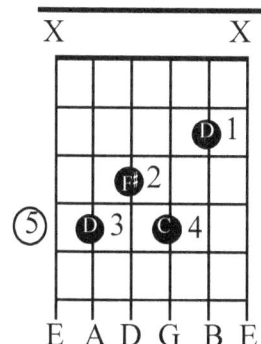

What's Next

This book only covers a few of the chords commonly used in traditional rock and folk, which is in turn only one small part of the larger picture of your development as a musician/guitarist. It is important to continue your exploration into the basics of music and music theory so you can have a better understanding of what you are actually doing with the music you are playing. For the guitar this is particularly true because many students just blindly learn chords and expect that this will be enough for them to build a musical ability on the guitar.

I frequently use the analogy of learning a new language when comparing the short sighted ideas people have about studying the guitar. For instance, if you were learning the English language, would you learn only those words which allow you to order a cup of coffee and say "thank you?" Of course not: you would want to understand the grammar of the language and the meaning of many words, so you could form your own sentences and communicate at least on a rudimentary level with an English speaking person. It is the same for music. You need to educate yourself to get a deeper understanding of the basic elements of music, so that you understand what you are playing. Then, you can use the musical information you have learned to create other combinations. You will then be able to communicate your musical ideas to others effortlessly and *it's all about communicating isn't it?* Learning music on this deeper level is harder, but not as difficult as you might think. By using the right textbooks you can eventually educate yourself to a level where music makes sense both aurally and theoretically.

If this seems like a path you would like to follow, I would recommend purchasing two books to get started. "New York Guitar Method Primer Book Two" and "New York Guitar Method Primer Ensemble Book Two." "Primer Book Two" provides students with an excellent foundation in theory, ear training, chord and scale comprehension on the guitar. It is a prerequisite for entering New York University's Summer Guitar Intensive Program and provides students studying independently with the tools they will need to successfully move on to New York Guitar Method Book One. "Primer Ensemble Book Two" presents a breakthrough approach for teaching guitarists how to sightread. Each chapter has eighth note, sixteenth note, single string, lines, and chord exercises. The book also includes modal jazz vamps and solos and is an excellent resource for lab/ensemble studies as it contains 3 and 4-part reading examples. Both these books give you a foundation that most students of music learn in their freshman year at college. It is now available to you in book form. The methods found in these two books are the techniques used in music colleges throughout the world. By working through these books you too, can properly educate yourself.

Further Thoughts on Practicing and Playing Music

This book may have been your first contact with learning how to make music. It is therefore important to share some thoughts on how to think about the relationship of the creative process with the technical process of learning to play an instrument. I always tell my students there are two sides to playing music; one is <u>creative,</u> and one is <u>technical</u>. For a beginning student it is very easy to lose track of one or the other. Student A will open this book and diligently work through all the exercises, learn the chords and chord progressions but find that their playing feels mechanical. On the other hand Student B will open this book to the first chord progression skipping all the information about technique, music theory, rhythm and learn to play it in a day or two and then just start creating new chord progressions by rearranging the chords, and trying new strumming patterns. Both approaches have their merits and their pitfalls. Student A has learned the necessary technical information, but is not spending enough time just being creative with the information. Student B is all creativity but finds over time that their hand hurts, their ideas stagnate, and they don't understand basic musical concepts. The answer to this dilemma is to work on both sides of the equation. Be creative with the information you learn in this book. Experiment with different combinations of chords, rhythms, strumming patterns. On the other hand learn how to play correctly so you can take full advantage of your talents. Learn your music theory so you understand how music is put together so you notice patterns and possibilities, and develop your rhythmic skills so you can explore many styles of music and interact with other musicians.

Another often overlooked aspect of playing an instrument is your <u>sound</u>. How does each chord that you play sound? Does every note of the chord ring out clearly? Are you picking the strings in order to make the nicest sound? Are you able to switch between chords smoothly so they connect to make a flow in a chord progression? These are questions you should ask yourself. By also spending time developing your own sound you will find you give any music your personal stamp and that people enjoy hearing you because they recognize you in your music.

Learning to <u>practice efficiently</u> is an art in itself. As an overall concept, break up your practicing with rest periods to give your hands and your mind a rest. The length of practice vs. rest will vary depending on the difficulty of the exercise you are working on. In general a 15-30 minute practice followed by a 10-15 minute rest is a good starting place.

Keep a <u>positive frame of mind</u>. It's easy to get discouraged when starting to play the guitar especially for the first time. Many people set up expectations based on their limited knowledge of music or peer pressure. From all my years as an instructor I have found widely ranging development patterns in students. The ones that end up playing the best are the ones who just keep working, asking questions, solving their problems and finding music to be something they just can't live without.

In this 21st century where the buzz words are "easy" and "instantly" remember that music is an art, not a fast food. It's not about finding the easiest and quickest way to play something by leaving out considerations of sound, technique, understanding of purpose (i.e. music theory) and internal connection with your musical self. We all know this instinctively, but it's important to say it and remember it, as you progress.

In closing I would like to tell you how I see music. Music is a complete universe with many wonderful and fascinating aspects. From the theories of why and how notes go together to the intricate world of rhythm, to the understanding of music from an aural perspective, music gives you a field of study that is vast and rewarding on every level. As you start to understand each musical kernel that makes up the whole, you will be rewarded by this extraordinary world. If you approach your studies as a life long quest, you will find that it gives you satisfaction, amazement, and most importantly, joy, as you hear and experience this ever unfolding musical cosmos.

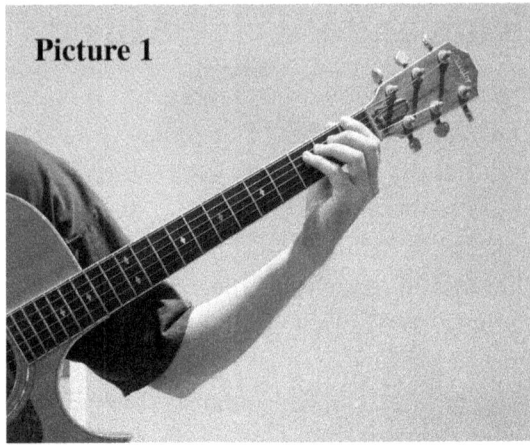

Picture 1

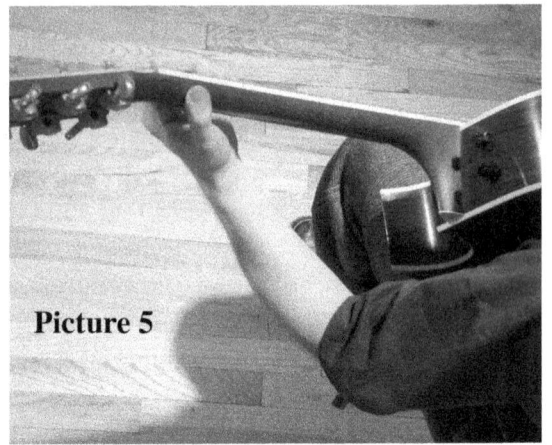

Picture 5

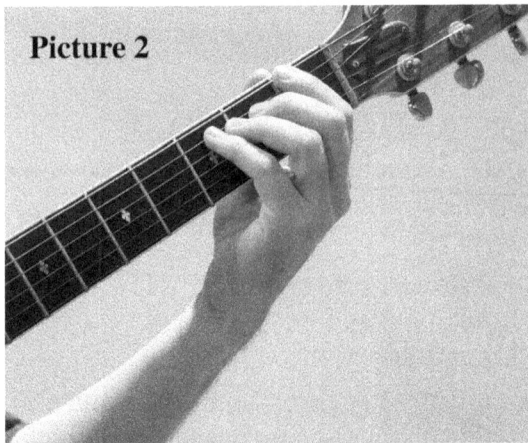

Picture 2

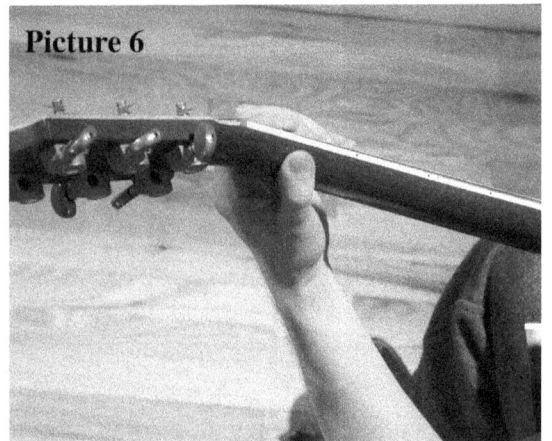

Picture 6

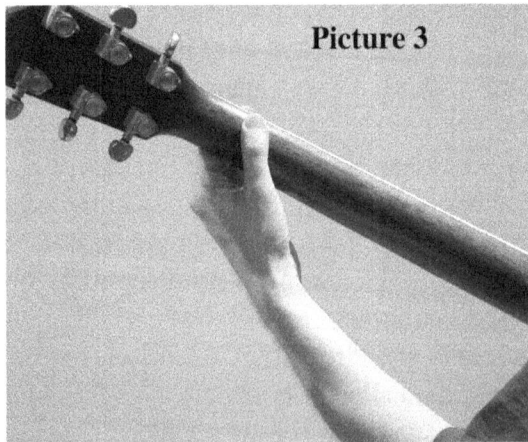

Picture 3

Picture 7

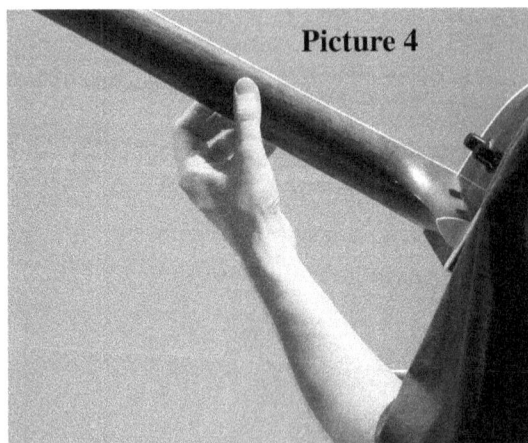

Picture 4

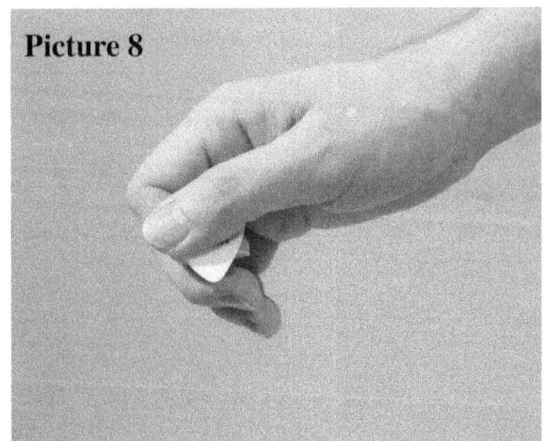

Picture 8

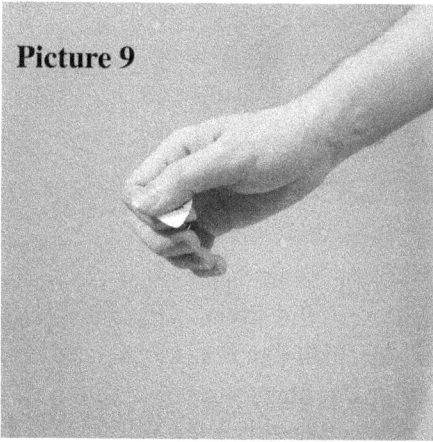

Picture 9

Picture 13

Picture 10

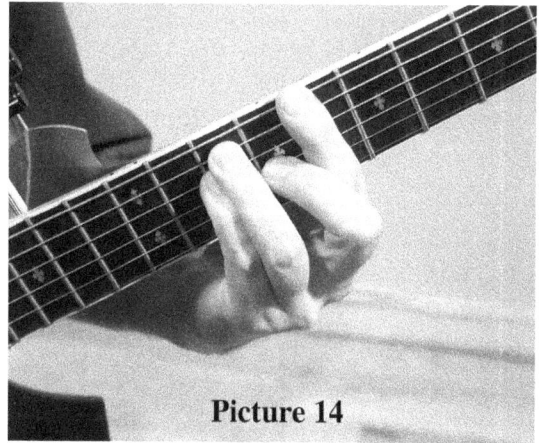

Picture 14

Picture 11

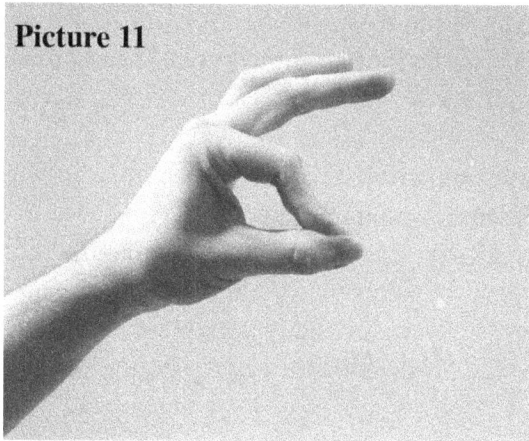

Picture 15

Picture 12

Picture 16

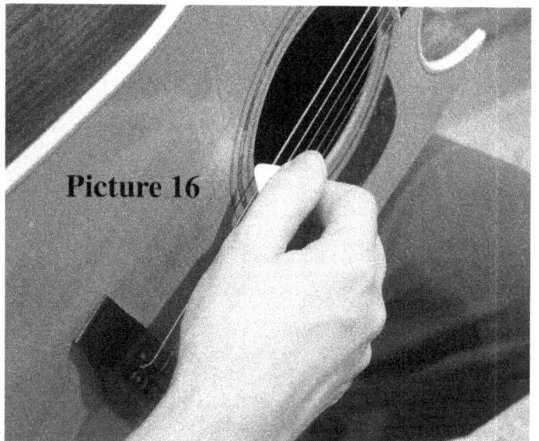

Scales 3 Notes per String

If you are a more advanced student or just a very dedicated student you should start right away to learn the scales on the next few pages. There are 10 scales shown here that represent the seven different modes of a major scale along with the Major and Minor Pentatonic and the Blues Scale. You can learn these scales in any order. Please note that the modes of major have been all listed in the key of C. This is done to help a student quickly learn the scales that they will need to know to improvise with modern chord progressions. All of these scales should be learned in all keys. With all of these scales you should practice them with the following consi- erations:

1.   Each scale should be learned by thinking the notes i.e. C,D,E... or by thinking the degrees C=1,D=2, etc., Do not just memorize a fingering pattern. After you have mastered the scale in every position. You should lear this scale form in all keys. Use Cycle 5 to move through the keys i.e. C then F, Bb, Eb, Ab, Db, Gb, B, E, A, D G. Remember always think the notes or the degrees.

2. When practicing the scales you need to hear these scales in the right "key" relationship. In the Member's Area of the www.muse-eek.com web site there are vamps that you can download in the "Help files for Vamps." Folder. Look at the chord type for each scale found in the upper left hand corner of each page and download th correct vamp. As you practice the scale have these vamps playing in the background. You don't have to play in time with the vamp they are only there to help your ear hear the scale in the right context. See number 3 for how to improvise over the vamps.

3. After practicing the scale thinking note names or degrees you should download a vamps from the muse-eek. com member's area. Again look for the folder "Help files for Vamps." As mentioned you will notice in the upper left hand corner of each page the chords types that each scale can be played over. Download the vamp a: sociated with each scale and use this vamp to improvise with the scale. This vamp can be the same vamp used to practice the scale as mentioned in number 2 or a different vamp. There are many vamps for each chord type
    If you are just starting with improvisation take a look at the "Help files for Improvisation" found in the Member's area to help you get started with improvisation.

Please note that the minor pentatonic is a mode of the major pentatonic. In other words a C Major Pentatonic is the same as an A minor Pentatonic. Although these scales have to same notes it is best to learn each as it's own key center and therefore know the notes not just a fingering pattern.

The Blues scale as mentioned on the scale page is based on key not chord. So you can put a blues scale over any chord progression that is all in one key center. You can use any of the one chord vamps in the Help files fc Vamps with a blues scale. It is recommend that you start with a Dominant chord or a minor chord. You could also use the many blues progressions MP3 found with chord progression 10.

C Major Scale (all 7 positions on guitar)

String	6			5			4			3			2			1		
Fingering	1	2	4	1	2	4	1	2	4	1	3	4	1	3	4	1	2	4
Fret	1	3	5	2	3	5	2	3	5	2	4	5	3	5	6	3	5	7

String	6			5			4			3			2			1		
Fingering	1	2	4	1	2	4	1	2	4	1	2	4	1	2	4	1	3	4
Fret	3	5	7	3	5	7	3	5	7	4	5	7	5	6	8	5	7	8

String	6			5			4			3			2			1		
Fingering	1	3	4	1	3	4	1	2	4	1	2	4	1	2	4	1	2	4
Fret	5	7	8	5	7	8	5	7	9	5	7	9	6	8	10	7	8	10

String	6			5			4			3			2			1		
Fingering	1	2	4	1	2	4	1	3	4	1	3	4	1	2	4	1	2	4
Fret	7	8	10	7	8	10	7	9	10	7	9	10	8	10	12	8	10	12

String	6			5			4			3			2			1		
Fingering	1	2	4	1	2	4	1	2	4	1	2	4	1	3	4	1	3	4
Fret	8	10	12	8	10	12	9	10	12	9	10	12	10	12	13	10	12	13

String	6			5			4			3			2			1		
Fingering	1	3	4	1	2	4	1	2	4	1	2	4	1	2	4	1	2	4
Fret	10	12	13	10	12	14	10	12	14	10	12	14	12	13	15	12	13	15

String	6			5			4			3			2			1		
Fingering	1	2	4	1	3	4	1	3	4	1	2	4	1	2	4	1	2	4
Fret	12	13	15	12	14	15	12	14	15	12	14	16	13	15	17	13	15	17

C Dorian Scale (all 7 positions on guitar)

String	6			5			4			3			2			1		
Fingering	1	2	4	1	2	4	1	2	4	1	2	4	1	2	4	1	3	4
Fret	1	3	5	1	3	5	1	3	5	2	3	5	3	4	6	3	5	6

String	6			5			4			3			2			1		
Fingering	1	3	4	1	3	4	1	2	4	1	2	4	1	2	4	1	2	4
Fret	3	5	6	3	5	6	3	5	7	3	5	7	4	6	8	5	6	8

String	6			5			4			3			2			1		
Fingering	1	2	4	1	2	4	1	3	4	1	3	4	1	2	4	1	2	4
Fret	5	6	8	5	6	8	5	7	8	5	7	8	6	8	10	6	8	10

String	6			5			4			3			2			1		
Fingering	1	2	4	1	2	4	1	2	4	1	2	4	1	3	4	1	3	4
Fret	6	8	10	6	8	10	7	8	10	7	8	10	8	10	11	8	10	11

String	6			5			4			3			2			1		
Fingering	1	3	4	1	2	4	1	2	4	1	2	4	1	2	4	1	2	4
Fret	8	10	11	8	10	12	8	10	12	8	10	12	10	11	13	10	11	13

String	6			5			4			3			2			1		
Fingering	1	2	4	1	3	4	1	3	4	1	2	4	1	2	4	1	2	4
Fret	10	11	13	10	12	13	10	12	13	10	12	14	11	13	15	11	13	15

String	6			5			4			3			2			1		
Fingering	1	2	4	1	2	4	1	2	4	1	3	4	1	3	4	1	2	4
Fret	11	13	15	12	13	15	13	15	12	14	15	13	15	16	13	15	17

C Phrygian Scale (all 7 positions on guitar)

String	6			5			4			3			2			1		
Fingering	1	3	4	1	3	4	1	2	4	1	2	4	1	2	4	1	2	4
Fret	1	3	4	1	3	4	1	3	5	1	3	5	2	4	6	3	4	6

String	6			5			4			3			2			1		
Fingering	1	2	4	1	2	4	1	3	4	1	3	4	1	2	4	1	2	4
Fret	3	4	6	3	4	6	3	5	6	3	5	6	4	6	8	4	6	8

String	6			5			4			3			2			1		
Fingering	1	2	4	1	2	4	1	2	4	1	2	4	1	3	4	1	3	4
Fret	4	6	8	4	6	8	5	6	8	5	6	8	6	8	9	6	8	9

String	6			5			4			3			2			1		
Fingering	1	3	4	1	2	4	1	2	4	1	2	4	1	2	4	1	2	4
Fret	6	8	9	6	8	10	6	8	10	6	8	10	8	9	11	8	9	11

String	6			5			4			3			2			1		
Fingering	1	2	4	1	3	4	1	3	4	1	2	4	1	2	4	1	2	4
Fret	8	9	11	8	10	11	8	10	11	8	10	12	9	11	13	9	11	13

String	6			5			4			3			2			1		
Fingering	1	2	4	1	2	4	1	2	4	1	3	4	1	3	4	1	2	4
Fret	9	11	13	10	11	13	10	11	13	10	12	13	11	13	14	11	13	15

String	6			5			4			3			2			1		
Fingering	1	2	4	1	2	4	1	2	4	1	2	4	1	2	4	1	3	4
Fret	11	13	15	11	13	15	11	13	15	12	13	15	13	14	16	13	15	16

*Use Lydian over a
CΔ7 or CΔ7#11 chord

C Lydian Scale (all 7 positions on guitar)

C Mixolydian Scale (all 7 positions on guitar)

String	6			5			4			3			2			1		
Fingering	1	2	4	1	2	4	1	2	4	1	2	4	1	3	4	1	3	4
Fret	1	3	5	1	3	5	2	3	5	2	3	5	3	5	6	3	5	6

String	6			5			4			3			2			1		
Fingering	1	3	4	1	2	4	1	2	4	1	2	4	1	2	4	1	2	4
Fret	3	5	6	3	5	7	3	5	7	3	5	7	5	6	8	5	6	8

String	6			5			4			3			2			1		
Fingering	1	2	4	1	3	4	1	3	4	1	2	4	1	2	4	1	2	4
Fret	5	6	8	5	7	8	5	7	8	5	7	9	6	8	10	6	8	10

String	6			5			4			3			2			1		
Fingering	1	2	4	1	2	4	1	2	4	1	3	4	1	3	4	1	2	4
Fret	6	8	10	7	8	10	7	8	10	7	9	10	8	10	11	8	10	12

String	6			5			4			3			2			1		
Fingering	1	2	4	1	2	4	1	2	4	1	2	4	1	2	4	1	3	4
Fret	8	10	12	8	10	12	8	10	12	9	10	12	10	11	13	10	12	13

String	6			5			4			3			2			1		
Fingering	1	3	4	1	3	4	1	2	4	1	2	4	1	2	4	1	2	4
Fret	10	12	13	10	12	13	10	12	14	10	12	14	11	13	15	12	13	15

String	6			5			4			3			2			1		
Fingering	1	2	4	1	2	4	1	3	4	1	3	4	1	2	4	1	2	4
Fret	12	13	15	12	13	15	12	14	15	12	14	15	13	15	17	13	15	17

C Aeolian Scale (all 7 positions on guitar)

String	6			5			4			3			2			1		
Fingering	1	3	4	1	2	4	1	2	4	1	2	4	1	2	4	1	2	4
Fret	1	3	4	1	3	5	1	3	5	1	3	5	3	4	6	3	4	6

String	6			5			4			3			2					
Fingering	1	2	4	1	3	4	1	3	4	1	2	4	1	2	4	1	2	4
Fret	3	4	6	3	5	6	3	5	6	3	5	7	4	6	8	4	6	8

String	6			5			4			3			2					
Fingering	1	2	4	1	2	4	1	2	4	1	3	4	1	3	4	1	2	4
Fret	4	6	8	5	6	8	5	6	8	5	7	8	6	8	9	6	8	10

String	6			5			4			3			2					
Fingering	1	2	4	1	2	4	1	2	4	1	2	4	1	2	4	1	3	4
Fret	6	8	10	6	8	10	6	8	10	7	8	10	8	9	11	8	10	11

String	6			5			4			3						1		
Fingering	1	3	4	1	3	4	1	2	4	1	2	4	1	2	4	1	2	4
Fret	8	10	11	8	10	11	8	10	12	8	10	12	9	11	13	10	11	13

String	6			5			4			3								
Fingering	1	2	4	1	2	4	1	3	4	1	3	4	1	2	4	1	2	4
Fret	10	11	13	10	11	13	10	12	13	10	12	13	11	13	15	11	13	15

String	6			5			4			3						1		
Fingering	1	2	4	1	2	4	1	2	4	1	2	4	1	3	4	1	3	4
Fret	11	13	15	11	13	15	12	13	15	12	13	15	13	15	16	13	15	16

182

*Use Locrian over a C-7b5 chord

C Locrian Scale (all 7 positions on guitar)

Fingering	1	2	4	1	3	4	1	3	4	1	2	4	1	2	4	1	2	4
Fret	1	2	4	1	3	4	1	3	4	1	3	5	2	4	6	2	4	6

Fingering	1	2	4	1	2	4	1	2	4	1	3	4	1	3	4	1	2	4
Fret	2	4	6	3	4	6	3	4	6	3	5	6	4	6	7	4	6	8

Fingering	1	2	4	1	2	4	1	2	4	1	2	4	1	2	4	1	3	4
Fret	4	6	8	4	6	8	4	6	8	5	6	8	6	7	9	6	8	9

Fingering	1	3	4	1	3	4	1	2	4	1	2	4	1	2	4	1	2	4
Fret	6	8	9	6	8	9	6	8	10	6	8	10	7	9	11	8	9	11

Fingering	1	2	4	1	2	4	1	3	4	1	3	4	1	2	4	1	2	4
Fret	8	9	11	8	9	11	8	10	11	8	10	11	9	11	13	9	11	13

Fingering	1	2	4	1	2	4	1	2	4	1	2	4	1	3	4	1	3	4
Fret	9	11	13	9	11	13	10	11	13	10	11	13	11	13	14	11	13	14

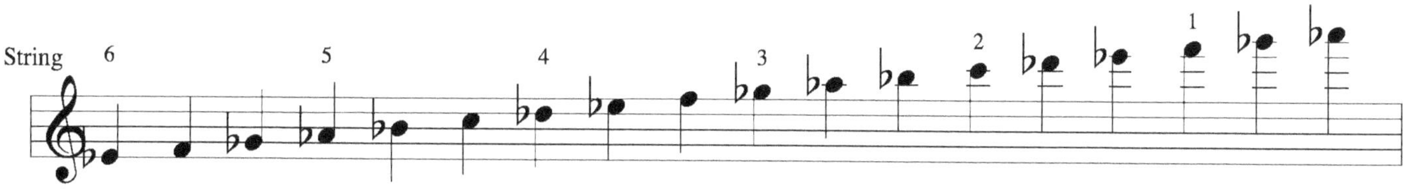

Fingering	1	3	4	1	2	4	1	2	4	1	2	4	1	2	4	1	2	4
Fret	11	13	14	11	13	15	11	13	15	11	13	15	13	14	16	13	14	16

C (Major) Pentatonic Scale
5 positions on guitar

String	6		5		4		3		2		1	
Fingering	1	3	1	3	1	4	1	4	1	3	1	3
Fret	3	5	3	5	2	5	2	5	3	5	3	5

String	6		5		4		3		2		1	
Fingering	1	4	1	3	1	3	1	3	1	4	1	4
Fret	5	8	5	7	5	7	5	7	5	8	5	8

String	6		5		4		3		2		1	
Fingering	1	3	1	4	1	4	1	3	1	3	1	3
Fret	8	10	7	10	7	10	7	9	8	10	8	10

String	6		5		4		3		2		1	
Fingering	1	3	1	3	1	3	1	4	1	4	1	3
Fret	10	12	10	12	10	12	9	12	10	13	10	12

String	6		5		4		3		2		1	
Fingering	1	4	1	4	1	3	1	3	1	3	1	4
Fret	12	15	12	15	12	14	12	14	13	15	12	15

Use Minor Pentatonic over a
C minor, C7 or C7sus4

A Blues Scale is based by key not by chord. Therefore figure out the key center for the chord progression and then use the appropriate blues scale.

C Blues Scale
(1, b3, 4, #4, 5, b7)

String	6		5		4			3		2				1	
Fingering	1	4	1	4	1	2	3	1	3	1	1	2	3	1	3
Fret	3	6	3	6	3	4	5	3	5	4	6	7	8	6	8

String	6		5				4	3				2		1			
Fingering	1	3	1	1	2	3	1	3	1	1	2	3	1	3	1	1	2	3
Fret	6	8	6	8	9	10	8	10	8	10	11	12	11	13	11	13	14	15

String	6		5			4		3				2		1			
Fingering	1	4	1	2	3	1	3	1	1	2	3	1	3	1	1	2	3
Fret	8	11	8	9	10	8	10	8	10	11	12	11	13	11	13	14	15

String	6			5	4				3		2					1	
Fingering	1	1	2	3	1	3	1	1	2	3	1	3	1	1	2	3	1	3
Fret	11	13	14	15	13	15	13	15	16	17	15	17	16	18	19	20	18	20

186

Books Available From
Muse Eek Publishing Company

The Bruce Arnold series of instruction books for guitar are the result of 30 years of teaching. Mr. Arnold, who teaches at New York University and Princeton University has listened to the questions and problems of his students, and written fifty books addressing the needs of the beginning to advanced student. Written in a direct, friendly and practical manner, each book is structured in such a way as to enable a student to understand, retain and apply musical information. In short, these books teach.

1st Steps for a Beginning Guitarist
Spiral Bound ISBN 1890944-90-4 Perfect Bound ISBN 1890944-93-9

1st Steps for a Beginning Guitarist is a comprehensive method for guitar students who have no prior musical training. Whether you are playing acoustic, electric or twelve-string guitar, this book will give you the information you need, and trouble shoot the various pitfalls that can hinder the self-taught musician. Includes pictures, videos and audio in the form of midifiles and mp3's.

Chord Workbook for Guitar Volume 1 (2nd edition)
Spiral Bound ISBN 0-9648632-1-9 Perfect Bound ISBN 1890944-50-5

A consistent seller, this book addresses the needs of the beginning through intermediate student. The beginning student will learn chords on the guitar, and a section is also included to help learn the basics of music theory. Progressions are provided to help the student apply these chords to common sequences. The more advanced student will find the reharmonization section to be an invaluable resource of harmonic choices. Information is given through musical notation as well as tablature.

Chord Workbook for Guitar Volume 2 (2nd edition)
Spiral Bound ISBN 0-9648632-3-5 Perfect Bound ISBN 1890944-51-3

This book is the Rosetta Stone of pop/jazz chords, and is geared to the intermediate to advanced student. These are the chords that any serious student bent on a musical career must know. Unlike other books which simply give examples of isolated chords, this unique book provides a comprehensive series of progressions and chord combinations which are immediately applicable to both composition and performance.

Music Theory Workbook for Guitar Series

The worlds most popular instrument, the guitar, is not taught in our public schools. In addition, it is one of the hardest on which to learn the basics of music. As a result, it is frequently difficult for the serious guitarist to get a firm foundation in theory.

Theory Workbook for Guitar Volume 1
Spiral Bound ISBN 0-9648632-4-3   Perfect Bound ISBN 1890944-52-1

This book provides real hands-on application of intervals and chords. A theory section written in concise and easy to understand language prepares the student for all exercises. Worksheets are given that quiz a student about intervals and chord construction using staff notation and guitar tablature. Answers are supplied in the back of the book enabling a student to work without a teacher.

Theory Workbook for Guitar Volume 2
Spiral Bound ISBN 0-9648632-5-1   Perfect Bound ISBN 1890944-53-X

This book provides real hands-on application for 22 different scale types. A theory section written in concise and easy to understand language prepares the student for all exercises. Worksheets are given that quiz a student about scale construction using staff notation and guitar tablature. Answers are supplied in the back of the book enabling a student to work without a teacher. Audio files are also available on the muse-eek.com website to facilitate practice and improvisation with all the scales presented.

Rhythm Book Series

These books are a breakthrough in music instruction, using the internet as a teaching tool! Audio files of all the exercises are easily downloaded from the internet.

Rhythm Primer
Spiral Bound ISBN 0-890944-03-3   Perfect Bound ISBN 1890944-59-9

This 61 page book concentrates on all basic rhythms using four rhythmic levels. All examples use one pitch, allowing the student to focus completely on time and rhythm. All exercises can be downloaded from the internet to facilitate learning. See http://www.muse-eek.com for details

Rhythms Volume 1
Spiral Bound ISBN 0-9648632-7-8   Perfect Bound ISBN 1890944-55-6

This 120 page book concentrates on eighth note rhythms and is a thesaurus of rhythmic patterns. All examples use one pitch, allowing the student to focus completely on time and rhythm. All exercises can be downloaded from the internet to facilitate learning. See http://www.muse-eek.com for details.

Rhythms Volume 2
Spiral Bound ISBN 0-9648632-8-6   Perfect Bound ISBN 1890944-56-4

This volume concentrates on sixteenth note rhythms, and is a 108 page thesaurus of rhythmic patterns. All examples use one pitch, allowing the student to focus completely on time and rhythm. All exercises can be downloaded from the internet to facilitate learning. See http://www.muse-eek.com for details.

Rhythms Volume 3
Spiral Bound ISBN 0-890944-04-1   Perfect Bound ISBN 1890944-57-2

This volume concentrates on thirty second note rhythms, and is a 102 page thesaurus of rhythmic patterns. All examples use one pitch, allowing the student to focus completely on time and rhythm. All exercises can be downloaded from the internet to facilitate learning. See http://www.muse-eek.com for details.

Odd Meters Volume 1
Spiral Bound ISBN 0-9648632-9-4   Perfect Bound ISBN 1890944-58-0

This book applies both eighth and sixteenth note rhythms to odd meter combinations. All examples use one pitch, allowing the student to focus completely on time and rhythm. Exercises can be downloaded from the internet to facilitate learning. This 100 page book is an essential sight reading tool. See http://www.muse-eek.com for details.

Contemporary Rhythms Volume 1
Spiral Bound ISBN 1-890944-27-0   Perfect Bound ISBN 1890944-84-X

This volume concentrates on eight note rhythms and is a thesaurus of rhythmic patterns. Each exercise uses one pitch which allows the student to focus completely on time and rhythm. Exercises use modern innovations common to twentieth century notation, thereby familiarizing the student with the most sophisticated systems likely to be encountered in the course of a musical career. All exercises can be downloaded from the internet to facilitate learning. See http://www.muse-eek.com for details.

Contemporary Rhythms Volume 2
Spiral Bound ISBN 1-890944-28-9   Perfect Bound ISBN 1890944-85-8

This volume concentrates on sixteenth note rhythms and is a thesaurus of rhythmic patterns. Each exercise uses one pitch which allows the student to focus completely on time and rhythm. Exercise use modern innovations common to twentieth century notation, thereby familiarizing the student with the most sophisticated systems likely to be encountered in the course of a musical career. All exercises can be downloaded from the internet to facilitate learning. See http://www.muse-eek.com for details.

Independence Volume 1
Spiral Bound ISBN 1-890944-00-9   Perfect Bound ISBN 1890944-83-1

This 51 page book is designed for pianists, stick and touchstyle guitarists, percussionists and anyone who wishes to develop the rhythmic independence of their hands. This volume concentrates on quarter, eighth and sixteenth note rhythms and is a thesaurus of rhythmic patterns. The exercises in this book gradually incorporate more and more complex rhythmic patterns making it an excellent tool for both the beginning and the advanced student.

Other Guitar Study Aids

Right Hand Technique for Guitar Volume 1
Spiral Bound ISBN 0-9648632-6-X   Perfect Bound ISBN 1890944-54-8

Heres a breakthrough in music instruction, using the internet as a teaching tool! This book gives a concise method for developing right hand technique on the guitar, one of the most overlooked and under-addressed aspects of learning the instrument. The simplest, most basic movements are used to build fatigue-free technique. Exercises can be downloaded from the internet to facilitate learning. See http://www.muse-eek.com for details.

Single String Studies Volume One
Spiral Bound ISBN 1-890944-01-7   Perfect Bound ISBN 1890944-62-9

This book is an excellent learning tool for both the beginner who has no experience reading music on the guitar, and the advanced student looking to improve their ledger line reading and general knowledge of each string of the guitar. Each exercise concentrates the students attention on one string at a time. This allows a familiarity to form between the written pitch and where it can be found on the guitar along with improving ones feel for jumping linearly across the fretboard. Exercises can be downloaded from the internet to facilitate learning. See http://www.muse-eek.com for details.

Single String Studies Volume Two
Spiral Bound ISBN 1-890944-05-X   Perfect Bound ISBN 1890944-64-5

This book is a continuation of Volume One, but using non-diatonic notes. Volume Two helps the intermediate and advanced student improve their ledger line reading and general knowledge of each string of the guitar. Each exercise concentrates the students attention on one string at a time. This allows a familiarity to form between the written pitch and where it can be found on the guitar along with improving ones feel for jumping linearly across the fretboard. Exercises can be downloaded from the internet to facilitate learning. See http://www.muse-eek.com for details.

Single String Studies Volume One (Bass Clef)
Spiral Bound ISBN 1-890944-02-5   Perfect Bound ISBN 1890944-63-7

This book is an excellent learning tool for both the beginner who has no experience reading music on the bass guitar, and the advanced student looking to improve their ledger line reading and general knowledge of each string of the bass. Each exercise concentrates a students attention of one string at a time. This allows a familiarity to form between the written pitch and where it can be found on the bass along with improving ones feel for jumping linearly across the fretboard. Exercises can be downloaded from the internet to facilitate learning. See http://www.muse-eek.com for details.

Single String Studies Volume Two (Bass Clef)
Spiral Bound ISBN 1-890944-06-8   Perfect Bound ISBN 1890944-65-3

This book is a continuation of Volume One, but using non-diatonic notes. Volume Two helps the intermediate and advanced student improve their ledger line reading and general knowledge of each string of the bass. Each exercise concentrates the students attention on one string at a time. This allows a familiarity to form between the written pitch and where it can be found on the bass along with improving ones feel for jumping linearly across the fretboard. Exercises can be downloaded from the internet to facilitate learning. See http://www.muse-eek.com for details.

Guitar Clinic
Spiral Bound ISBN 1-890944-45-9   Perfect Bound ISBN 1890944-86-6

Guitar Clinic contains techniques and exercises Mr. Arnold uses in the clinics and workshops he teaches around the U.S.. Much of the material in this book is culled from Mr. ArnoldÕs educational series, over thirty books in all. The student wishing to expand on his or her studies will find suggestions within the text as to which of Mr. Arnold's books will best serve their specific needs. Topics covered include: how to read music, sight reading, reading rhythms, music theory, chord and scale construction, modal sequencing, approach notes, reharmonization, bass and chord comping, and hexatonic scales.

The Essentials: Chord Charts, Scales, and Lead Patterns for the Guitar
Saddle Stitched (Stapled) ISBN 1-890944-94-7

This book is truly essential to the aspiring guitarist. It includes the most commonly played chords on the guitar in all keys, plus a bonus of the most commonly used scales and lead patterns. You can quickly learn all the chords, scales and lead patterns you need to know to play your favorite songs-and solo over them, too! The Essentials doesn't stop there, though. It also includes chord progressions to help you learn how to chord songs in folk, country, rock, blues and other popular styles. The books contain loads of easy to understand diagrams of chords, scales and lead patterns so you will be up and running in no time!

<h2>Sight Singing and Ear Training Series</h2>

The world is full of ear training and sight reading books, so why do we need more? This sight singing and ear training series uses a different method of teaching relative pitch sight singing and ear training. The success of this method has been remarkable. Along with a new method of ear training these books also use CDs and the internet as a teaching tool! Audio files of all the exercises are easily downloaded from the internet at www. muse-eek.com By combining interactive audio files with a new approach to ear training a studentÕs progress is limited only by their willingness to practice!

A Fanatic's Guide to Ear Training and Sight Singing
Spiral Bound ISBN 1-890944-19-X   Perfect Bound ISBN 1890944-75-0

This book and CD present a method for developing good pitch recognition through sight singing. This method differs from the myriad of other sight singing books in that it develops the ability to identify and name all twelve pitches within a key center. Through this method a student gains the ability to identify sound based on it's relationship to a key and not the relationship of one note to another (i.e. interval training as commonly taught in many texts). All note groupings from one to six notes are presented giving the student a thesaurus of basic note combinations which develops sight singing and note recognition to a level unattainable before this Guide's existence.

Key Note Recognition
Spiral Bound ISBN 1-890944-30-3   Perfect Bound ISBN 1890944-77-7

This book and CD present a method for developing the ability to recognize the function of any note against a key. This method is a must for anyone who wishes to sound one note on an instrument or voice and instantly know what key a song is in. Through this method a student gains the ability to identify a sound based on its relationship to a key and not the relationship of one note to another (i.e. interval training as commonly taught in many texts). Key Center Recognition is a definite requirement before proceeding to two note ear training.

LINES Volume One: Sight Reading and Sight Singing Exercises
Spiral Bound ISBN 1-890944-09-2   Perfect Bound ISBN 1890944-76-9

This book can be used for many applications. It is an excellent source for easy half note melodies that a beginner can use to learn how to read music or for sight singing slightly chromatic lines. An intermediate or advanced student will find exercises for multi-voice reading. These exercises can also be used for multi-voice ear training. The book has the added benefit in that all exercises can be heard by downloading the audio files for each example. See http://www.muse-eek.com for details.

LINES Volume Two: Sight Reading and Sight Singing Exercises
Spiral Bound ISBN 1-594899-88-6   Perfect Bound ISBN 1594899-99-1

Recommended for those who have completed volume one, volume two introduces more complex harmonic material. This book can be used for many applications. It is an excellent source for easy quarter note melodies that a beginner can use to learn how to read music or for sight singing slightly chromatic lines. An intermediate or advanced student will find exercises for multi-voice reading. These exercises can also be used for multi-voice ear training. The book has the added benefit in that all exercises can be heard by downloading the audio files for each example. See http://www.muse-eek.com for details.

Ear Training ONE NOTE: Beginning Level
Spiral Bound ISBN 1-890944-12-2   Perfect Bound ISBN 1890944-66-1

This Book and Audio CD presents a new and exciting method for developing relative pitch ear training. It has been used with great success and is now finally available on CD. There are three levels available depending on the student's ability. This beginning level is recommended for students who have little or no music training.

Ear Training ONE NOTE: Intermediate Level
Spiral Bound ISBN 1-890944-13-0   Perfect Bound ISBN 1890944-67-X

This Audio CD and booklet presents a new and exciting method of developing relative pitch ear training. It has been used with great success and is now finally available on CD. This intermediate level is recommended for students who have had some music training but still find their skills need more development.

Ear Training ONE NOTE: Advanced Level
Spiral Bound ISBN 1-890944-14-9   Perfect Bound ISBN 1890944-68-8

This Audio CD and booklet presents a new and exciting method of developing relative pitch ear training. It has been used with great success and is now finally available on CD. There are three levels available depending on the student's ability. This advanced level is recommended for students who have worked with the intermediate level and now wish to perfect their skills.

Ear Training TWO NOTE: Beginning Level Volume One
Spiral Bound ISBN 1-890944-31-9   Perfect Bound ISBN 1890944-69-6

This Book and Audio CD continues the method of developing relative pitch ear training as set forth in the "Ear Training, One Note" series. There are six volumes in the beginning level series. Through practice, the student eventually gains the ability to recognize the key and the names of any two notes played simultaneously. Volume One concentrates on 5ths. Prerequisite: a strong grasp of the One Note method.

Ear Training TWO NOTE: Beginning Level Volume Two
Spiral Bound ISBN 1-890944-32-7   Perfect Bound ISBN 1890944-70-X

This Book and Audio CD continues the method of developing relative pitch ear training as set forth in the "Ear Training, One Note" series. There are six volumes in the beginning level series. Through practice, the student eventually gains the ability to recognize the key and the names of any two notes played simultaneously. Volume Two concentrates on 3rds. Prerequisite: a strong grasp of the One Note method.

Ear Training TWO NOTE: Beginning Level Volume Three
Spiral Bound ISBN 1-890944-33-5   Perfect Bound ISBN 1890944-71-8

This Book and Audio CD continues the method of developing relative pitch ear training as set forth in the "Ear Training, One Note" series. There are six volumes in the beginning level series. Through practice, the student eventually gains the ability to recognize the key and the names of any two notes played simultaneously. Volume Three concentrates on 6ths. Prerequisite: a strong grasp of the One Note method.

Ear Training TWO NOTE: Beginning Level Volume Four
Spiral Bound ISBN 1-890944-34-3   Perfect Bound ISBN 1890944-72-6

This Book and Audio CD continues the method of developing relative pitch ear training as set forth in the "Ear Training, One Note" series. There are six volumes in the beginning level series. Through practice, the student eventually gains the ability to recognize the key and the names of any two notes played simultaneously. Volume Four concentrates on 4ths. Prerequisite: a strong grasp of the One Note method.

Ear Training TWO NOTE: Beginning Level Volume Five
Spiral Bound ISBN 1-890944-35-1   Perfect Bound ISBN 1890944-73-4

This Book and Audio CD continues the method of developing relative pitch ear training as set forth in the "Ear Training, One Note" series. There are six volumes in the beginning level series. Through practice, the student eventually gains the ability to recognize the key and the names of any two notes played simultaneously. Volume Five concentrates on 2nds. Prerequisite: a strong grasp of the One Note method.

Ear Training TWO NOTE: Beginning Level Volume Six
Spiral Bound ISBN 1-890944-36-X   Perfect Bound ISBN 1890944-74-2

This Book and Audio CD continues the method of developing relative pitch ear training as set forth in the "Ear Training, One Note" series. There are six volumes in the beginning level series. Through practice, the student eventually gains the ability to recognize the key and the names of any two notes played simultaneously. Volume Six concentrates on 7ths. Prerequisite: a strong grasp of the One Note method.

Comping Styles Series

This series is built on the progressions found in Chord Workbook Volume One. Each book covers a specific style of music and presents exercises to help a guitarist, bassist or drummer master that style. Audio CDs are also available so a student can play along with each example and really get "into the groove."

Comping Styles for the Guitar Volume Two FUNK
Spiral Bound ISBN 1-890944-07-6   Perfect Bound ISBN 1890944-60-2

This volume teaches a student how to play guitar or piano in a funk style. 36 Progressions are presented: 12 keys of a Major and Minor Blues plus 12 keys of Rhythm Changes A different groove is presented for each exercise giving the student a wide range of funk rhythms to master. An Audio CD is also included so a student can play along with each example and really get "into the groove." The audio CD contains "trio" versions of each exercise with Guitar, Bass and Drums.

Comping Styles for the Bass Volume Two FUNK
Spiral Bound ISBN 1-890944-08-4   Perfect Bound ISBN 1890944-61-0

This volume teaches a student how to play bass in a funk style. 36 Progressions are presented: 12 keys of a Major and Minor Blues plus 12 keys of Rhythm Changes A different groove is presented for each exercise giving the student a wide range of funk rhythms to master. An Audio CD is also included so a student can play along with each example and really get "into the groove." The audio CD contains "trio" versions of each exercise with Guitar, Bass and Drums.

Jazz and Blues Bass Line
Spiral Bound ISBN 1-890944-15-7   Perfect Bound ISBN 1890944-16-5

This book covers the basics of bass line construction. A theoretical guide to building bass lines is presented along with 36 chord progressions utilizing the twelve keys of a Major and Minor Blues, plus twelve keys of Rhythm Changes. A reharmonization section is also provided which demonstrates how to reharmonize a chord progression on the spot.

Time Series

The Doing Time series presents a method for contacting, developing and relying on your internal time sense: This series is an excellent resource for any musician who is serious about developing strong internal sense of time. This is particularly useful in any kind of music where the rhythms and time signatures may be very complex or free, and there is no conductor.

THE BIG METRONOME
Spiral Bound ISBN 1-890944-37-8   Perfect Bound ISBN 1890944-82-3

The Big Metronome is designed to help you develop a better internal sense of time. This is accomplished by requiring you to "feel time" rather than having you rely on the steady click of a metronome. The idea is to slowly wean yourself away from an external device and rely on your internal/natural sense of time. The exercises presented work in conjunction with the three CDs that accompany this book. CD 1 presents the first 13 settings from a traditional metronome 40-66; the second CD contains metronome markings 69-116, and the third CD contains metronome markings 120-208. The first CD gives you a 2 bar count off and a click every measure, the second CD gives you a 2 bar count off and a click every 2 measures, the 3rd CD gives you a 2 bar count off and a click every 4 measures. By presenting all common metronome markings a student can use these 3 CDs as a replacement for a traditional metronome.

Doing Time with the Blues Volume One
Spiral Bound ISBN 1-890944-17-3   Perfect Bound ISBN 1890944-78-5

The book and CD presents a method for gaining an internal sense of time thereby eliminating dependence on a metronome. The book presents the basic concept for developing good time and also includes exercises that can be practiced with the CD. The CD provides eight 8 minute tracks at different tempos in which the time is delineated every 2 bars, and with an extra hit every 12 bars to outline the blues form. The student may then use the exercises presented in the book to gain control of their execution or improvise to gain control of their ideas using this bare minimum of time delineation.

Doing Time with the Blues Volume Two
Spiral Bound ISBN 1-890944-18-1   Perfect Bound ISBN 1890944-79-3

This is the 2nd volume of a four volume series which presents a method for developing a musicians internal sense of time, thereby eliminating dependence on a metronome. This 2nd volume presents different exercises which further the development of this time sense. This 2nd volume begins to test even a professional level players ability. The CD provides eight 8 minute tracks at different tempos in which the time is delineated every 4 bars with an extra hit every 12 bars to outline the blues form. New exercises are also included that can be practiced with the CD. This series is an excellent resource for any musician who is serious about developing an internal sense of time.

Doing Time with 32 Bars Volume One
Spiral Bound ISBN 1-890944-22-X   Perfect Bound ISBN Spiral Bound ISBN 1890944-80-7

The book and CD presents a method for gaining an internal sense of time thereby eliminating dependence on a metronome. The book presents the basic concept for developing good time and also includes exercises that can be practiced with the CD. The CD provides eight 8 minute tracks at different tempos in which the time is delineated every 2 bars, with an extra hit every 32 to outline the 32 bar form. The student may then use the exercises presented in the book to gain control of their execution or improvise to gain control of their ideas using this bare minimum of time delineation.

Doing Time with 32 Bars Volume Two
Spiral Bound ISBN 1-890944-23-8   Perfect Bound ISBN Spiral Bound ISBN 1890944-81-5

This is the 2nd volume of a four volume series which presents a method for developing a musicians internal sense of time, thereby eliminating dependence on a metronome.. This 2nd volume presents different exercises which further the development of this time sense. This 2nd volume begins to test even a professional level players ability. The CD provides eight 8 minute tracks at different tempos in which the time is delineated every 4 bars with an extra hit every 32 bars to outline the 32 bar form. New exercises are also included that can be practiced with the CD. This series is an excellent resource for any musician who is serious about developing an internal sense of time.

Other Workbooks

Music Theory Workbook for All Instruments, Volume 1: Interval and Chord Construction
Spiral Bound ISBN 1594899-51-7   Perfect Bound ISBN 1890944-46-7

This book provides real hands-on application of intervals and chords. A theory section written in concise and easy to understand language prepares the student for all exercises. Worksheets are given that quiz a student about intervals and chord construction using staff notation. Answers are supplied in the back of the book enabling a student to work without a teacher.

Jazz Piano Vocabulary by Roberta Piket, Volume 1: The Major Scale
Spiral Bound ISBN 1594899-51-7   Perfect Bound ISBN 1594899-51-7

This is the 1st volume in a series designed to help the student of jazz piano learn and apply jazz scales by mastering each scale and its uses in improvisation. Each book focuses on a different scale, illustrating the scale in all twelve keys with complete fingerings. Also provided are chords and left hand voicings to match, exercises and études to apply the material to improvising, ideas for further study and listening, and detailed suggestions on how to prace the material. Volume 1 also includes a detailed primer in note reading, basic theory, and rhythmic notation.

Jazz Piano Vocabulary by Roberta Piket, Volume 2: The Dorian Mode
Spiral Bound ISBN 1890944-96-3   Perfect Bound ISBN 1890944-98-X

The 2nd volume in the series, this book focuses on the Dorian scale and applies it to improvising on minor seventh chords. The Dorian scale is presented in all twelve keys with complete fingerings. The book also contains left hand voicings, exercises, many examples, an étude to help apply the material, ideas for further study, an extended discography, and detailed instruction and practice tips.

Jazz Piano Vocabulary by Roberta Piket, Volume 3: The Phrygian Mode
Spiral Bound ISBN 1594899-53-3 Perfect Bound ISBN 1594899-54-1

For students who have covered the basics in Volume 1,2 and 5, this book focuses in the Phrygian and Spanish Phrygian scales. It discusses "modern" jazz chords such as the "Phrygian" chord (susb9). The scale is presented in all 12 keys with fingerings. It also provides a detailed treatise on a modal approach to chord voicings, practice tips and a Phrygian étude.

Jazz Piano Vocabulary by Roberta Piket, Volume 4: The Lydian Mode
Spiral Bound ISBN 1594899-55-X Perfect Bound ISBN 1594899-56-8

Volume 4 features the Lydian scale in all twelve keys; two octaves up and down with complete piano fingerings. Chords are presented with left hand voicings that work with the scale (along with fingerings) Also included are exercises to develop the concept of melodic phrasing in improvisation, examples of the use of the Lydian scale in the jazz repertoire, and detailed instructions on how to practice the material. Added feature: author can be contacted online if questions arise.

Jazz Piano Vocabulary by Roberta Piket, Volume 5: The Mixolydian Mode
Spiral Bound ISBN 1594899-57-6 Perfect Bound ISBN 1594899-58-4

This book focuses on the Mixolydian scale and applies it to improvising on dominant seventh and dominant seventh sus chords. The scale is presented in all twelve keys with fingerings. The book also contains an introduction to approach notes, an explanation and étude on twelve bar blues form, left hand voicings, exercises, melodic examples, instruction and practice tips.

New York Guitar Method Volume 1
Spiral Bound ISBN 159489-987-8 Perfect Bound ISBN 159489-900-2

This series of books distills several of our previous publications into a method currently in use at New York University for the Summer Guitar Intensive Program. Content is geared towards both the straight ahead player seeking to understand previous styles of playing, or the avant-garde enthusiast looking to expand into uncharted territory. Material concentrates on essential information the student must master in order to become a professional guitarist in the heavily competitive New York City music scene. While the book is set up as a 3 week intensive course of study for NYU, it can also be used as the basis for a regular 15 week semester program, should others wish to use it in that manner. Additional features facilitate its use by teachers as well as students studying on their own. This resource consists of a DVD, two Ear Training CDs, and a Chord Vamps CD, all included in each book.

New York Guitar Method Volume 2
Spiral Bound ISBN 159489-901-0 Perfect Bound ISBN 159489-902-9

This is the second book in our series currently in use at New York University for the Summer Guitar Intensive Program. A continuation of Volume 1, Volume 2 focuses on approach notes and discusses how to apply approaches to jazz lines in order to create the signature sounding lines of bebop through the contemporary sounding lines of the modern masters.

New York Guitar Method Ensemble Book 1
Spiral Bound ISBN 159489-905-3   Perfect Bound ISBN 159489-906-1

This series of books combines many of our previous publications into a method currently in use at New York University for their Summer Guitar Intensive Program. Our Ensemble Method presents a break-through approach for teaching guitarists how to sightread. Each chapter has eighth note, sixteenth note, single string, lines, and chord exercises. The book also includes jazz and classical reading études and is an excellent resource for lab/ensemble studies as it contains 3 and 4-part reading examples.

New York Guitar Method Ensemble Book 2
Spiral Bound ISBN 159489-907-X   Perfect Bound ISBN 159489-908-8

A contuation of Volume One, Volume Two focuses on reading jazz solos that demonstrate the many uses of approach notes as discussed in the accompanying New York Guitar Method Volume 2. The book also includes jazz and classical reading études and is an excellent resource for lab/ensemble studies as it contains 3 and 4-part reading examples.

New York Guitar Method Primer Book 1
Spiral Bound ISBN 159489-911-8   Perfect Bound ISBN 159489-912-6

This book provides students with an excellent foundation in theory, ear training, chord and scale comprehension on the guitar. It is a prerequisite for entering New York University's Summer Guitar Intensive Program and provides students studying independently with the tools they will need to successfully move on to Primer Book 2.

New York Guitar Method Primer Book 2
Spiral Bound ISBN 159489-915-0   Perfect Bound ISBN 159489-916-9

This book provides students with an excellent foundation in theory, ear training, chord and scale comprehension on the guitar. It is a prerequisite for entering New York University's Summer Guitar Intensive Program and provides students studying independently with the tools they will need to successfully move on to New York Guitar Method Book 1.

New York Guitar Method Primer Ensemble Book 2
Spiral Bound ISBN 159489-913-4   Perfect Bound ISBN 159489-914-2

This book is a prerequisite for entering New York University's Summer Guitar Intensive Program and provides students studying independently with the tools they will need to successfully move on to Volume 1. Our Ensemble Method presents a breakthrough approach for teaching guitarist how to sightread. Each chapter has eighth note, sixteenth note, single string, lines, and chord exercises. The book also includes modal jazz vamps and solos and is an excellent resource for lab/ensemble studies as it contains 3 and 4-part reading examples.

Set Theory for Improvisation
Spiral Bound ISBN 159489-926-6   Perfect Bound ISBN 159489-927-4

"Set Theory for Improvisation" examines the use and organization of pitch class sets for improvisation and composition. Two through twelve note pitch class sets are explored and their application to the harmony and melody shown through multiple examples. The companion series "Set Theory for Improvisation Ensemble" is recommended as both a overall musical development tool and as a sight reading gold mine. For all instruments.

Set Theory for Improvisation Ensemble Method

This series of books explores the relationships of post tonal theory to contemporary improvisation. The ensemble method gives examples of applying post tonal theory to contemporary improvisation in the form of études. Each étude explores the melodic possibilities using various combinations of note groupings, rhythms, metric level, melodic range and density. There are 12 études in each book, one in each key which can be played over a variety of chords. These études range from highly diatonic to non-diatonic examples depending on the organization of the material. For all instruments.

Set Theory for Improvisation Ensemble Method: Hexatonic 027 027
Spiral Bound ISBN 159489-920-7   Perfect Bound ISBN 159489-921-5

Set Theory for Improvisation Ensemble Method: Hexatonic 027 016
Spiral Bound ISBN 159489-922-3   Perfect Bound ISBN 159489-923-1

Set Theory for Improvisation Ensemble Method: Hexatonic 027 026
Spiral Bound ISBN 159489-924-X   Perfect Bound ISBN 159489-925-8

E-Books

The Bruce Arnold series of instructional E-books is for the student who wishes to target specific areas of study that are of particular interest. Many of these books are excerpted from other larger texts. The excerpted source is listed for each book. These books are available on-line at www.muse-eek.com as well as at many e-tailers throughout the internet. These books can also be purchased in the traditional book binding format. (See the ISBN number for proper format)

Chord Velocity: Volume One, Learning to switch between chords quickly
E-book ISBN 1-890944-88-2   Traditional Book Binding ISBN 1-890944-97-1

The first hurdle a beginning guitarist encounters is difficulty in switching between chords quickly enough to make a chord progression sound like music. This book provides exercises that help a student gradually increase the speed with which they change chords. Special free audio files are also available on the muse-eek.com website to make practice more productive and fun. Within a few weeks, remarkable improvement can be achieved using this method. This book is excerpted from "1st Steps for a Beginning Guitarist Volume One."

Guitar Technique: Volume One, Learning the basics to fast, clean, accurate and fluid performance skills.
E-book ISBN 1-890944-91-2   Traditional Book Binding ISBN 1-890944-99-8

This book is for both the beginning guitarist or the more experienced guitarist who wishes to improve their technique. All aspects of the physical act of playing the guitar are covered, from how to hold a guitar to the specific way each hand is involved in the playing process. Pictures and videos are provided to help clarify each technique. These pictures and videos are either contained in the book or can be downloaded at www.muse-eek.com This book is excerpted from "1st Steps for a Beginning Guitarist Volume One."

Accompaniment: Volume One, Learning to Play Bass and Chords Simultaneously
E-book ISBN 1-890944-87-4   Traditional Book Binding ISBN 1-890944-96-3

The techniques found within this book are an excellent resource for creating and understanding how to play bass and chords simultaneously in a jazz or blues style. Special attention is paid to understanding how this technique is created, thereby enabling the student to recreate this style with other pieces of music. This book is excerpted from the book "Guitar Clinic."

Beginning Rhythm Studies: Volume One, Learning the basics of reading rhythm and playing in time.
E-book ISBN 1-890944-89-0   Traditional Book Binding 1-890944-98-X

This book covers the basics for anyone wishing to understand or improve their rhythmic abilities. Simple language is used to show the student how to read and play rhythm. Exercises are presented which can accelerate the learning process. Audio examples in the form of midifiles are available on the muse-eek.com website to facilitate learning the correct rhythm in time. This book is excerpted from the book "Rhythm Primer."

www.ingramcontent.com/pod-product-compliance
Lightning Source LLC
Chambersburg PA
CBHW062041090426

42740CB00016B/2985